IMAGES
of America

SPORTS MEMORIES OF SONOMA COUNTY

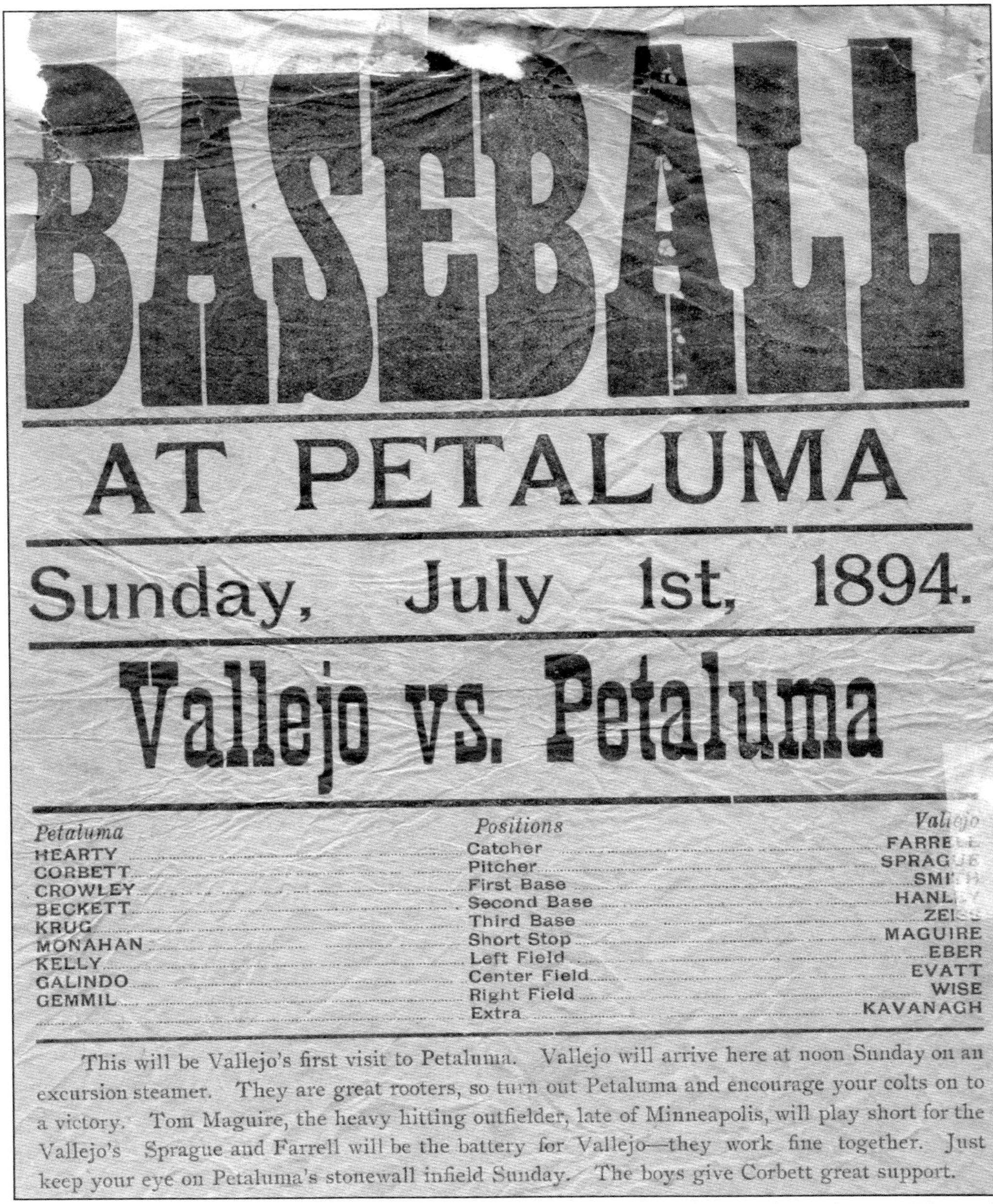

BASEBALL

AT PETALUMA

Sunday, July 1st, 1894.

Vallejo vs. Petaluma

Petaluma	*Positions*	*Vallejo*
HEARTY	Catcher	FARRE[illegible]
CORBETT	Pitcher	SPRAG[illegible]
CROWLEY	First Base	SMI[illegible]
BECKETT	Second Base	HANL[illegible]
KRUG	Third Base	ZEI[illegible]
MONAHAN	Short Stop	MAGUIRE
KELLY	Left Field	EBER
GALINDO	Center Field	EVATT
GEMMIL	Right Field	WISE
	Extra	KAVANAGH

This will be Vallejo's first visit to Petaluma. Vallejo will arrive here at noon Sunday on an excursion steamer. They are great rooters, so turn out Petaluma and encourage your colts on to a victory. Tom Maguire, the heavy hitting outfielder, late of Minneapolis, will play short for the Vallejo's Sprague and Farrell will be the battery for Vallejo—they work fine together. Just keep your eye on Petaluma's stonewall infield Sunday. The boys give Corbett great support.

An 1894 placard announced a July 1 baseball game between Vallejo and Petaluma. "This will be Vallejo's first visit to Petaluma. Vallejo will arrive here at noon Sunday on an excursion steamer. They are great rooters, so turn out Petaluma and encourage your colts on to a victory... keep your eye on Petaluma's stonewall infield Sunday. The boys give Corbett (the pitcher) great support."

Game called at 2:30 o'clock p.m. Street cars run direct to the grounds.
admission 25 cents boys 10 cts. Ladies free.

(After all the promotional efforts, Vallejo did not show up for the game.) Petaluma Museum.

IMAGES
of America

SPORTS MEMORIES OF SONOMA COUNTY

Lee Torliatt

ARCADIA
PUBLISHING

ISBN 978-0-7385-2056-8

Published by Arcadia Publishing
Charleston, South Carolina

Printed in the United States of America

Library of Congress Catalog Card Number: 2002101623

For all general information contact Arcadia Publishing at:
Telephone 843-853-2070
Fax 843-853-0044
E-Mail sales@arcadiapublishing.com
For customer service and orders:
Toll-Free 1-888-313-2665

Visit us on the Internet at www.arcadiapublishing.com

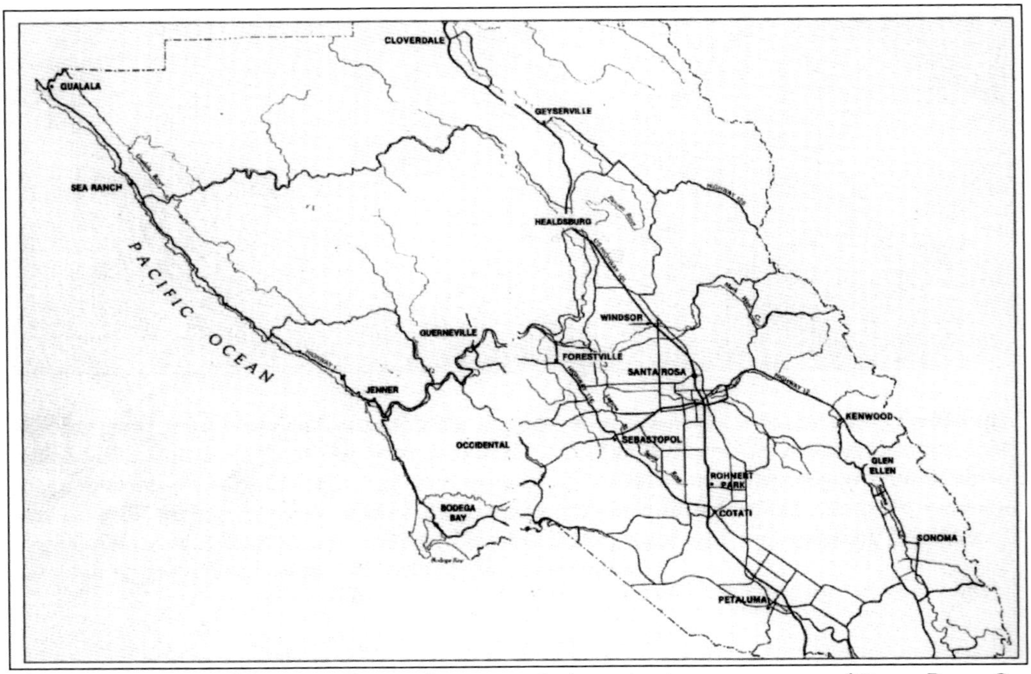

The sports centers of Sonoma County have mainly been in the county seat of Santa Rosa, Sebastopol in the west, Healdsburg in the north, Sonoma to the east, and Petaluma to the south.

Contents

ACKNOWLEDGMENTS

Heinie Abel
Darla Budworth
Paula Burks
John Bussman
Mike Capitani
Courtney Clements
Wes Colgan Jr.
Mike Daniels
Ralph DeMarco
Marie Djordjevich
Vida and Brad Evart
Walt Foster
Dick Gray
Virginia Hein
Audrey Herman
Holly Hoods
Tony Hoskins
Duke Iversen
Tom Kasovich
Lucy Kortum
Harry Lapham
Marie Laskelle
John and Gaye LeBaron
Guido Lorenzini
Vonnie Matthews
Ray Owen
Al Pisenti
Don Ramatici
Debi Riddle
Warren Rile
Clarence Ruonavaara
Liz Schuck
Diane Smith
June Maher Smith
Eric Stanley
Lorne Swanets
Brook Tauzer
Bob and Mary Testorelli
George Tomasini
Charles and Althea Torliatt
Cindy Torliatt
Ryo Torliatt
Jim Underhill Jr.
Bill and Ann Verity
Chandler Verity
Nicholas Verity
Bev Wallstrum

INTRODUCTION

The greats.

The near-greats.

The not-so-greats.

They included Ralph Rose, Ernie Nevers, Biff Hoffman, Mad Bull, Ralph Stone, Wilbur Reine, Guido Lorenzini, Elsie Parrott, Helen Wightman, Bill Charlesworth, Jack "Eagle Eye" Sindall, Fred "The Fox" Klemenok, Kid Noriel, Dick "The Wheel" Gray, Nodgie "Two Yards" Ganizzi, George Duke, Duke Iversen, Duke Radcliffe, Lefty Wetch, Lefty Ristau, and thousands more, including quite a few Maronis. They have all contributed to the rich sports history of Sonoma County.

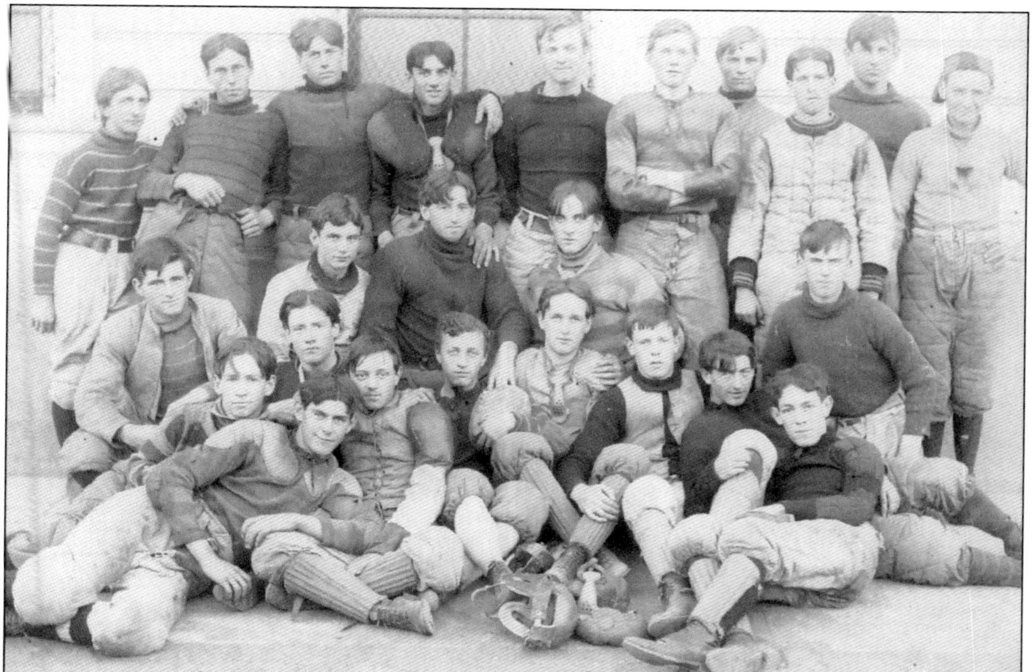

With helmets, pads, and a variety of equipment options, the Santa Rosa High School football squad gathered at the beginning of the 1903 season. Handwritten identifications indicate the team included Mallory, Malcolm Youker, Parsons, Ashby, Dodge, Jacob, Marshall, Meir, G. Briggs, Hogeboom, Snider, Rathbone, P. Smith, Lemmon, C. Briggs, More, Miller, Neugriler, Gray, Roy Hitchcock, Ned Wilson, McKinley, Burris, and Dornell. Donald Gray appears to be the third person from the left, sitting in the front row. Courtesy of the Sonoma County Museum.

The games ranged from the familiar—football, baseball, track, and basketball—to the fairly exotic. Who would have expected ice hockey in Sonoma County? Or a car racing a horse?

The geographic focus is on the five main towns in old Sonoma County: Santa Rosa in the center, Sebastopol to the west, Healdsburg to the north, Sonoma to the east, and Petaluma to the south.

It's been said that historians should leave a little time between historic events and the present. This book covers the first recorded sports events in the mid-19th century to 1952, leaving a 50-year gap between "then and now."

It's not possible to mention all the great teams, players, or memorable incidents of our past, but hats off to all of those, male and female, who have donned a uniform, worked up a sweat, and contributed to this story.

The photos for this book came from Sonoma County museums, libraries, and private collections. The text came mainly from research of newspapers, yearbooks, and interviews with those who were on the scene in days past. The histories of 19th and 20th-century Santa Rosa by Gaye LeBaron, Joann Mitchell, Dee Blackman, and Harvey Hansen were also helpful.

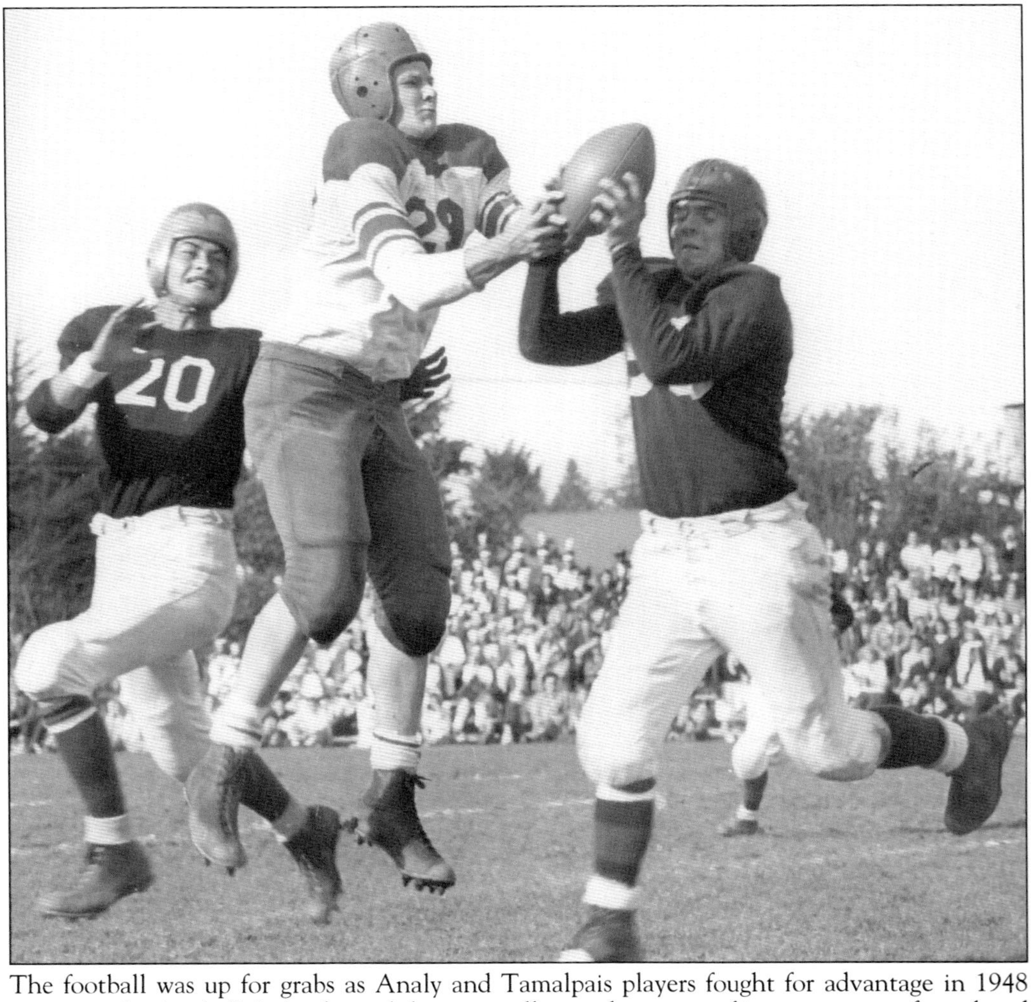

The football was up for grabs as Analy and Tamalpais players fought for advantage in 1948 game won by Analy 7-6. Analy, with lower enrollment than most of its opponents, often played spoiler in the North Bay League of the late 1940s. Courtesy of the Walt Foster collection.

One

THE EARLY DAYS

Sport can be defined as any activity that gives enjoyment or recreation. It can require more or less vigorous bodily exertion carried on according to some set of rules. Settlers from many parts of the world brought traditional diversions with them to Sonoma County. These included horse racing, boxing, bicycling, baseball, football, basketball, track, tennis, and hunting and fishing. Santa Rosa had a track for horse racing in 1857, and a Jockey Club was formed in 1860. Healdsburg and Cloverdale offered spring races in 1861, featuring "some fine two-year-old quarterstock." By 1869, a mile course was being built on Mr. Bailhache's land near Healdsburg. A large crowd showed up at the Agricultural Park Course in Petaluma in September 1876 to watch W.V. Smith in a 50-mile race against time. Santa Rosa boasted a covered grandstand with a capacity for 500 by 1880. Anteeo, a trotting stallion from the stables of Isaac DeTurk, appeared at tracks in many parts of California. The famed pacer, Lou Dillon, bred in Santa Rosa, became the first harness horse to cover a mile track in less than two minutes.

There was early interest in boxing. In 1863, two years before the Marquis of Queensbury provided the world with a set of rules for the sport, two combatants battled on the banks of the Petaluma Creek south of town.

Johnny Lazarus and Peter Daley "agreed to maul and be mauled until the word 'quit,' for a stake of $2,000. After some 40 rounds, during which...Johnny 'got in lightly' three or four times on Pete's 'kissers,' 'peepers,' and 'smeller,' causing the 'claret' to circulate somewhat freely, and Pete's returning the compliment by punching Johnny on the 'conk,' in the 'bread basket,' etc... the umpires deciding Daley to be the winner."

Healdsburg fans cheered hometown-boy Chris Merchant, the amateur heavyweight champion of the Pacific Coast, in the 1870s.

Santa Rosa's first bicycling club, the Wheelmen, took part in cross-country expeditions and Bay Area racing events from the 1880s. The Noonan brothers, Henry and Ben, and Jesse Williamson competed in Bay Area events. Proving the superiority of man over machines, Ben Noonan raced a train from Santa Rosa to Sebastopol, breezing in the winner in 16 minutes. By 1895, in addition to road runs, Healdsburg's Wheelmen held races at Matheson's Park, which drew up to 500 fans but "there was no more than a $1,000 wagered on any of the races."

Baseball was being played in America by the 1830s, and Santa Rosa fielded a team in 1861. In the 1870s, a Santa Rosa team took on opponents from other towns, and the games got pretty wild. In one case, the Santa Rosa Olympics outslugged Petaluma 57 to 46. One Sunday around 1890, Healdsburg players boarded a "band wagon" pulled by a crack pair of horses driven by J. C. O'Connor. When a front wheel came off, the horses bolted and the players ended up in the street in front of the Occidental Hotel. With cuts, aches, pains, and "blood in their eyes," the players marched onto the field and upended "their keen contenders...to the tune of 7 to 6." The headline in the Santa Rosa newspaper read, "HEALDSBURG BEAT COUNTY SEATERS ON CRUTCHES."

Charles Wolcott was credited with adding a catcher's mask and glove to the Healdsburg team's equipment. Before the arrival of the protective gear, the catcher stood far back of the plate and caught the ball on the bounce.

Teams came in by train to play the locals, and there were numerous special events. A National League game was played in Santa Rosa in 1897 and a few years later the Boston Bloomer Girls lost to the Santa Rosa men's team, 13-8. Healdsburg played Sebastopol and other opponents in the 1890s. Petaluma had teams called the Maroons, Alerts, and Merchants.

Early football seemed to include quite a bit of rugby. In some cases, five points were awarded for touchdowns, the standard reward for a "try" or goal in rugby. Santa Rosa fielded its first football team at Pacific Methodist College in the early 1880s, and by early 1893 Petaluma High School proudly applied a 24-0 "coat of whitewash" to Santa Rosa. The Rose City coach, high school principal Clement C. Young, became California's governor but the team did not do as well, failing to win a game. Since home field was a vacant lot on E Street with no bleachers, fans stood or sat on the ground.

In late 1893, Petaluma hosted a team from San Francisco and "got the better of an unfinished game." Following an injury "and the desire of the visiting team to catch the 4:10 train back to San Francisco, the game was declared closed." It was said Petaluma had its best teams in 1892 and 1893.

The spirit of high school football extended into the broader community. "A goodly number of young gentlemen met at the office of Geo. C. Codding" in January 1893 to form a football club. Suggestions for a team mascot included a rooster, a cross-eyed pig, and a yellow dog. By Thanksgiving 1894, Healdsburg was eagerly awaiting its Thanksgiving football game with Petaluma.

When Santa Rosa High School moved into a new building in 1896, it had 250 students, 6 teachers, and 2 sports, football and track. A track field day at the Pierce Brothers' racetrack in Santa Rosa in 1897 attracted high school teams from Petaluma, Healdsburg, Ukiah, and Santa Rosa. Events included hurdles, a mile walk, a mile run, dashes, field events, and bicycle races. When three runners finished in a bunch in the 100-yard dash, they were required to run it a second time.

Women played some of the earliest basketball games. There were girls' teams in Petaluma and Santa Rosa in 1897.

Sports' bickering between Santa Rosa and Petaluma goes back at least to the early 1890s. A Petaluma-Santa Rosa high school football game, scheduled for December 31, 1892, was delayed when Santa Rosa asked for a postponement. After more delays, Petaluma sources did little to conceal their contempt, concluding, "Santa Rosa High School is not at all prepared to cope with Petaluma high school football."

Complaints aside, when the teams finally played in mid-January 1893, the Petaluma newspaper proudly clucked that a 24-0 "Coat of Whitewash" had been applied to the Santa Rosans.Players suffered on a "slimy and muddy field" but were served an elegant banquet at the Congregation Church presented by the "young ladies of the Petaluma High School and other assistants."

By 1893, Petaluma had three wins over their northern rivals, and one writer wondered "whether it is the richness of our milk, the pureness of our homemade flour, or the strength of the Petaluma cheese" that made Petaluma athletes superior.

One of the first major track meets, drawing high school teams from Petaluma, Ukiah, Healdsburg, and Santa Rosa, was held in Santa Rosa in June 1897. The grandstand was "comfortably filled" by the 2 p.m. starting time, and included "a great many young ladies...most of them wearing the black and orange of the Santa Rosa High School."

The judges, J.S. Sweet of Santa Rosa, I.H. Gunn of Healdsburg, and Fred Martin of Petaluma, found themselves in a dilemma when a knot of runners crossed the finish line in the 100-yard dash. Unable to pick a winner, they had the three top finishers run the race over again.

There was a full schedule of track and field events, including a mile walk, won by Scott of Petaluma in 8 minutes, 14 seconds. Petaluma also won the mile run, in a somewhat faster time.

A mile bicycle race was included, won by Ben Noonan of Santa Rosa.

Petaluma took team honors, trailed by Ukiah and Santa Rosa.

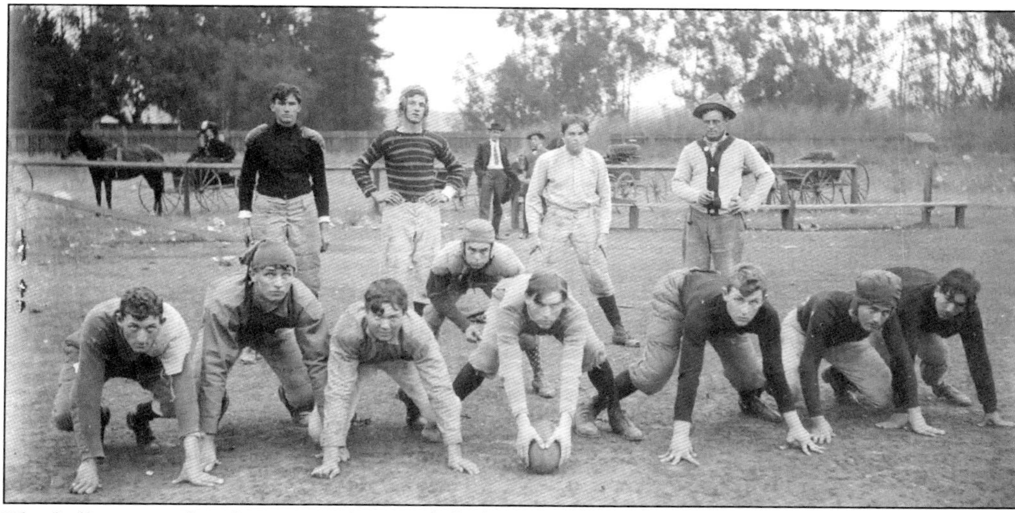

The ball was too fat, there weren't enough helmets, some of the players looked a little disheveled, but you had to start somewhere, and this was the Santa Rosa High School football team *c.* 1900. Critics considered the game, more like rugby than football, as too rough for young boys to play. Courtesy of the Sonoma County Museum.

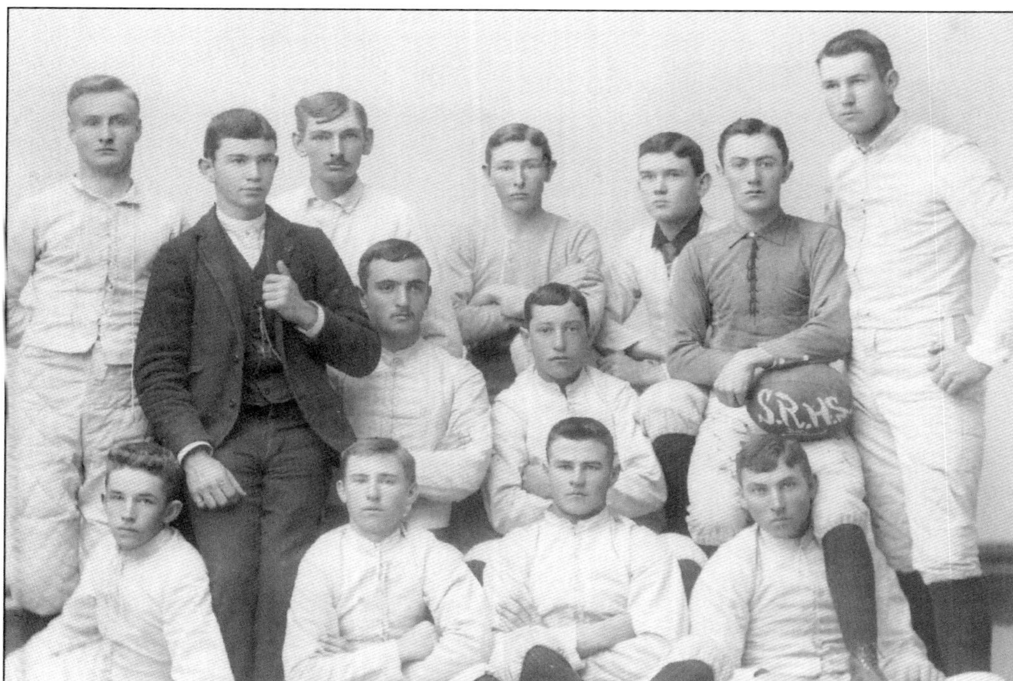

The Santa Rosa High School football team, vintage 1892-93, had little success against natural rival Petaluma. Members of the 1892 Santa Rosa team were center Paul Coulter, guard R. Hathaway, left guard Carl Yobo, tackles Fred Kinley and Virgil Hoffra, end Oscar Reeves, end Lane Ferguson, quarterback and captain Strout, halfback J. Godman, halfback James Near, fullback Murphy (not in picture), substitutes Shorty Winkler and Charles McPike, and manager Glenn Murdock. Courtesy of the Mike Capitani collection.

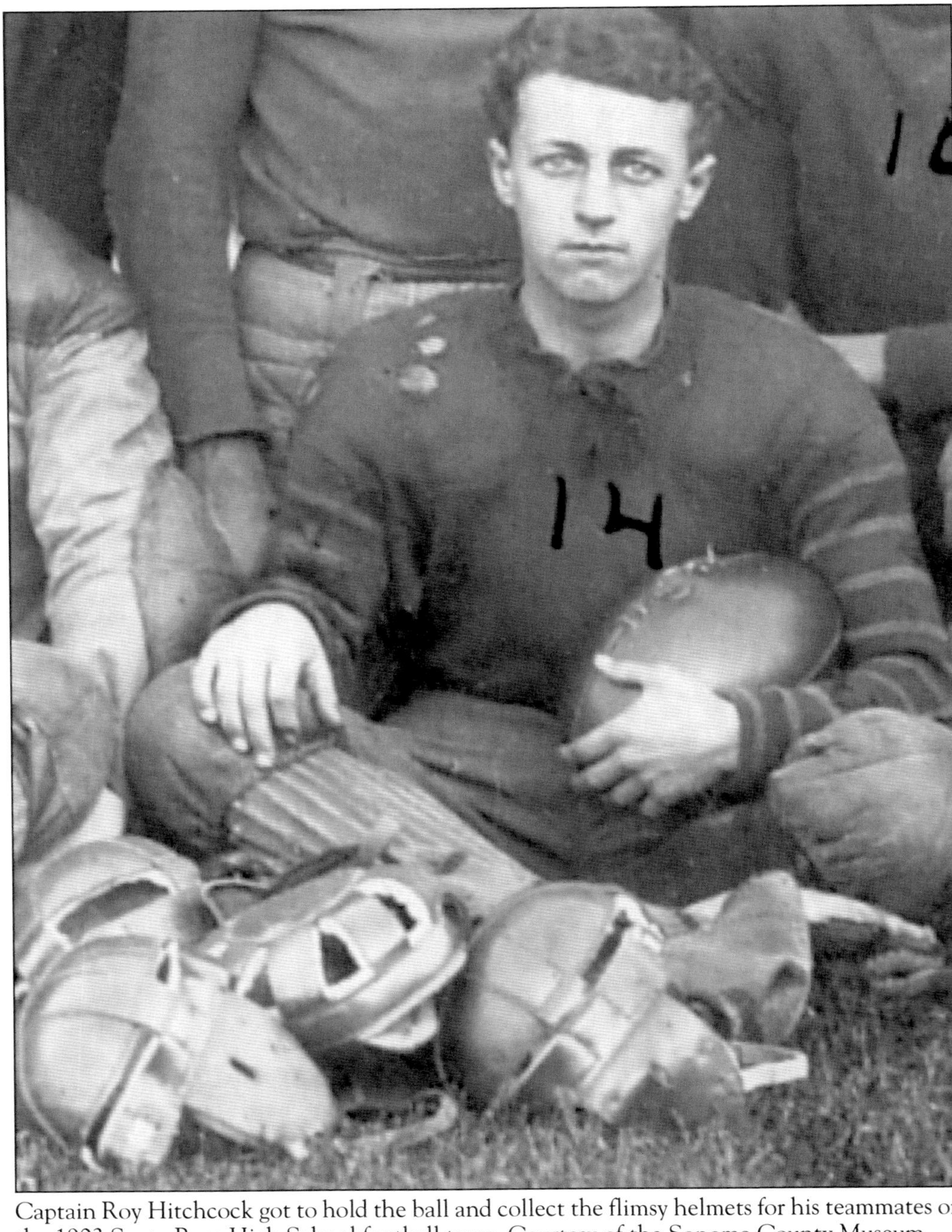

Captain Roy Hitchcock got to hold the ball and collect the flimsy helmets for his teammates on the 1903 Santa Rosa High School football team. Courtesy of the Sonoma County Museum.

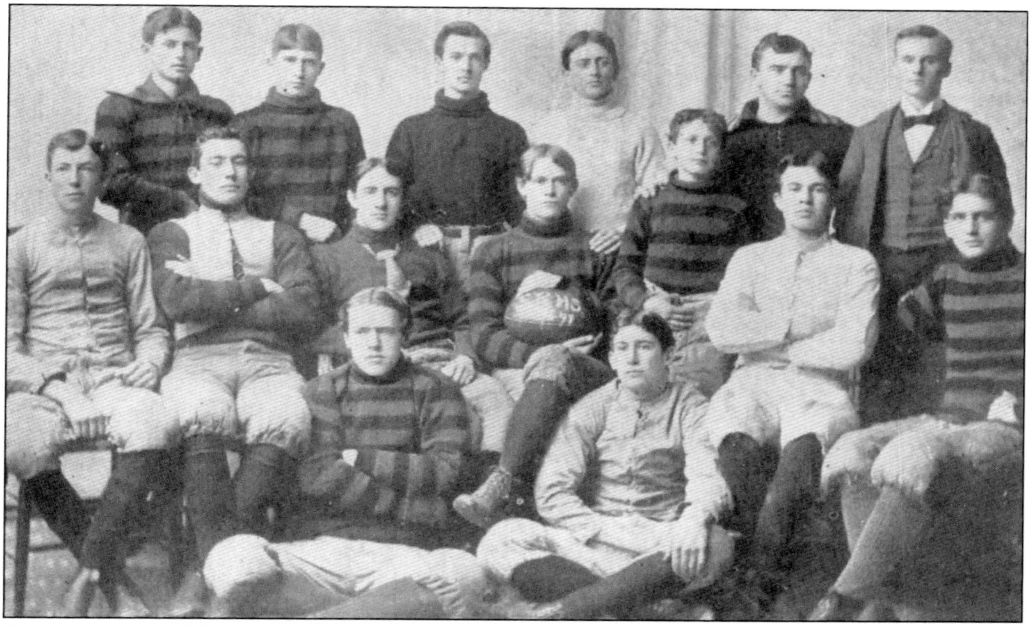

A rare picture of the 1896 Santa Rosa High School football team appeared in the 1923 Echo Yearbook. In late 1896, the Panthers beat Pacific Methodist College twice, 20-4 and 28-0. Halfback Maddux scored all four touchdowns in the first game. The 12-man Santa Rosa team went to Ukiah December 26 and overwhelmed the inexperienced Mendocino County team 42-4. Team members included captain H. Rogers, J. Steele, H. Steele, Maddux, Will McGregor, Grayson Pedigo, Eveleth, Thompson, Strout, Kohler ,and Wooley.

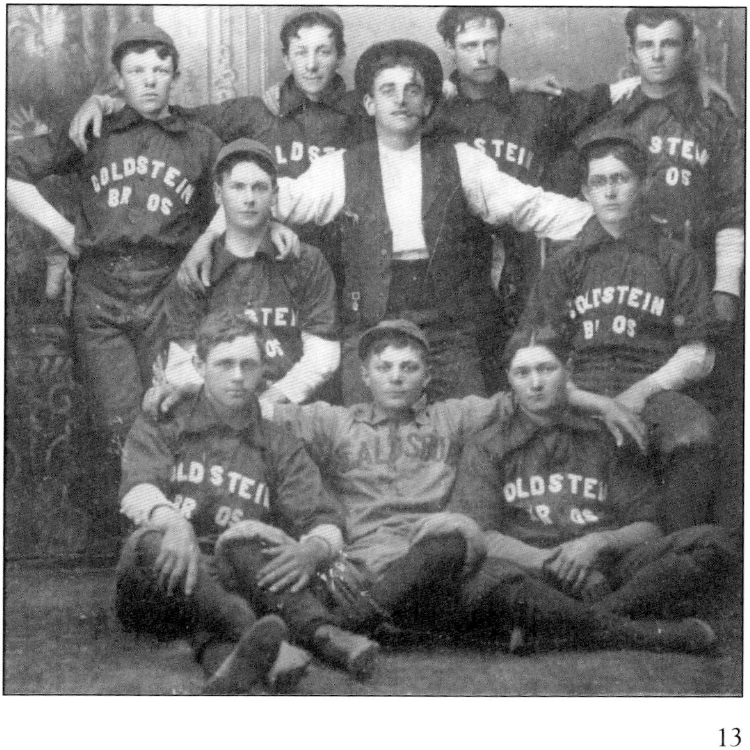

Goldstein Bros. of Healdsburg put a hearty group of young horsehiders on the field in 1900. Pictured are, back row from the left: Dutch Huebner, Pike Passalacqua, William Neely, and Frank Early; (middle row) Ted Lynch, Louis Foppiano, and John Miller; (front), Louis Belvail, Monk Teauffer, and Louis Bacigalupi. Courtesy of the Healdsburg Museum.

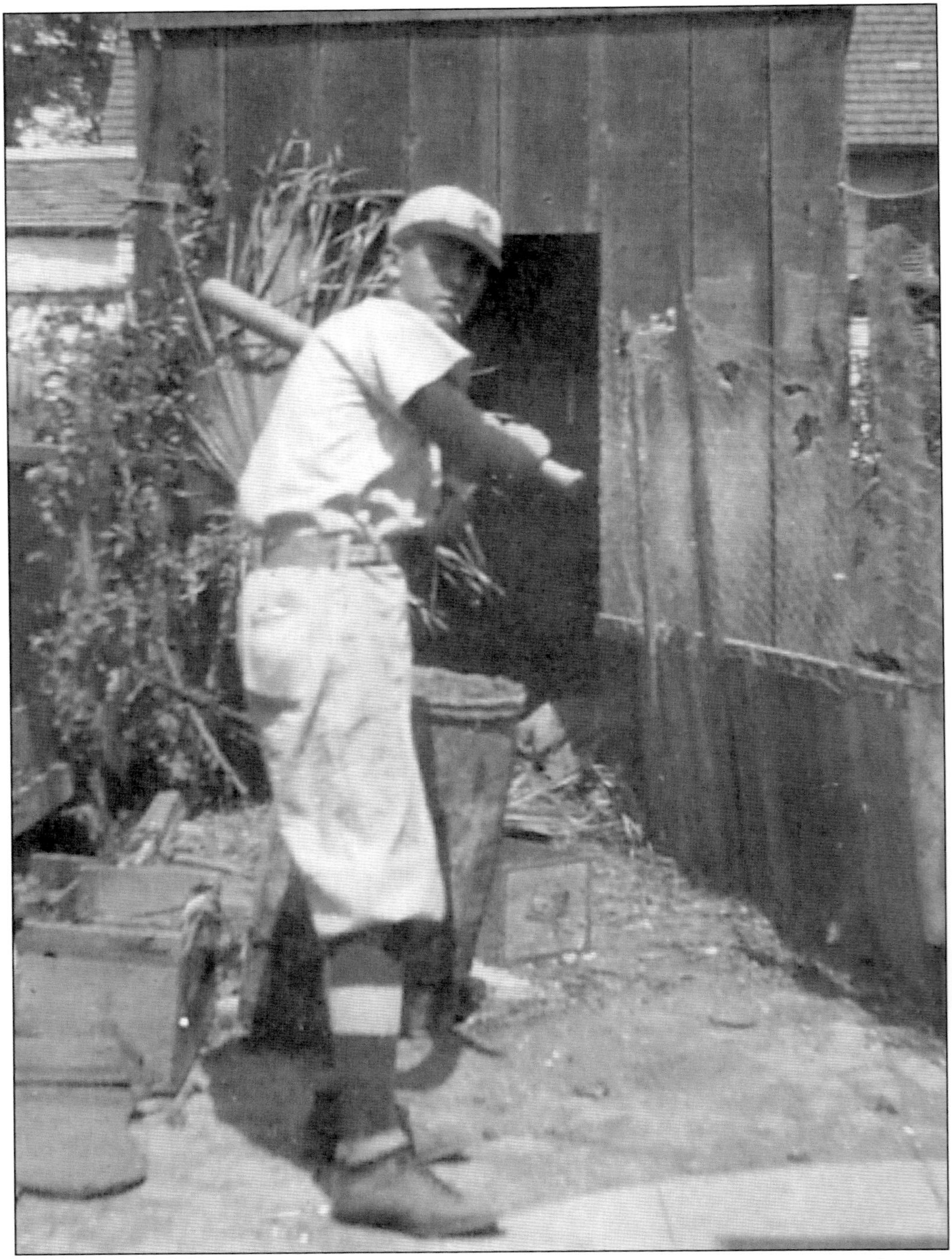

Since equipment and places to play were in short supply early in the 20th century, Mert Stewart and other innovative players often set up makeshift sites for batting practice. Stewart, a catcher, played for teams in and around Petaluma before moving to San Francisco. His skills helped him get a job with a San Francisco bank and a place on the bank's team. Courtesy of the Torliatt collection.

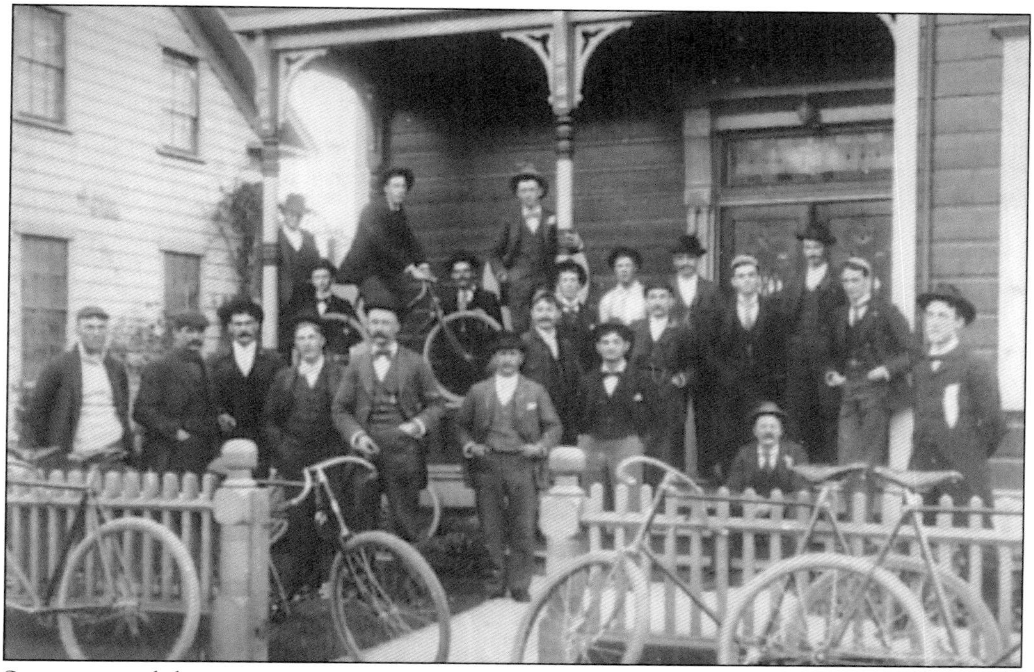

Since automobiles were not readily available, the young sports of the day got their travel and exercise activity in by pumping their bicycles through the rural hills and valleys of Sonoma County with frequent journeys to the ocean. The Santa Rosa Wheelmen gathered at their Cherry Street Clubhouse in the 1890s. Healdsburg also had an active bike group.

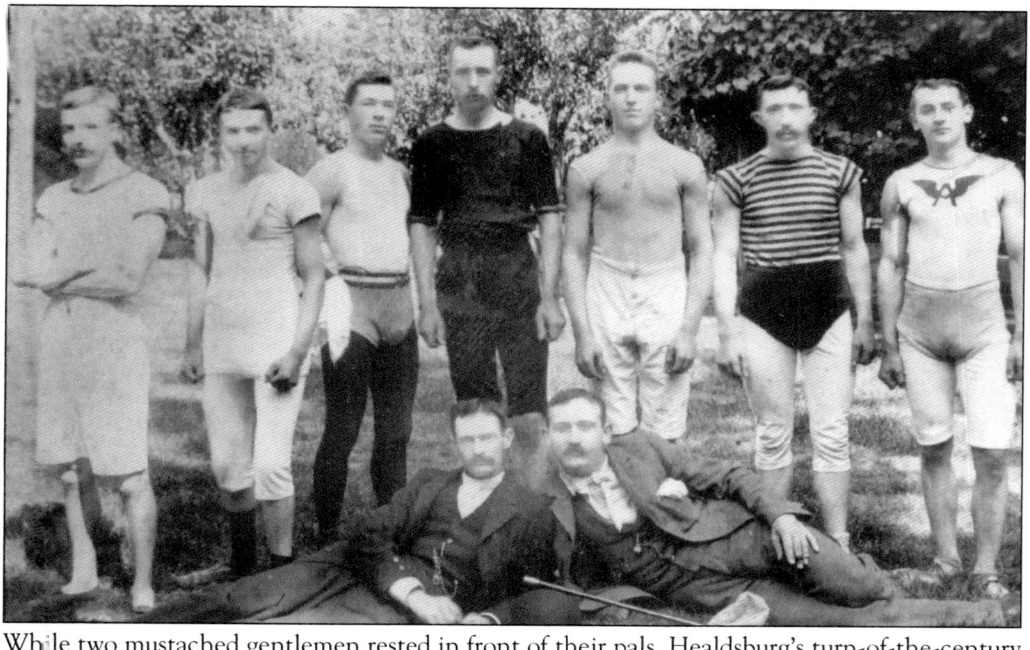

While two mustached gentlemen rested in front of their pals, Healdsburg's turn-of-the-century running club got ready to rack up some miles on nearby country roads. William Vollmer is third from left. Courtesy of the Sonoma County Museum.

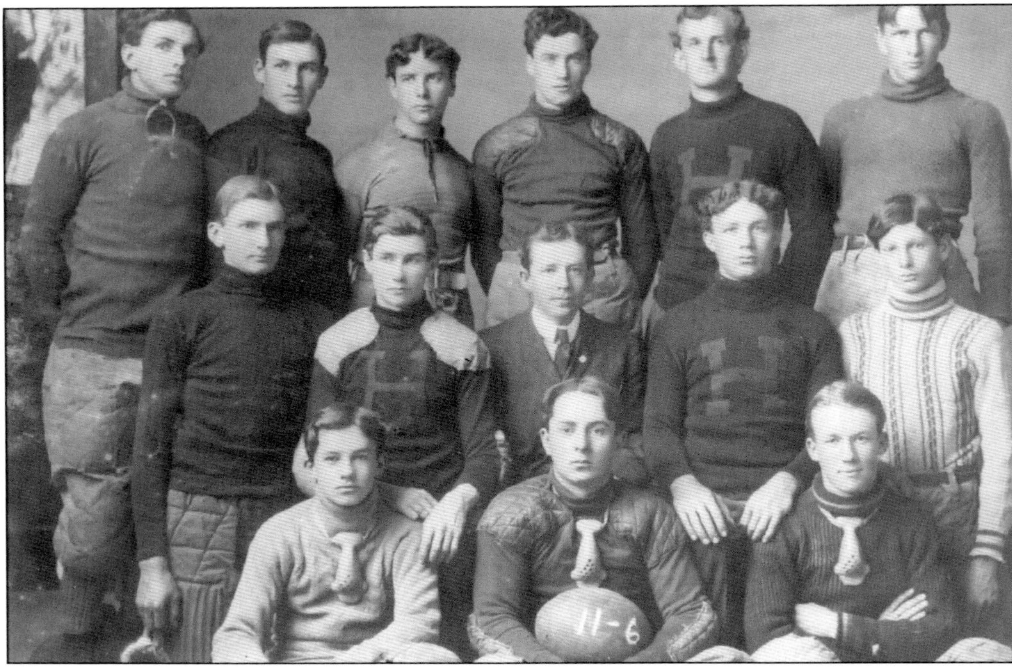

The 1906 Healdsburg High School football team is pictured here, from left: (front row) Fred Young, P. Mostrom, and H. Arresbury; (middle) Ray Vitousek, Melville McDonald, Dr. Fred Kinley, Floyd Bailey, and Moody; (back) Rodney McClure, Thurman Wiscarver, Burt McDonald, Lester McDonough, Ray Welch, and Frank Widlund. It's believed Coach Kinley played on the Santa Rosa High School squad *c.* 1892. Courtesy of the Sonoma County Museum.

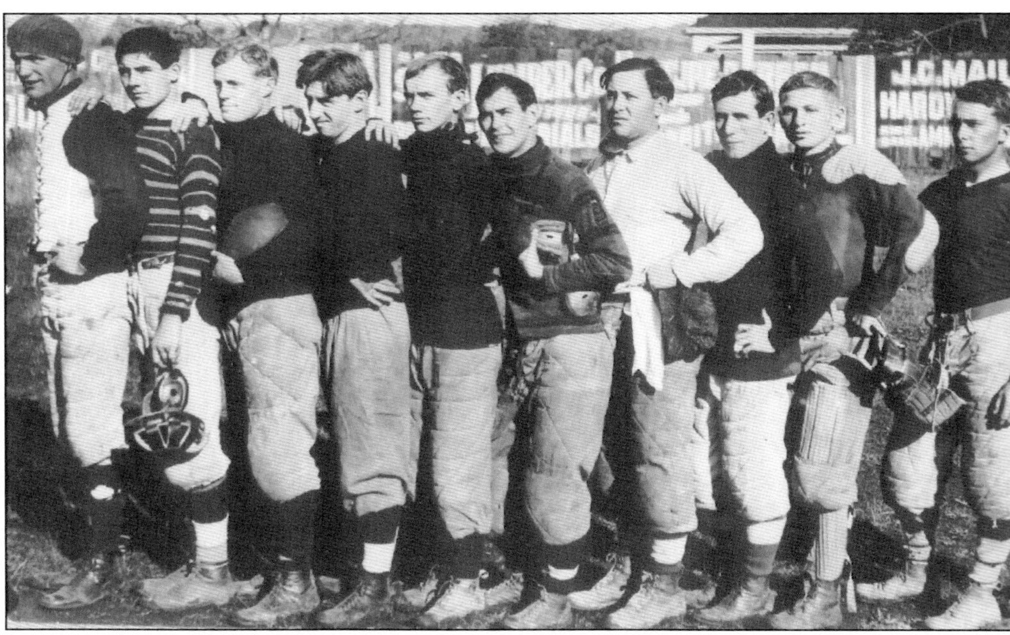

Enthusiastic members of the Santa Rosa Alumni football team lined up for action *c.* 1905. Courtesy of the Sonoma County Museum.

Two

FOOTBALL

Football was played sporadically from 1900 on, often around Thanksgiving or in the depths of winter. Santa Rosa High School blanked the visiting red and white of Healdsburg 11-0 on New Years Day 1901. On Thanksgiving Day 1902, Healdsburg hosted the Santa Rosa Business College team in Healdsburg. Healdsburg's future Olympian Ralph Rose got in his licks, punishing Santa Rosa runners in a losing effort.

In 1905, Healdsburg played four games. Doctor Fred Kinley, a boyish-looking dentist who played at Santa Rosa High School in the 1890s, was volunteer coach. Lester McDonough was his star runner, scoring four touchdowns against Santa Rosa Business College.

Because of injuries, the difficulty of recruiting enough people to fill 11-man teams, and other factors, football was played only sporadically at many schools.

Football came back strong in the 1920s. The first strong man was mighty Ernie Nevers, an import from Wisconsin who carried Santa Rosa to new heights in 1920. The semi-pro Santa Rosa Bonecrushers, led by Nevers, became state champions in 1928 and rolled to titles again in 1929 and 1930. Santa Rosa Junior College was "Great in '38," celebrating its 20th birthday with its first gridiron championship. The Cubs produced dominant teams again in 1949 and 1950.

Starting with a bunch of World War II veterans, the Petaluma Leghorns of the late 1940s and early '50s dominated the local scene, at one point going on a run of 26 games without a defeat. The Santa Rosa-Petaluma high school rivalry culminated in 1952 with a showdown battle that Petaluma won in the rain, 19-0.

The big names included Nevers, who went on to Stanford and an all-star pro career; Biff Hoffman, a running back from Petaluma who followed Nevers to Stanford; and Duke Iversen, a burly Petaluman who turned blocking and tackling into an art at University of Oregon and with two pro teams.

Football's comeback began in 1919 when Major Victor Hodge marched onto the scene to bring order, discipline, and the gridiron sport back to Santa Rosa High School. The team didn't win a game in 1919 but the following year Ernie Nevers arrived and put Santa Rosa on the football map, leading the team to a Northwest Section title.

The powerful Nevers made an immediate impression on his neighbors when he arrived in Rincon Valley from remote Superior, Wisconsin. Old-time writer Aubrey Brandon, who made his football debut at age seven as Nevers' center in pickup games, wrote:

"I played football with Ernie Nevers...in Rincon Valley where I grew up. Ernie and my brother Herb were the same age, and 10 years older than I.

"When any spare moment presented itself, Rincon Valley had a football game. The teams would form into two groups with Ernie and me (I was a skinny 7 at the time) on one side and 10 to 15 'big guys' on the other. The game was called, 'Stop Ernie.' I would center the ball to him and run as fast as I could to get out of the way while the opposing side would try to stop this tow-headed hurricane. I can still see this mass of humanity moving irresistibly forward with tacklers hanging on for dear life trying to bring this one-man holocaust to earth."

At Santa Rosa High, the future all-American quickly became the talk of the town. He "had an educated toe and was accurate in forward passing, a good plunging line bucker and...brilliant open-field man." Santa Rosa won seven games and the league title. In playoffs, the Panthers ran into mighty Berkeley, losing 61-0.

Playing its first season in 1924, St. Helena made the mistake of putting Santa Rosa on its schedule. The Panthers scored a touchdown every three plays, winning 141-0.

The big, bad Bonecrushers ran off 32 straight wins and brought 3 state amateur football championships to Santa Rosa. Ernie Nevers was the star attraction but the defense made it easy, allowing only 20 points the entire 1928 season. Howard Lawson, a bulging 260-pounder, anchored the line. His family had recently gone into business at the ocean resort at Dillon's Beach.

The Crushers won the state crown with a 22-0 victory over Modesto at Merced. Captain Hogan fell on a fumbled punt for the first score and the Santa Rosans never looked back.

The Bonecrushers sailed through the 1929 season undefeated. When the Santa Rosans heard Antioch had claimed the state title, "they took their uniforms out of mothballs," went to Kezar Stadium (in San Francisco on January 5, 1930) and "wiped up the turf with Antioch." Nevers scored twice in a 25-6 win while fan favorite Nodgie "Two Yards" Ganizzi rambled for 48 yards on 3 carries.

Menacing Duke Iversen came on the scene in Petaluma in the 1930s. His father told him, "You can play football on Saturdays but you have to clean the chicken house first." Many foes wish dad had kept him at home. It's said that Vallejo coach Colin Kilby once found a way to neutralize the menacing Petaluman. During a Vallejo-Petaluma game, Kilby allegedly sent in a little-used substitute to pick a fight with Iversen. Both players were ejected and Petaluma had to play the rest of the game without their punishing ground gainer. The game ended in a 0-0 tie.

Years of frustration ended in 1938 as the Santa Rosa Junior College Bear Cubs football team won the Northern California "B" Conference championship, the first conference title in the school's football history. Petaluma's Gene Benedetti blocked for speedsters Bob Acorne and Ken Battaglia as the Bear Cubs won seven games, including four in the league.

Santa Rosa Junior College had a banner sports year in 1949-50. Halfback Bill Charlesworth set a national Jaycee record in 1949, scoring 23 touchdowns as his team rolled to 11 wins to take the conference title. Coach Bill Neel's Cubs rolled up 442 points while giving up only 118.

The 1950 footballers gave an encore performance at the mid-century mark. "Nifty in 50," the team, finishing the season undefeated and untied with 12 wins and 462 points scored, beat LaSalle-Peru, Illinois 41-6 in the Gold Dust Bowl at Vallejo.

In 1952, Santa Rosa High rid itself of nine years of frustration by beating Vallejo 42-0. The victory set up a match between two unbeaten powerhouses, Santa Rosa and Petaluma. Santa Rosa boasted one of the most explosive offenses ever to perform in the North Bay. Len Read did the passing with running help from Warren Rile, Lary Robbins, and Chet Hamamoto. Petaluma relied on a big line and powerful running backs such as Jim Eaglin, Fred Brock, Ken Conley, and Duane Butler.

The teams played in a steady downpour before 5,000 fans. Quarterback D.R. Mobley threw two touchdown passes that carried Petaluma to a 19-0 victory.

The semi-pro Petaluma Leghorns played an Armistice Day game against the University of San Francisco Ramblers in 1946. Because a large crowd showed up, the team decided to play a full season in 1947. Fans were pleased when the Leghorns "fowled-up" Santa Rosa's Bonecrushers, 77-0. The next year, the teams met again in Santa Rosa. Halfback Bill Bottasso scored twice and lineman Guido Lorenzini kicked the extra point as the Crushers upset the Petalumans, 14-13.

After the game, angry Petaluma fans accused Santa Rosa of wetting down the field. A Santa Rosa coach responded that sprinklers had been left on overnight by mistake. A war of words followed in local newspapers for weeks.

By 1949, the Leghorns were a fixture in Sonoma County. Quarterback Fred "The Fox" Klemenok led the team to 12 wins, marred only by a loss and a tie. The team went on a streak of 26 wins without a loss. Coach Gene Benedetti retired in 1950 with a record of 40 wins, 6 losses, and 2 ties.

The team continued to play into the late 1950s.

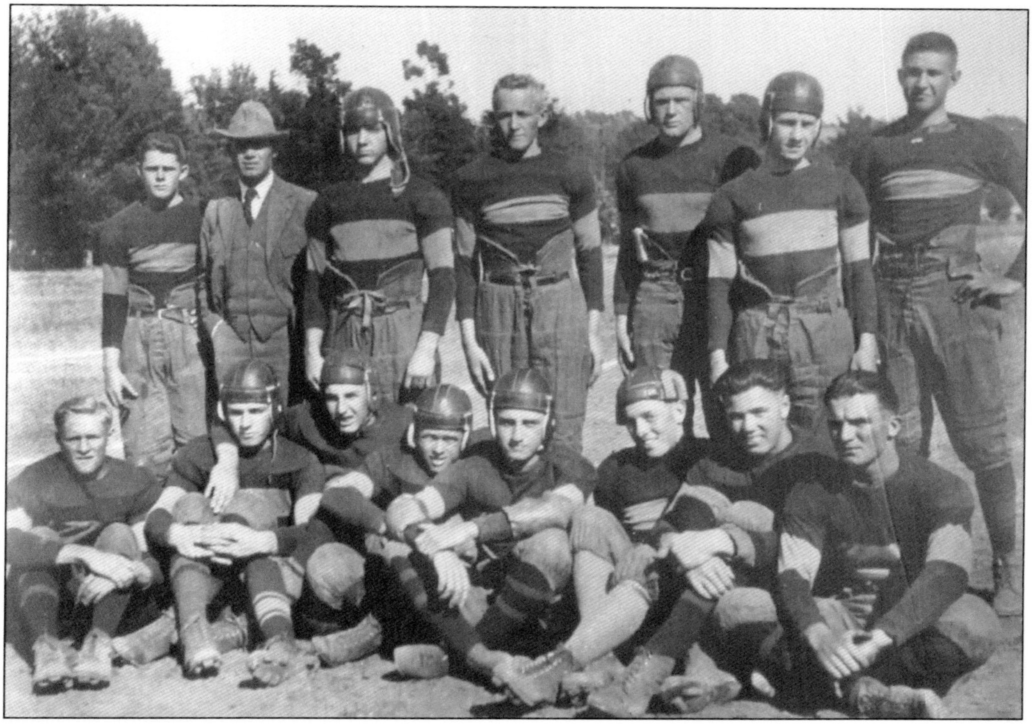

The 14-man Santa Rosa High School football team, bolstered by the arrival of power-running Ernie Nevers, went from winless in 1919 to champions in 1920. Pictured are: (back row) Stacey Lee, Coach Hodge, Joe Dearing, Tom Grace, Ernie Nevers, Al Lucas and Jerry Griffin; (front) Gale Johnson, Rosy Penry, Vinton Peter, Vern Stocker, Fred Feliz, Bill Cowan, Perce Anderson, and Cliff Morrill. One player went on to college at St. Mary's and most of the others to Stanford or UC Berkeley. Courtesy of the Santa Rosa High School Foundation.

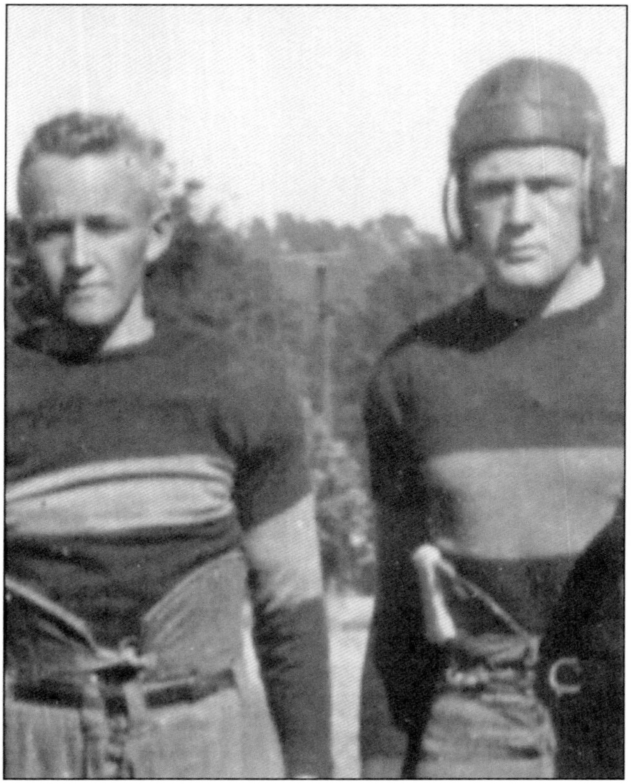

Tom Grace, left, member of a prominent Santa Rosa family, and Ernie Nevers, a menacing giant from the wilds of northern Wisconsin, teamed up to turn Santa Rosa football into a winning program in 1920. Courtesy of the SRHS Foundation.

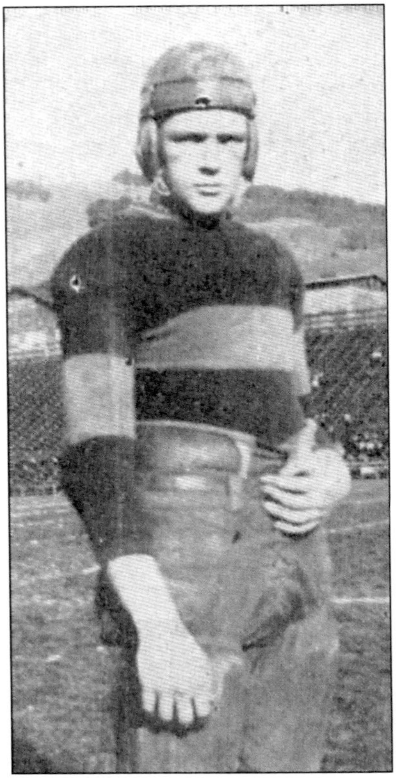

Nevers was an impressive sight in his Santa Rosa High School uniform. With his ability to pass, kick, run, and tackle, the big fullback from Wisconsin opened up a "golden era" in Santa Rosa sports. Later, at Stanford, he came close to beating the Four Horsemen of Notre Dame almost single-handedly in the Rose Bowl.

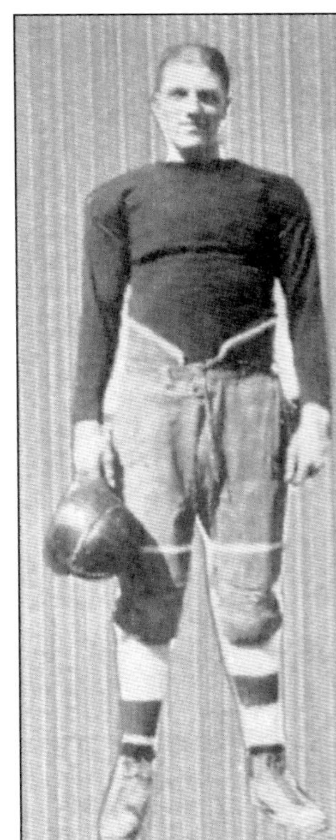

Biff Hoffman played for Petaluma High when the Trojans returned to a regular football schedule in 1921. The team won only one game while losing six, but fullback Hoffman impressed all with his speed and power. Following in the footsteps of Ernie Nevers, Hoffman became a triple-threat passing, running, and kicking star for coach Pop Warner at Stanford. Hoffman earned All-America honors in 1928 and was an outstanding discus thrower, winning an NCAA title. In his biggest game, an upset that "shocked the east coast," the upstart Stanford squad blanked mighty Army 26-0 at Yankee Stadium in New York.

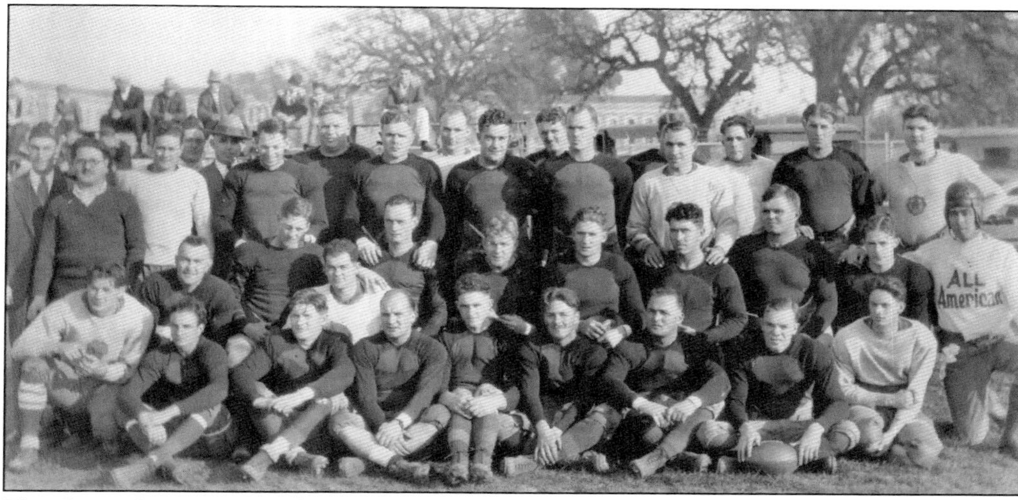

The Santa Rosa Bonecrushers were tough on offense and defense, winning state semi-pro championships three years in a row from 1928 to 1930. In 1928, the team went undefeated, winning the state American Legion crown with a sturdy defense and the offensive bursts of All-American Ernie Nevers, Bunny Belden, and Nodgie "Two Yards" Ganizzi. Some of these players have been identified. They are: (front, seated) sixth from left, John Trinity Houscona; seventh from left, Dick Blewett; (middle row) fifth from left, Nevers; fourth from right, lineman Joe Jackson; (back row) seventh from left, 260-pound lineman Howard Lawson. Courtesy of the Mike Daniels collection.

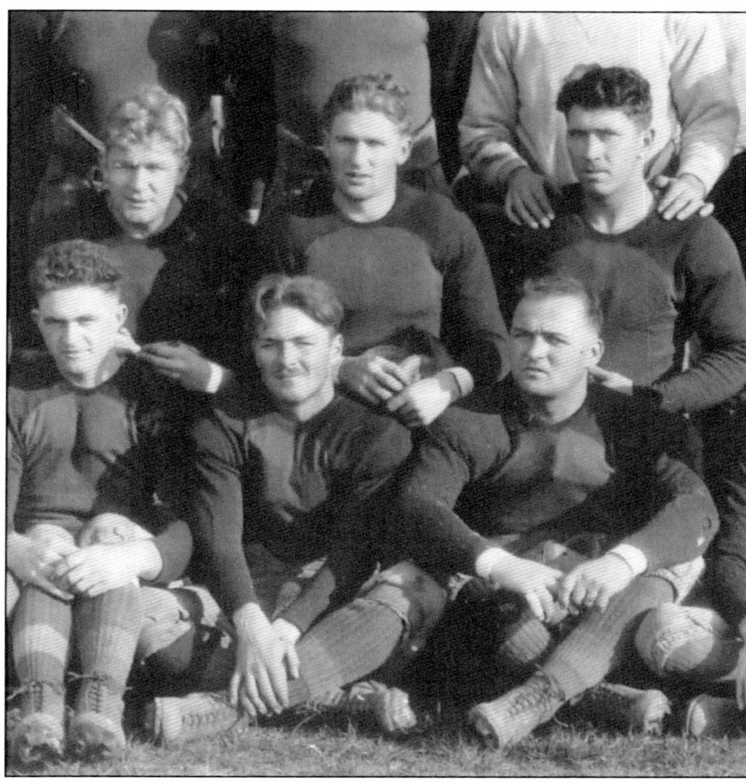

Nevers (top row, left) served as assistant coach at Stanford in 1928, and then joined the Bonecrushers for the stretch drive to a state championship. He suited up again for the title game at the end of the 1929 season. Courtesy of the Daniels collection.

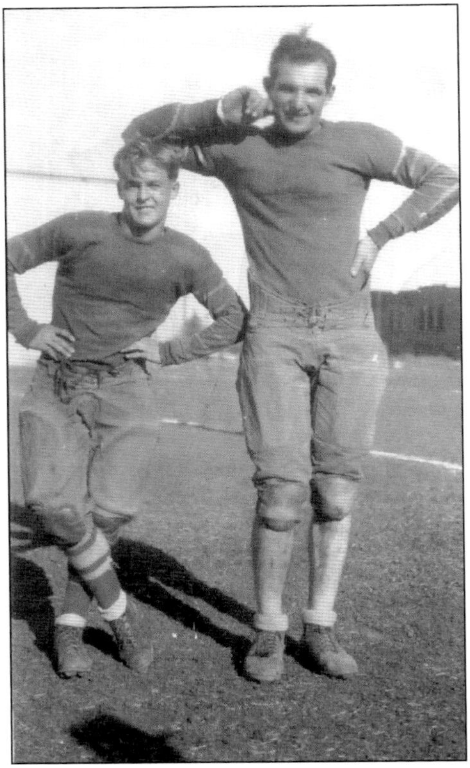

Future police chief Melvin (Dutch) Flohr (right) ran interference for future Justice of the Peace Rollie Webb at Petaluma High School in the 1920s. After playing at Santa Clara, the 6-foot, 4-inch Flohr came back to Sonoma County where he became Santa Rosa's police chief. Although the Bonecrushers disbanded in the early 1930s, Flohr and other local players put a new team, the Blue Eagles, on the field in 1933. The Eagles won five games and lost two.

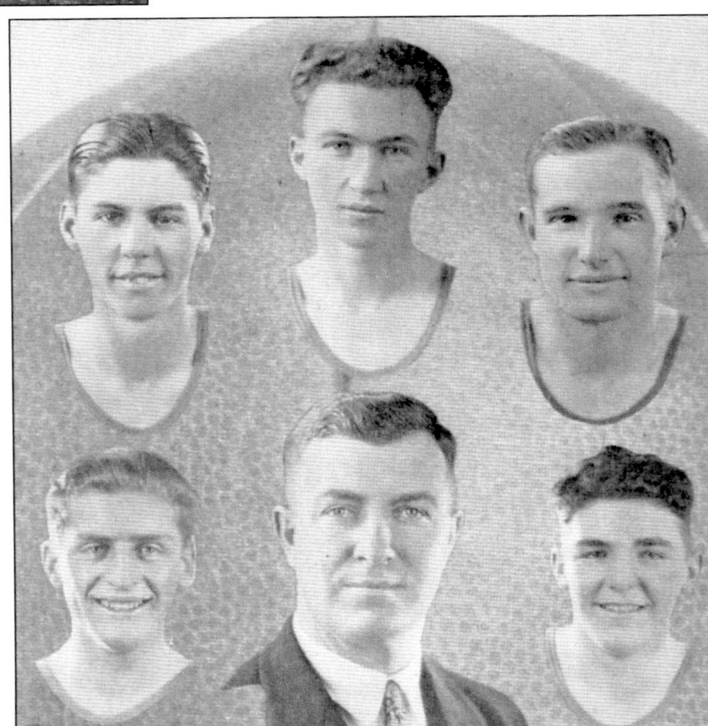

Melvin (Dutch) Flohr, top right, and Ralph Stone, lower right (next to Coach Cap Schuster), toiled for the Petaluma High School Trojans in 1926-27, first on the football team, and later on the championship basketball squad. Both were good enough to get bids to college—lineman Flohr at Santa Clara and end Stone at UC Berkeley. Stone played football in the Olympics in 1932, had bit parts in Hollywood movies, and came home to make a career as a businessman and financier. Flohr, later a police chief, joined Stone on the Blue Eagles semi-pro team in 1933.

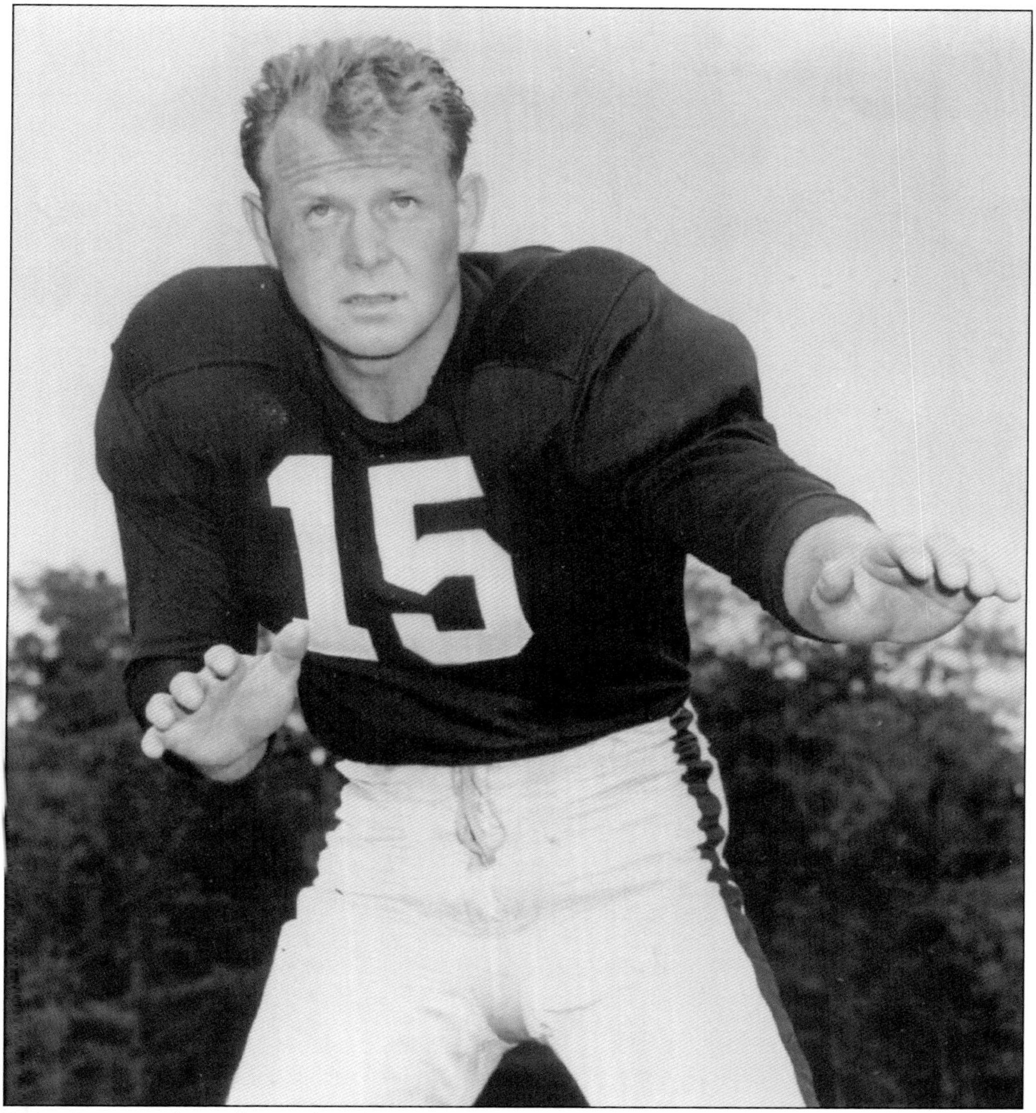

Duke Iversen cleaned out the chicken house first before donning pads to play football for Petaluma High School in the 1930s. A powerful runner, blocker, and tackler, Iversen later played at University of Oregon and professionally with the New York Yankees. When Iversen was at Petaluma, one opposing coach allegedly sent a raw sub in to pick a fight with the Trojan star to get him thrown out of the game. Courtesy of the Duke Iversen collection.

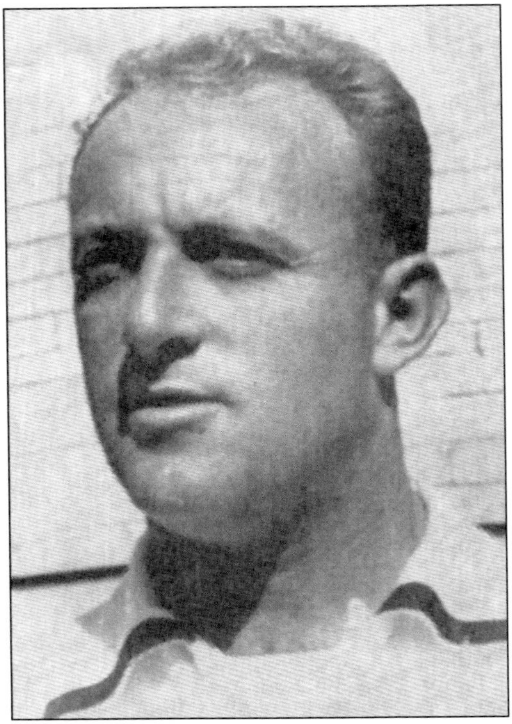

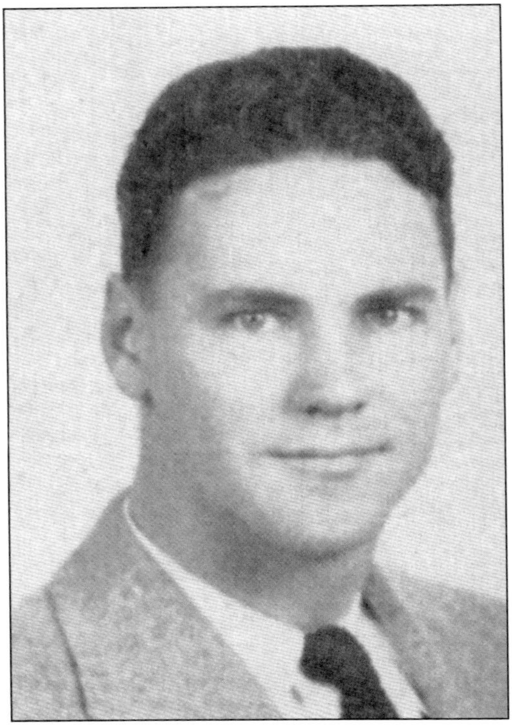

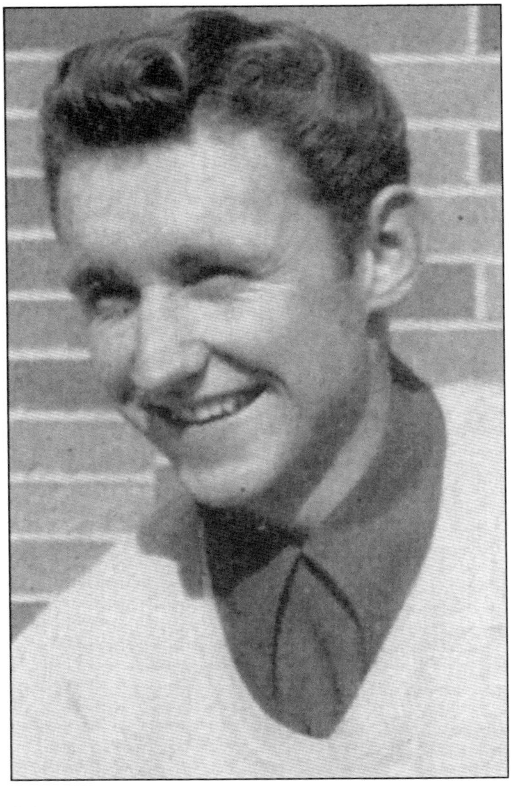

Top Left: Bob Acorne used his speed to his advantage at Petaluma High School, then helped Santa Rosa Junior College win its first football championship in 1938. With veteran Acorne running and pal Gene Benedetti blocking, the Bear Cubs tied for the title again in 1939. After World War II, Acorne and Benedetti helped organize the Petaluma Leghorns club football team.

Top Right: Halfback Bill Charlesworth set a national record by scoring 23 touchdowns for the Bear Cubs in 1949. He shared All-Conference honors with teammates Jack Bonetti, Fred Yost, Don Clare, Tsar Calfee, Ted Dunbar, and Dave Devoto. Courtesy of the Sonoma County Library.

Bottom Left: Shifty halfback Art Liebscher helped Santa Rosa Jr. College's "Nifty in '50" team roll to 12 wins, including a 41-6 triumph over LaSalle-Peru, Illinois, in the Gold Dust Bowl game in Vallejo in December 1950. Liebscher scored twice against Sacramento on 80-yard runs in the season's biggest game. He also led the running attack against LaSalle-Peru.

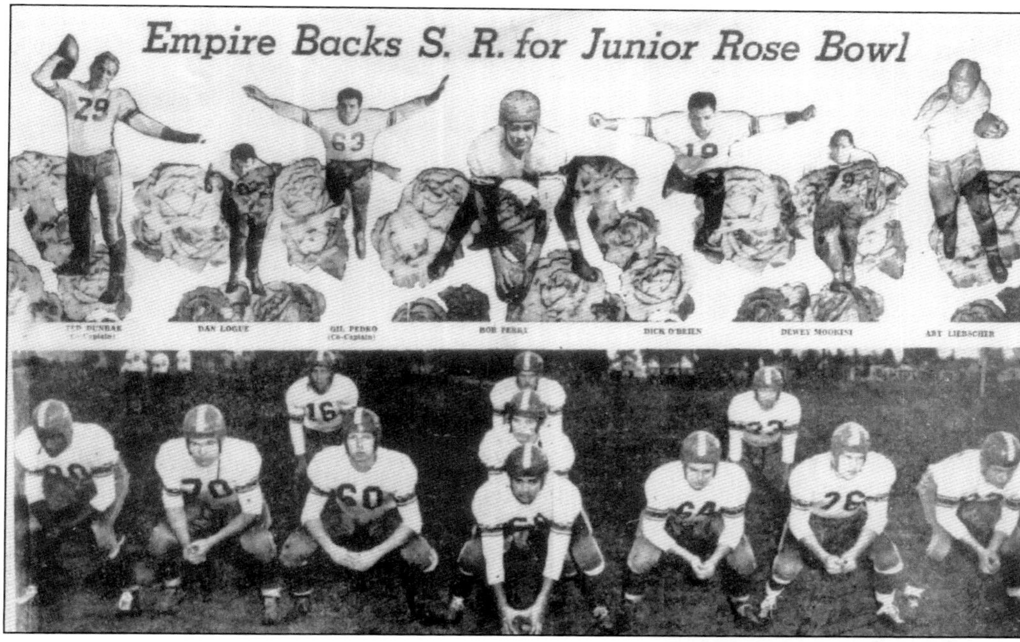

Although Santa Rosa JC was unbeaten in 12 games in 1950, a desired invitation to the Junior Rose Bowl never came. Unfortunately for LaSalle-Peru, the Bear Cubs showed up for the Gold Dust Bowl, beating the Illinois team 41-6. The upper section of the collage shows quarterback and co-captain Ted Dunbar, Dan Logue, co-captain Gil Pedro, Bob Perry, Dick O'Brien, Dewey Mookini, and Art Liebscher. The lower portion shows the starting team, consisting of linemen Marion Sims, Logue, Bill Wallace, Bob Perry, Jim Cusick, Grove Bolles, and Dave Devoto; backs quarterback Ted Dunbar with Jack Retzloff, Gailard Radcliffe, and Art Liebscher behind him. Courtesy of the Sonoma County Museum.

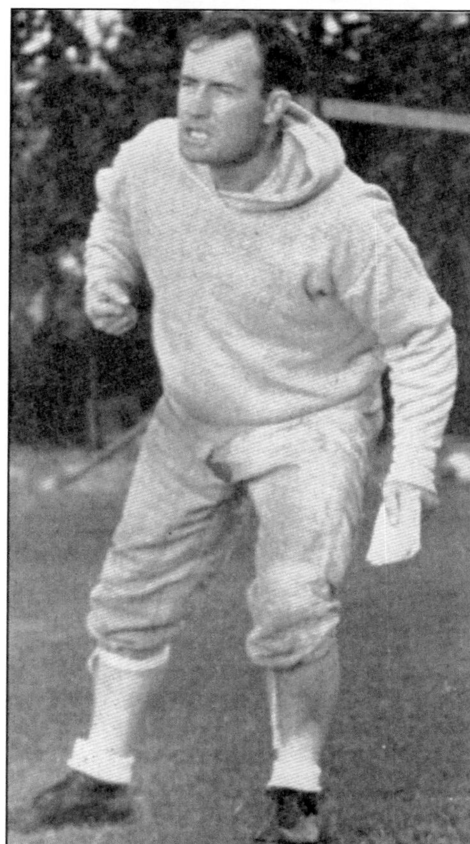

Is he doing a fire dance, putting a curse on opponents, or putting the Santa Rosa JC football squad through a routine drill? Probably the latter, since it was coach Cook Sypher's job to get his gridders in shape for the 1939 season. Dick Blewett, the school's first paid coach, came to SRJC in 1928, and was joined by Sypher in 1936.

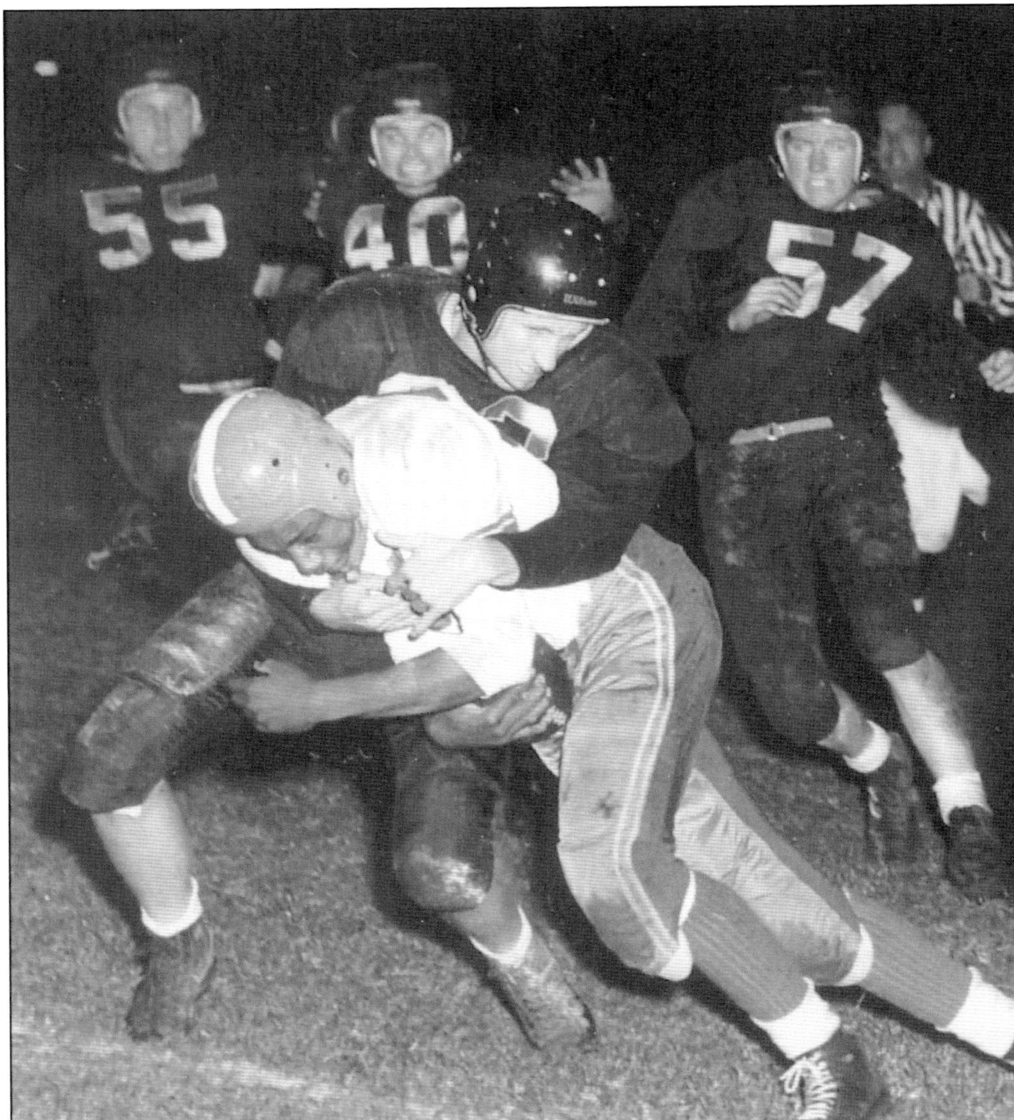

The irresistible force met the immovable object as the Bear Cubs' All-Conference end Marion Sims, surrounded by defenders, tried to grind out yards in a 1950 football game. The Cubs had little trouble scoring, rolling up 462 points while yielding only 62 to opponents, and putting 11 players on the conference first and second teams: Bob Perry, Ted Dunbar, Dave Devoto, Gil Pedro, Art Liebscher, Sims, Gailard Radcliffe, George Najarian, Jack Retzloff, Elvin Case, and Dick O'Brien. Courtesy of the SRJC collection.

Opposite: During football games, her name was Rosco and she prowled the field whipping up cheers for the Santa Rosa Bear Cubs. With the headpiece removed, she turned into a pert young lady who obviously enjoyed her secret identity with the junior college sports program. The mascot cheered on Santa Rosa teams, especially during "Big Game" week against Marin JC. Courtesy of the SRJC collection.

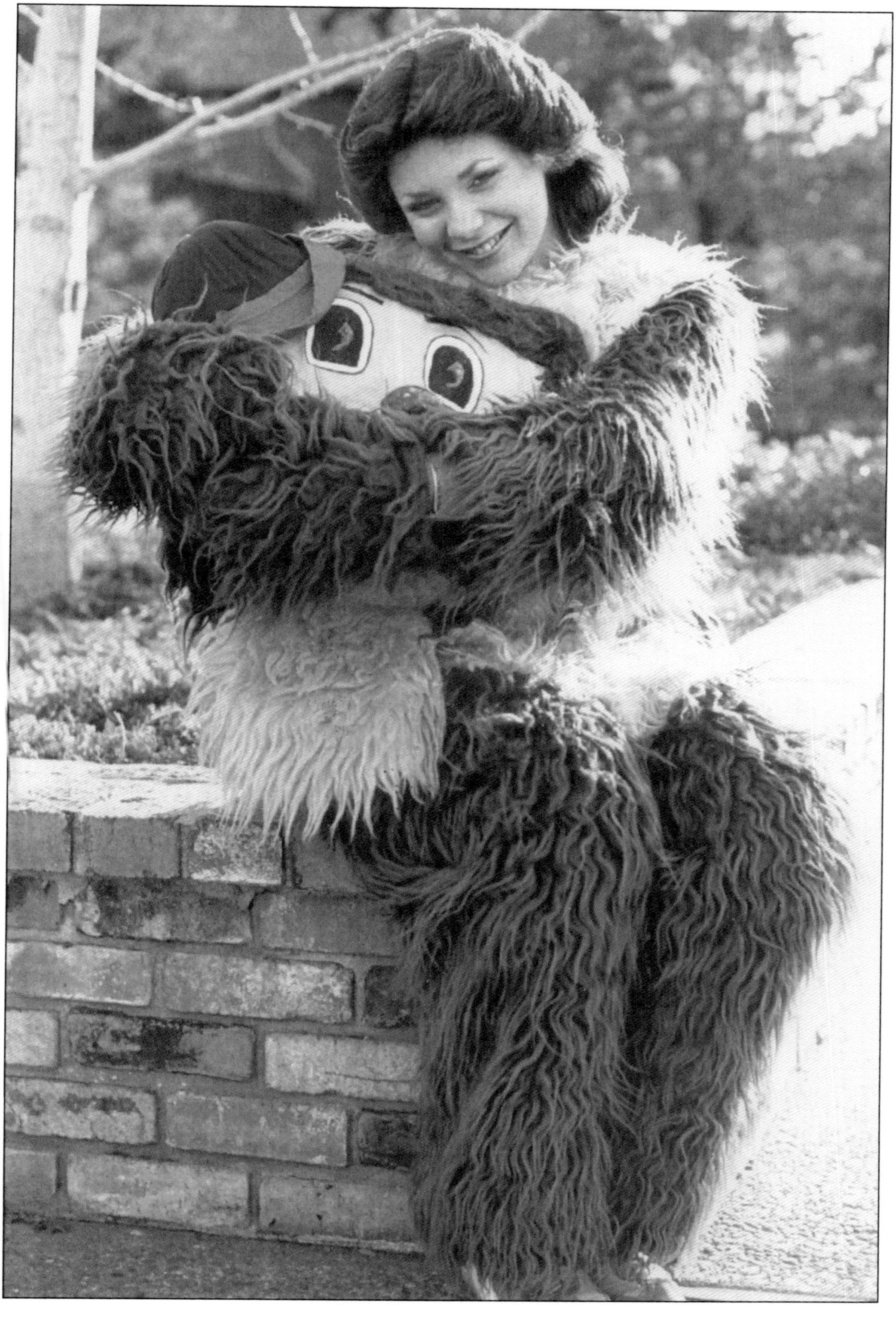

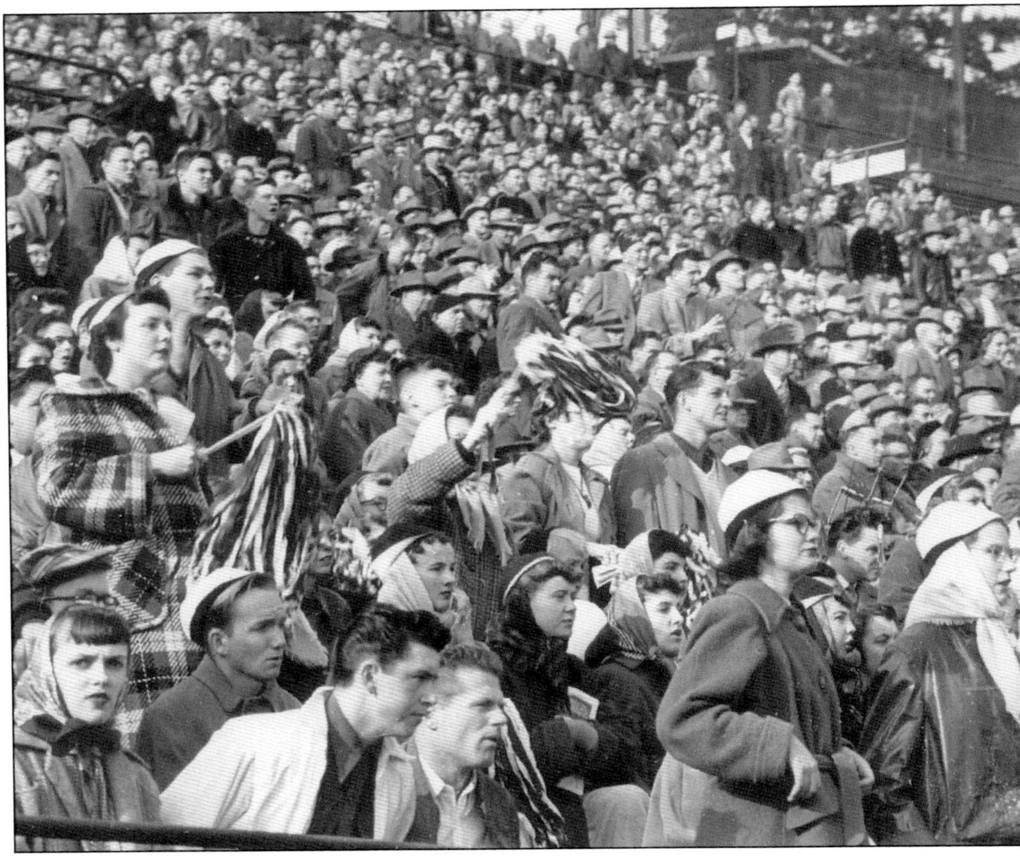

After two championship seasons, Santa Rosa's football team slipped to four wins, six losses and a tie in 1951. Fans gave it their best but had little to cheer about as the Bear Cubs lost in Everett, Washington 66-28. Courtesy of the SRJC collection.

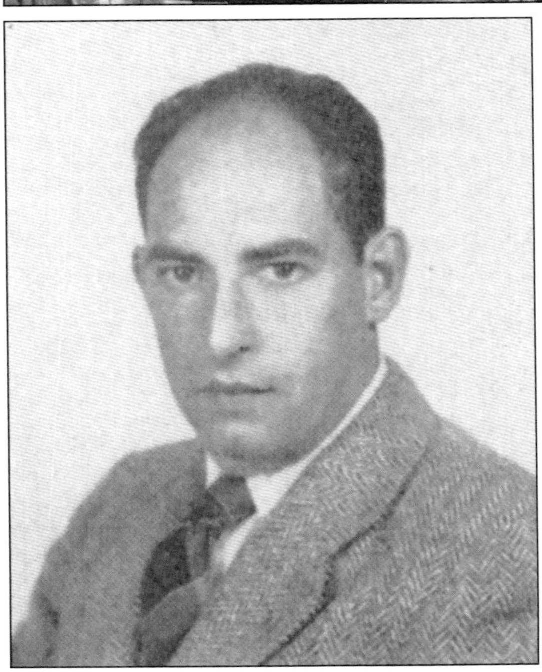

Bill Neel, fresh from the Pappy Waldorf staff at UC Berkeley, turned Santa Rosa Jr. College into a football powerhouse with titles in 1949 and 1950 and a runaway victory in the 1950 Gold Dust Bowl. Courtesy of the Sonoma County Library.

During this 1949 action, Bear Cubs defender Dick O'Brien downed a Vallejo runner in a 66-0 victory. With help from O'Brien and other defenders, quarterback Ted Dunbar and scatback Bill Charlesworth led the attack for the Bear Cubs. Courtesy of the Sonoma County Library.

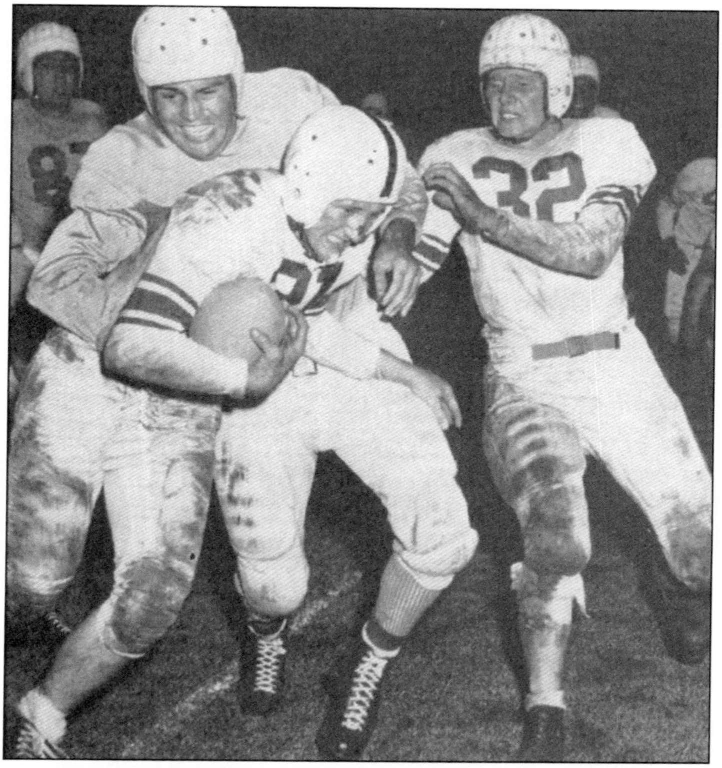

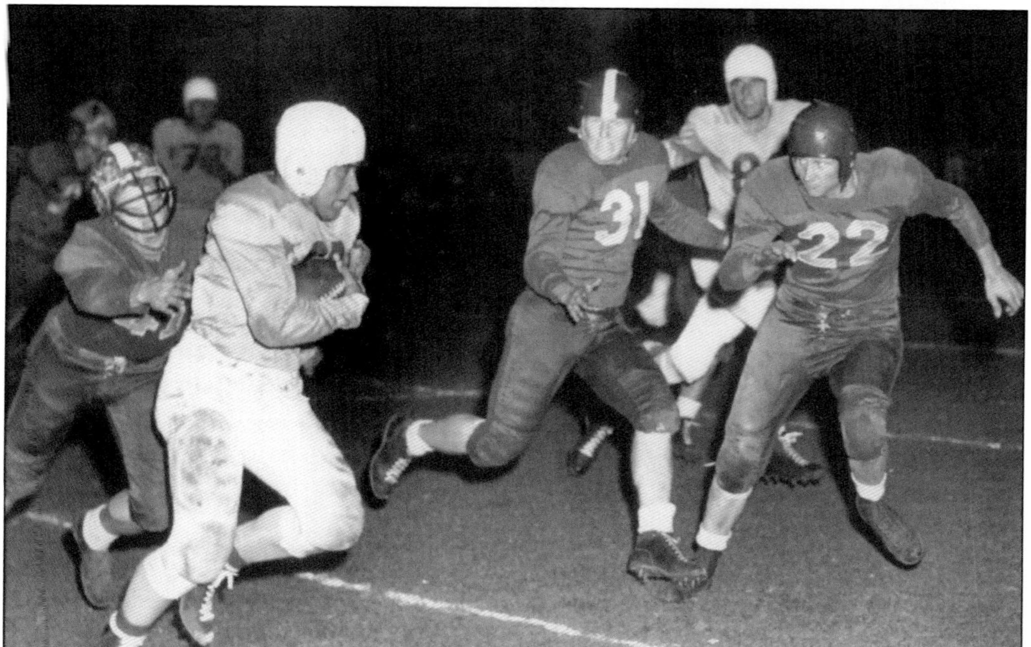

Lineman and team captain Don Clare got a chance to play a little offense, running back an intercepted pass in the 66-0 rout of Vallejo. Courtesy of the SRJC collection.

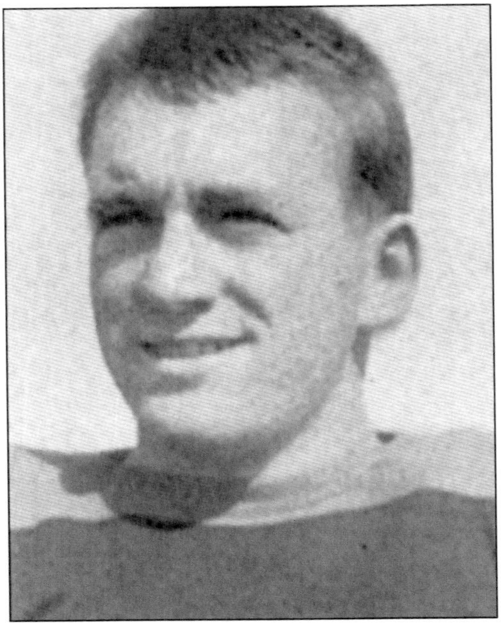

Joe Kelly, Santa Rosa High School football captain, "won one for dad" in 1933. After his father died in the hospital the day of the game, Kelly raced to the field to lead his team to a 12-7 victory over Analy. Observers said Kelly "played like a maniac" in tribute to his father.

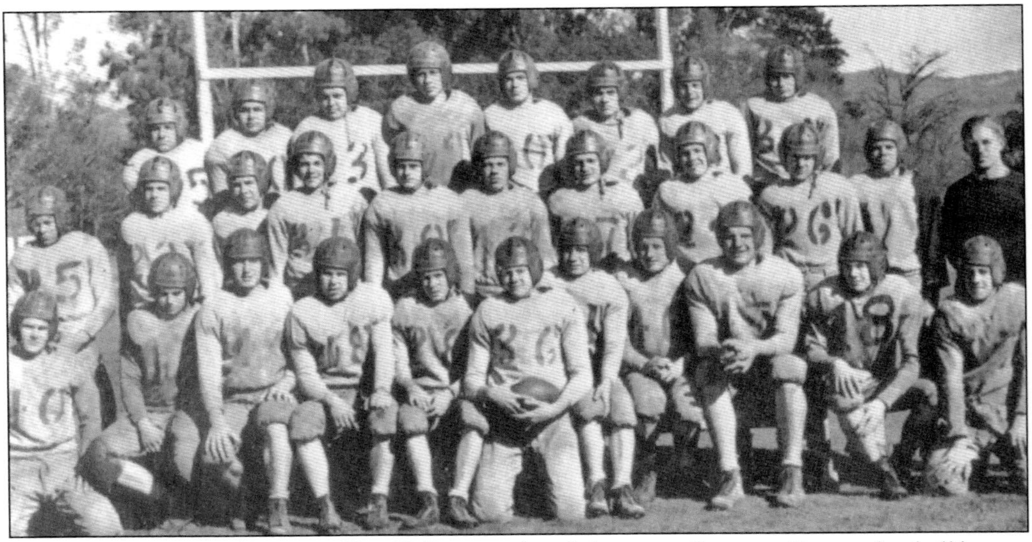

Ernie Nevers, Biff Hoffman, and Joe Kelly were already longtime Sonoma County football heroes by the time Sonoma High School fielded its first team in 1944. With nearly 30 candidates turning out, the team opened the season with a 13-6 win over the Petaluma Ramblers. By 1951, with Clarence Edsall coaching and elusive Dean Kime running, Sonoma won the North Bay League Section II championship. Team members, pictured here in 1944, are: (back row, from left) Rick Maffioli, Robert Ruise, Dick Such, Norman Krebs, Kenneth Phillips, Bill Oliver, Jack Winschell, and Jim Jangula; (middle) Ed Ernest, Robert Knox, Don Sample, Thomas Craig Smith, Norman Rider, Dale Stokes, Frank LaHaye, Kai Grant Thomsen, George Custer, George Block, and coach Clarence Pyke; (front) Gilbert Sample, Joseph Martini, John Rich, Robert Larson, George McGimsey, Lester Lahr, Gonzalo Escamilla Monarque, Angelo Pedroncelli, Charles (Porky) Bishop, Earn Horne, and Donald Simpson. Courtesy of the Sonoma Depot Park Museum.

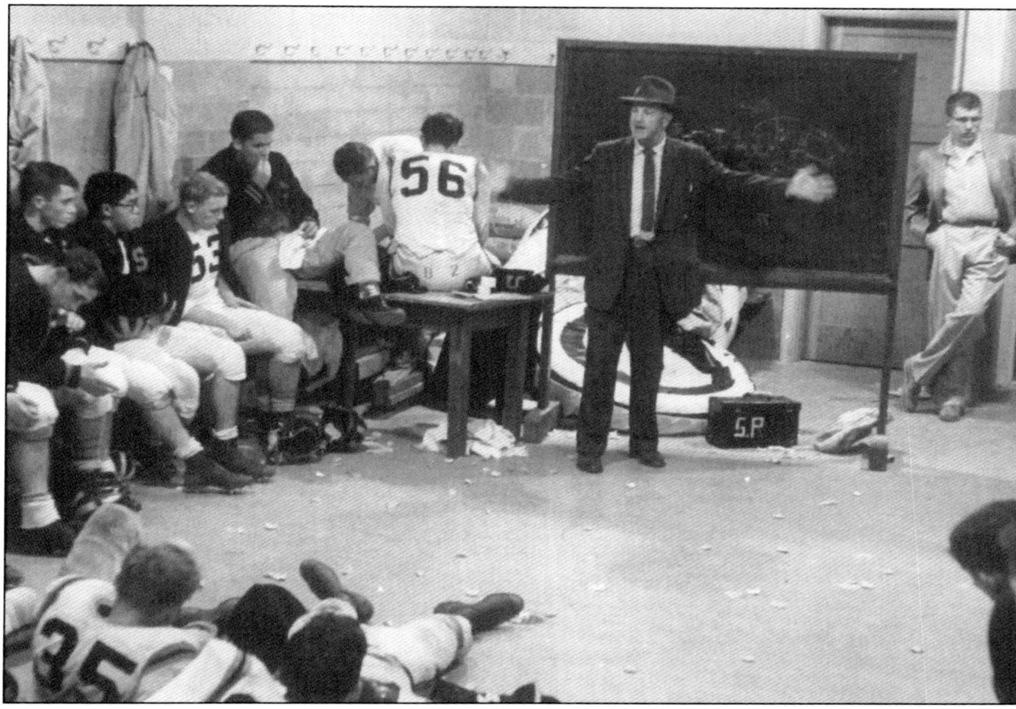

Battered but hardly beaten, Santa Rosa Panthers football team listened to a halftime pep talk by master motivator Jimmy Underhill. Underhill not only knew how to get his team in the right mood for winning, but was known to use psychological techniques on his opponent, such as bringing his team on the field at the very last minute before the end of the halftime break. Underhill was a bruising halfback at St. Mary's College in the 1920s. Coaching at Santa Rosa High, he won five football championships and five baseball titles. Courtesy of John LeBaron.

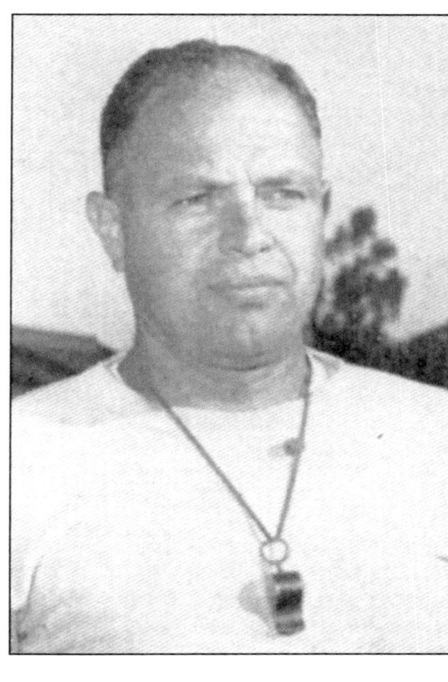

Coach Bill Abbey put a note on the locker room bulletin board in 1950 that read, "The last time we beat Santa Rosa, our seniors were in the fourth grade." The motivational message worked as the Trojans beat their traditional rival and went on to win the North Bay League title. Abbey went undefeated in 1952, winning another NBL crown. Between 1950 and 1953, his teams were champions three times.

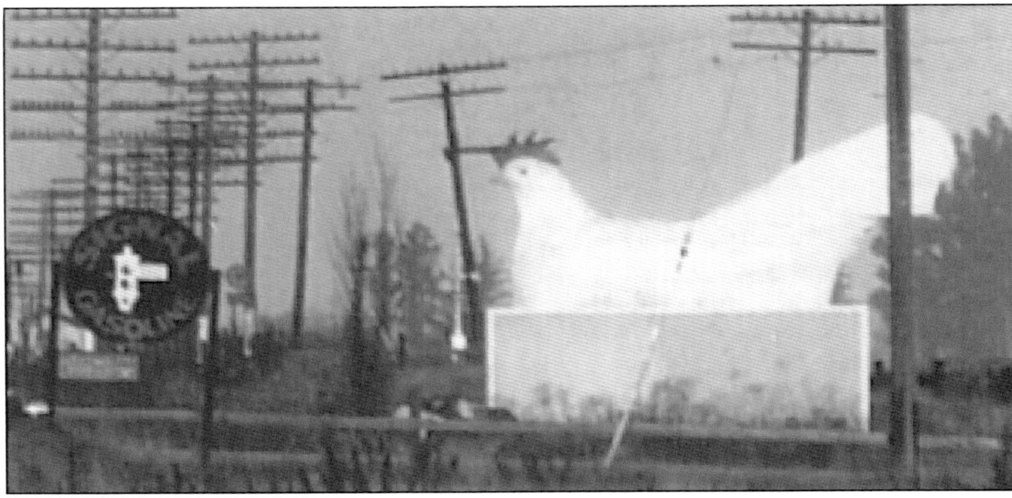

The Petaluma chicken stood at the south end of the Egg City, a symbol of all that was hated by neighboring towns, some in Marin County, others north in Santa Rosa. The clucker was a frequent target of attack, especially during the football season. In 1938, somebody planted a bomb in the bird's innards. The fowl blew to pieces, leaving patrons at the nearby Colony Club wondering what the bartender had put in their drinks. Bewildered motorists zig-zagged around chunks of stucco, twisted wire, and sticks that littered the road. Courtesy of the Virginia Hein collection, Petaluma Museum.

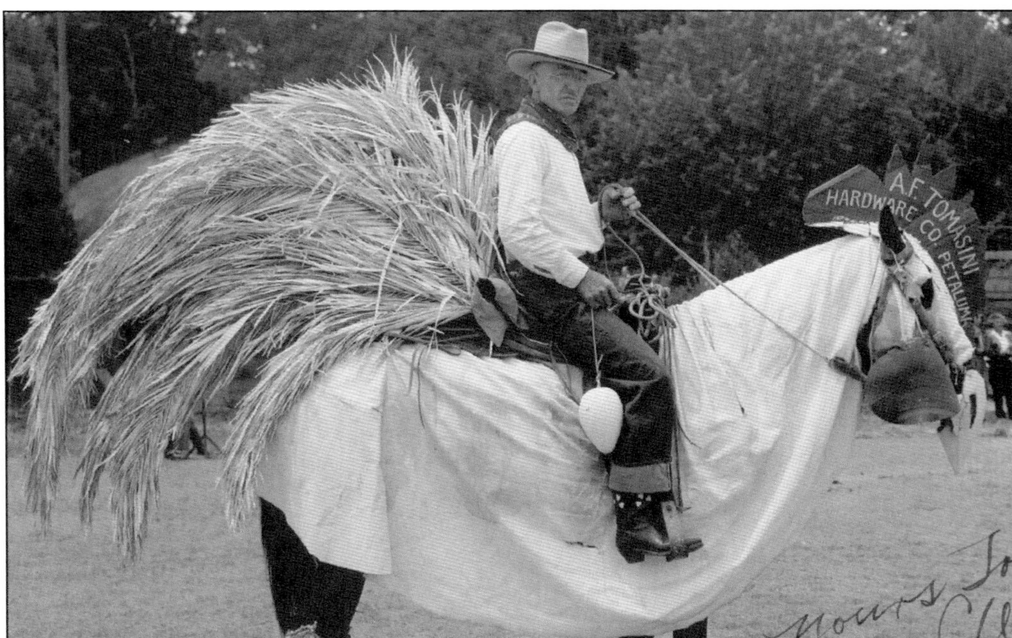

No doubt about it, Petalumans had a fixation about chickens, to such an extent that some people even decorated their horses to look like the Egg City's favorite fowl. James Wayne, representing Tomasini Hardware Store, rode a "horse dressed as a chicken" in a 1945 parade. The sight of a Petaluma chicken, real or imagined, often drew the ire of teenagers from nearby towns. Courtesy of the George Tomasini collection.

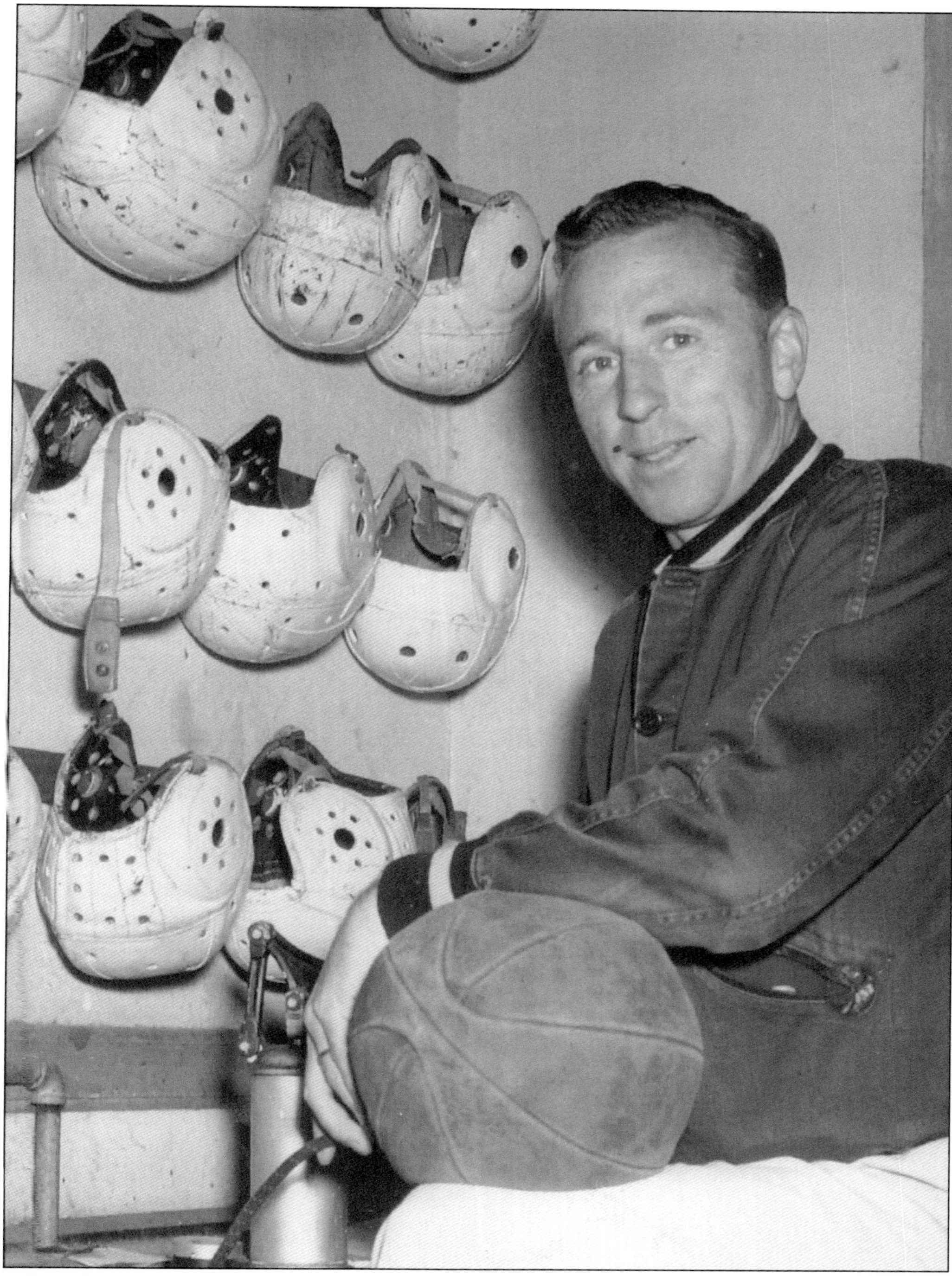

When the seasons changed, Analy's adaptable coach Walt Foster hung up the football helmets and pumped up a basketball to start the cage season. In small schools like Analy, many athletes played several sports, sometimes participating in two different sports on the same day. The helmets on the wall bear little resemblance to modern helmets in terms of padding and facial protection. Courtesy of the Foster collection.

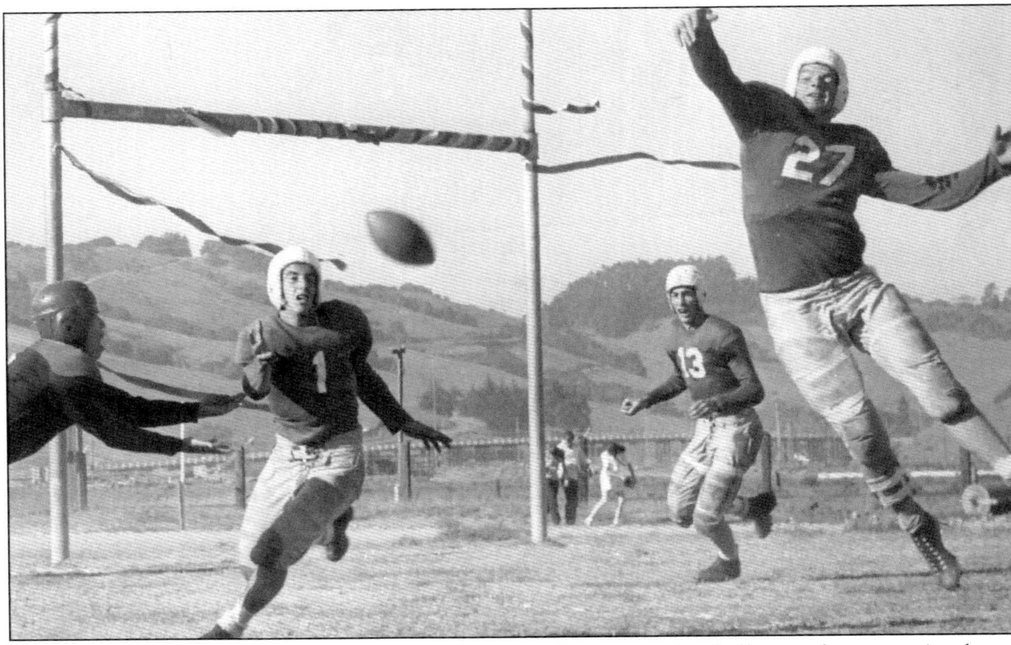

It could have been the Swan Lake ballet, but actually it was a football game between Analy and Tamalpais High Schools in 1947. Wolfe and Garcia provided the footwork, while Wester looked on in awe and a Tamalpais receiver looked on in despair. Courtesy of the Foster collection.

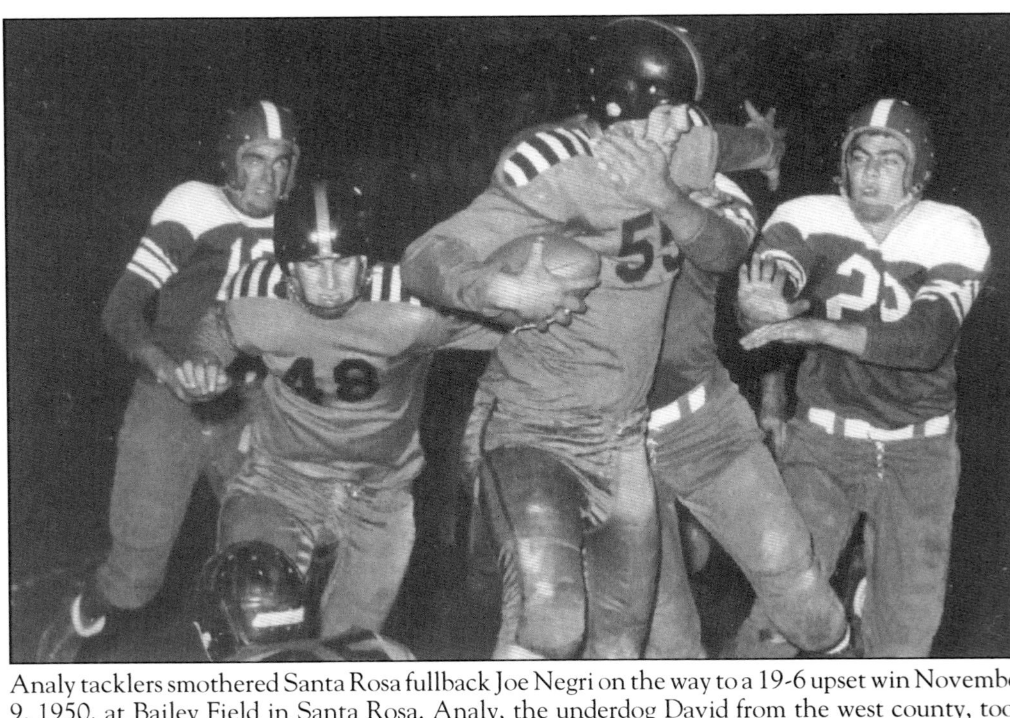

Analy tacklers smothered Santa Rosa fullback Joe Negri on the way to a 19-6 upset win November 9, 1950, at Bailey Field in Santa Rosa. Analy, the underdog David from the west county, took pride in upending the Goliath from the county seat in Santa Rosa. Two years earlier, Analy, a 20-point underdog, tied the Panthers 13-13. Courtesy of the Foster collection.

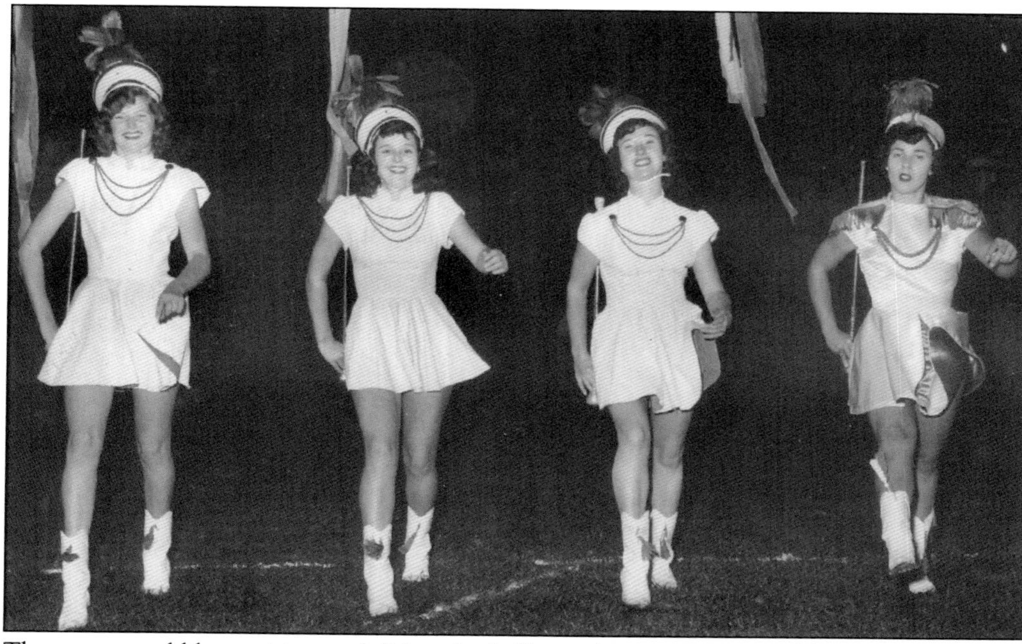

The games could be exciting or dull but the halftime shows were irresistible, especially if they involved an attractive quartet of ladies, such as the Analy majorettes of 1952. Strutting their stuff are, from left, Irma Allred, Barbara Fowler, Darlene Purcell, and Frances Frigerio. Courtesy of the Foster collection.

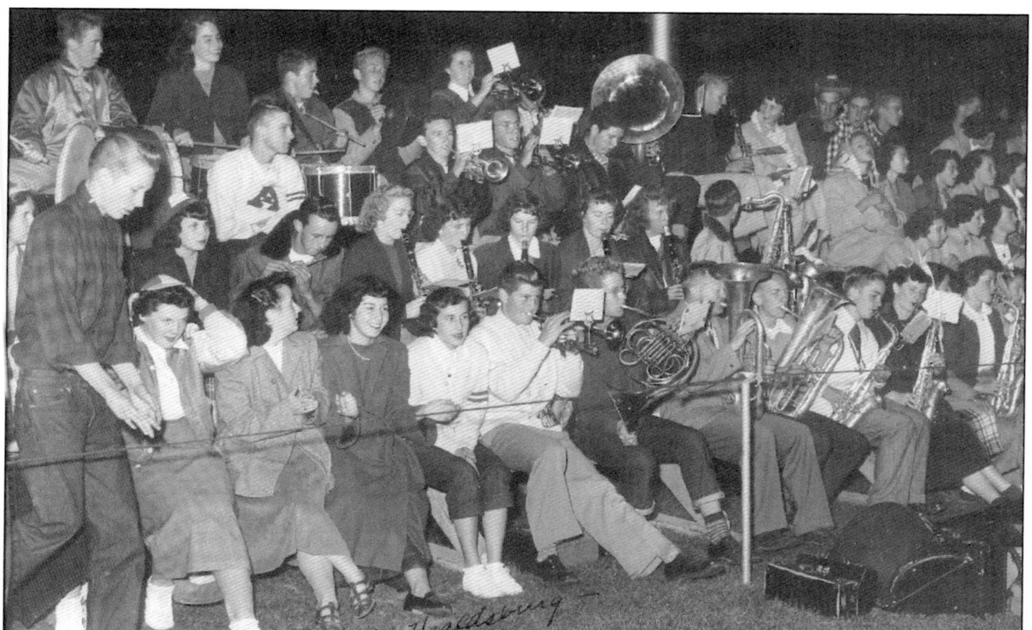

The action was hot and heavy on the sidelines when prep teams got together to fight it out on the football field for a year's worth of "bragging rights." The Analy band and rooting section did its bit at an Analy-Healdsburg game.

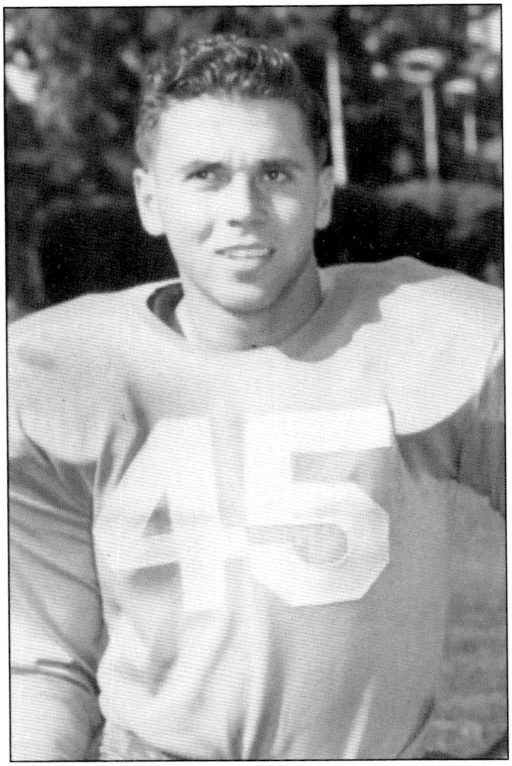

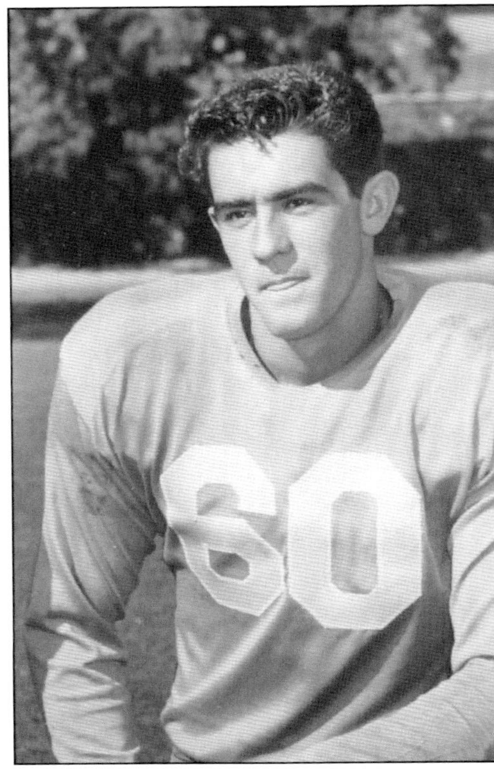

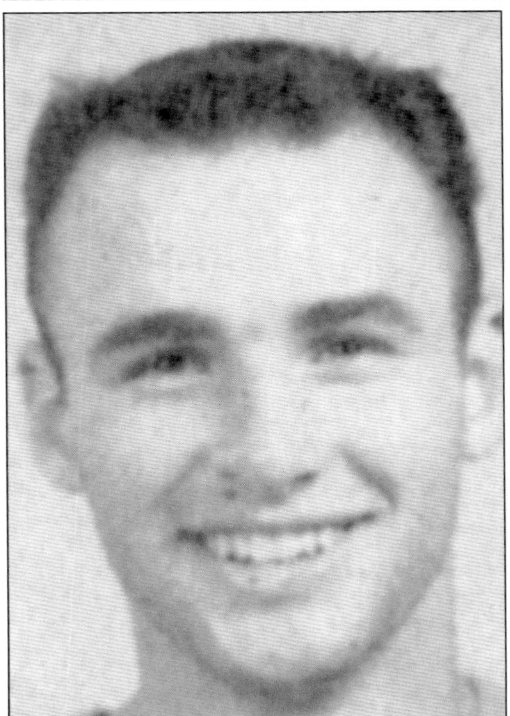

Top Left: Fullback Bill Schleth helped Petaluma High's ball control game in 1950. When Santa Rosa threatened to upset the Trojans, Schleth broke a 51-yard touchdown run that won the game for the Egg City team. He later played at Santa Rosa Junior College. Courtesy of the SRJC collection.

Top Right: Guard Tom Louderback played at Petaluma and Santa Rosa Jr. College and eventually became an outstanding lineman with the Oakland Raiders. He's seen here at SRJC in 1951. Courtesy of the SRJC collection. .

Bottom Left: Halfback Jim Eaglin led the Petaluma Trojans' running attack that helped the 1952 team to a 9-0 record. The following year, Eaglin returned to help Petaluma to another league crown. Courtesy of the Petaluma Museum.

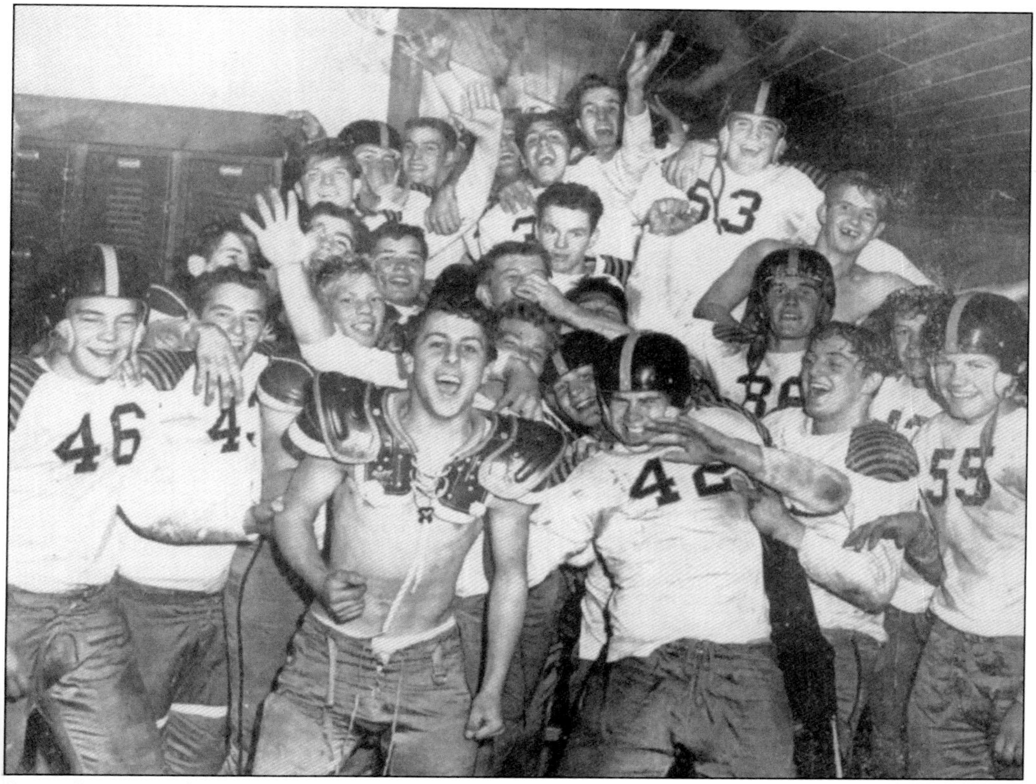

Santa Rosa Panthers football team celebrated the end of nine years of frustration after a 42-0 win over Vallejo. Topless halfback Fred Giannini led the cheers. Among identifiable players are: fullback Doug Camilli (46); guard Jim Michaels (43); Giannini; center Don Read (42); Paul Litka and tackle Arlin Schneider in front row; a row back, to the left of the player holding his nose is Hans Rothert; holding his nose is Pete Mazzucchi; to his right Chet Hamamoto (top of head visible) and halfback Warren Rile; above Hamamoto is Dick Underhill, son of Coach Jimmy Underhill and to his right Dick Codding showing his tooth gap; behind Underhill is Frank Giannini and to his right Bob Stone (53); and at the top is Don Trowbridge. The backfield of Lary Robbins, Len Read, Chet Hamamoto, and Warren Rile combined to form perhaps the greatest scoring machine in the school's history, until a rainy November night when they were blanked 19-0 by Petaluma. Courtesy of the SRHS Foundation.

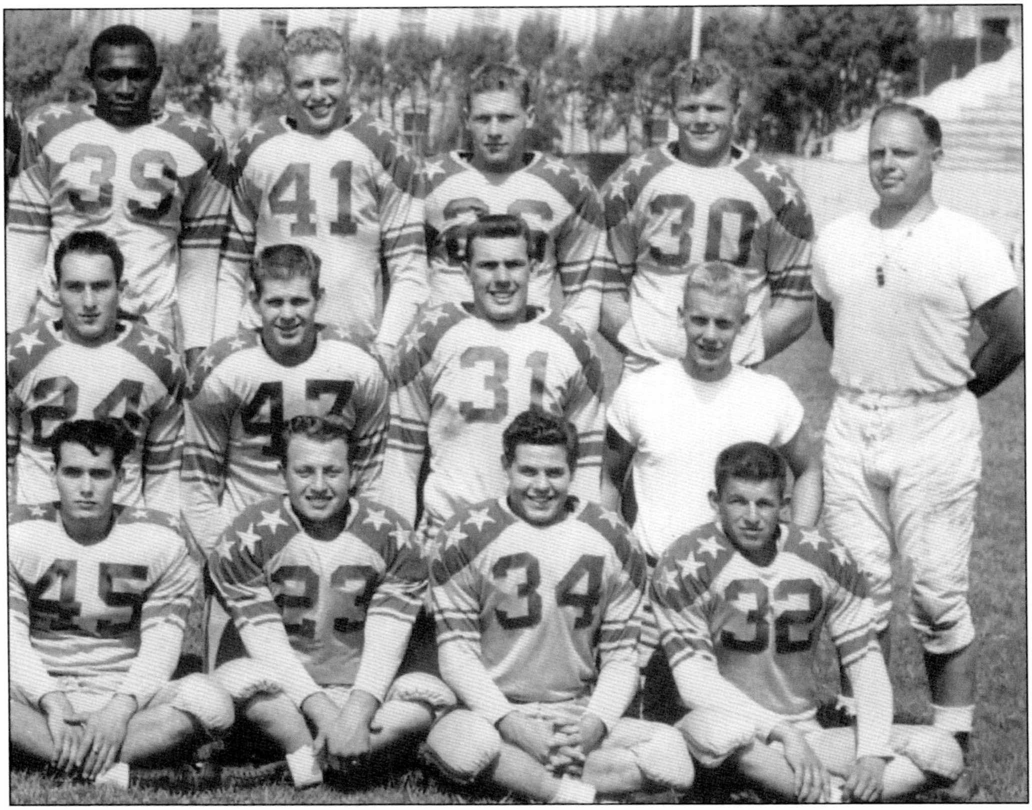

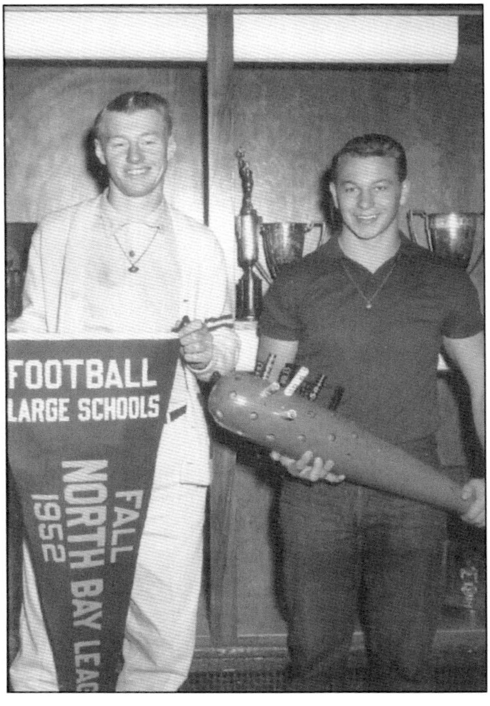

It was a thrill for several Sonoma County football stars to take part in the North-South prep game in Los Angeles in 1953. Bolstering the north team was, front row, from the left, speedy Santa Rosa halfback Warren Rile and Petaluma lineman Frances Garzoli. In the second row, second from the left, is Santa Rosa center Don Read. Don Bossert, to the left of Read, also played in the game and later became a coach at Analy High School. At the far right is Petaluma coach Bill Abbey, who piloted the Trojans to a North Bay League championship in 1952 with a 19-0 win over Santa Rosa. Courtesy of the Rile collection.

Don Paulsen (left) and quarterback D.R. Mobley hold up pennant and club, symbolic of Petaluma High School's victory over Santa Rosa in the championship game in 1952. Mobley threw two touchdown passes to lead the Trojans to a 19-0 victory. Courtesy of Alan Miner collection.

Defying gravity, Petaluma High's cheerleaders rose to new heights on a pleasant day in the fall of 1952. How did the young folks manage to hang in the air like that? A spy suggested it might have had something to do with airbrushing a ladder out of the picture. The cheerleaders, from the top, are Alan Milner, Twyla Rowley, Jonna Roth, and Alvin Stein. Courtesy of the Petaluma Museum.

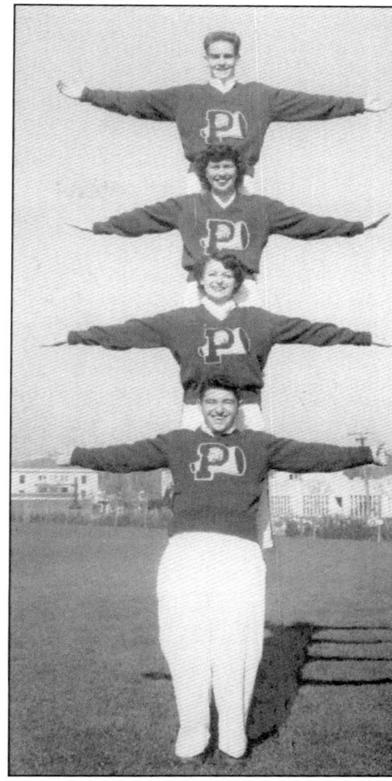

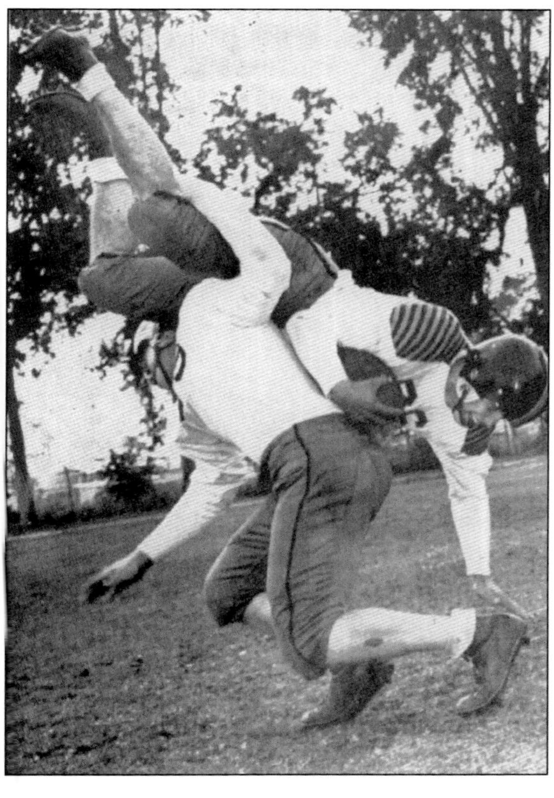

Santa Rosa halfback Warren Rile saw the world upside-down after he was upended during a practice in 1952 by teammate Arlin Schneider. Few tacklers had success against the versatile Rile, especially when the Panther halfback led a 42-0 romp over archrival Vallejo. The Panthers scored 275 points in their first seven games. Courtesy of the 1953 Echo yearbook.

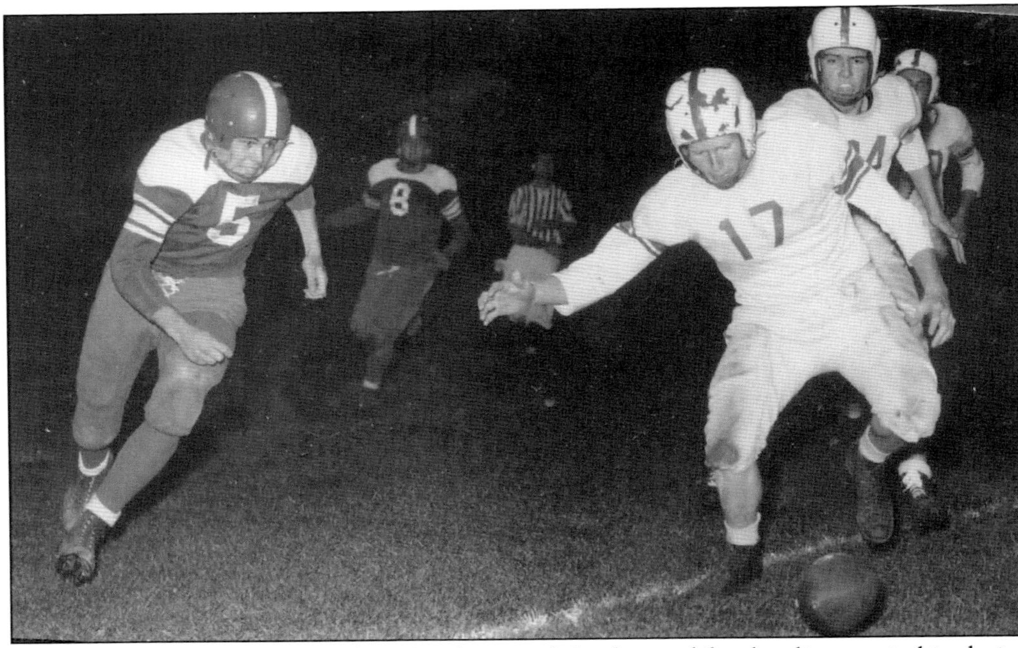

"Hey, there's the ball." Players from Petaluma and Analy raced for the slippery pigskin during their 1951 game at Analy. The west county Tigers made it tough on their traditional rivals, the Santa Rosa Panthers, holding the "big city" boys to a 0-0 tie, but Petaluma got most of the bounces in a 47-6 win. Courtesy of the Foster collection.

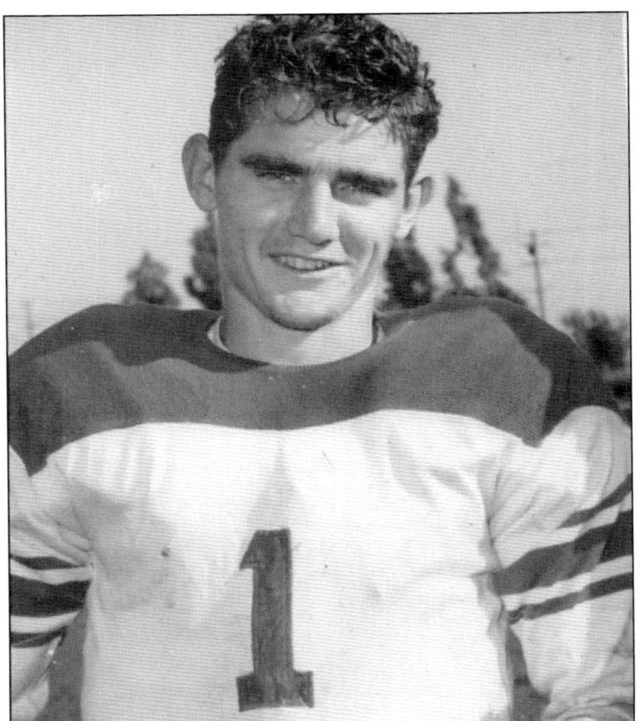

Quarterback Mike Parmeter was a key man in leading the Analy football attack in the late 1940s. It was a Parmeter-to-Bill-Scheidecker pass that keyed a 13-13 tie against heavily-favored Santa Rosa in 1948. Courtesy of the Foster collection.

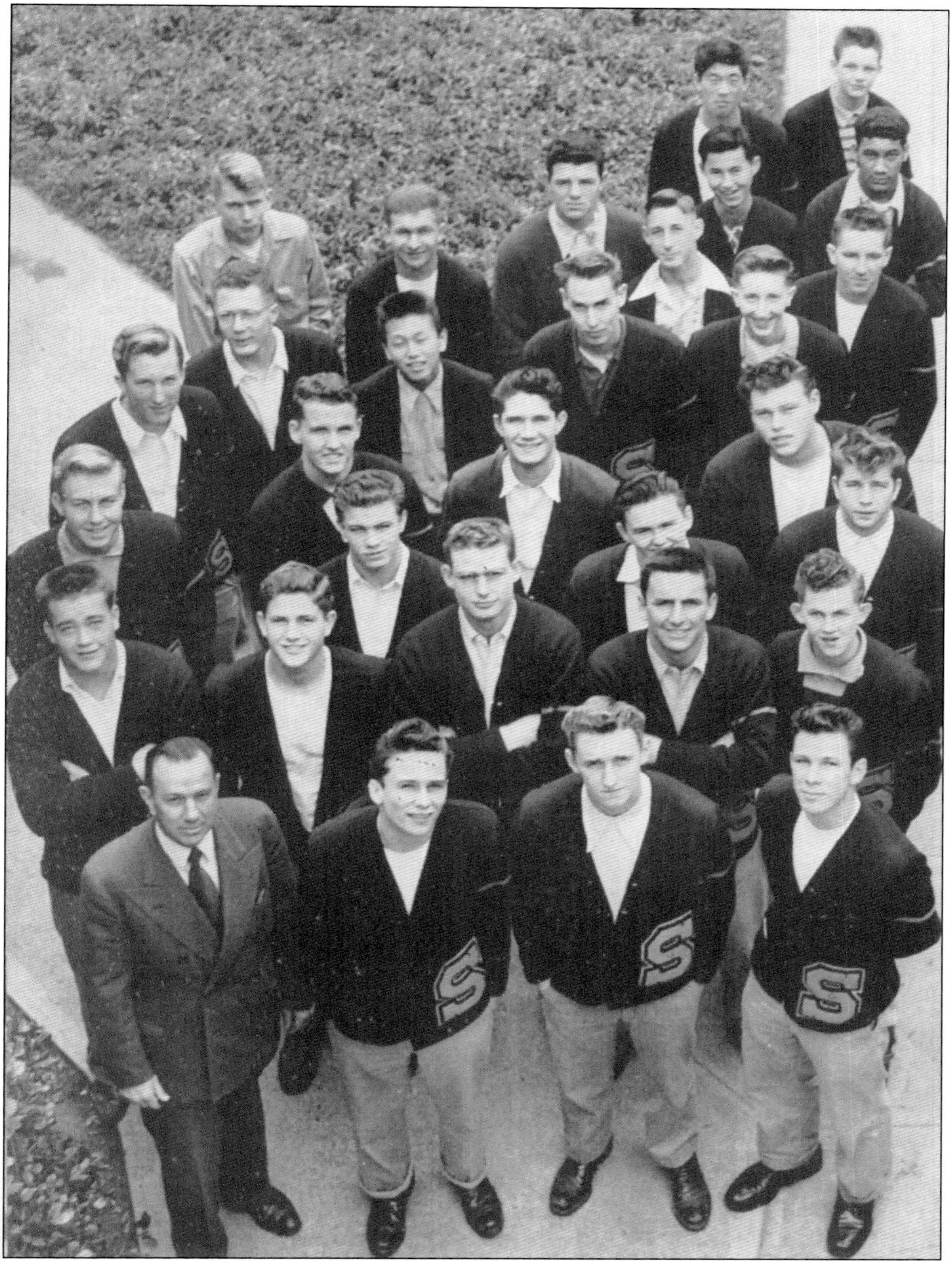

An eagle-eye view caught the Santa Rosa Block S Society with advisor Orb Fortier in 1950. Courtesy of the 1950 Echo yearbook.

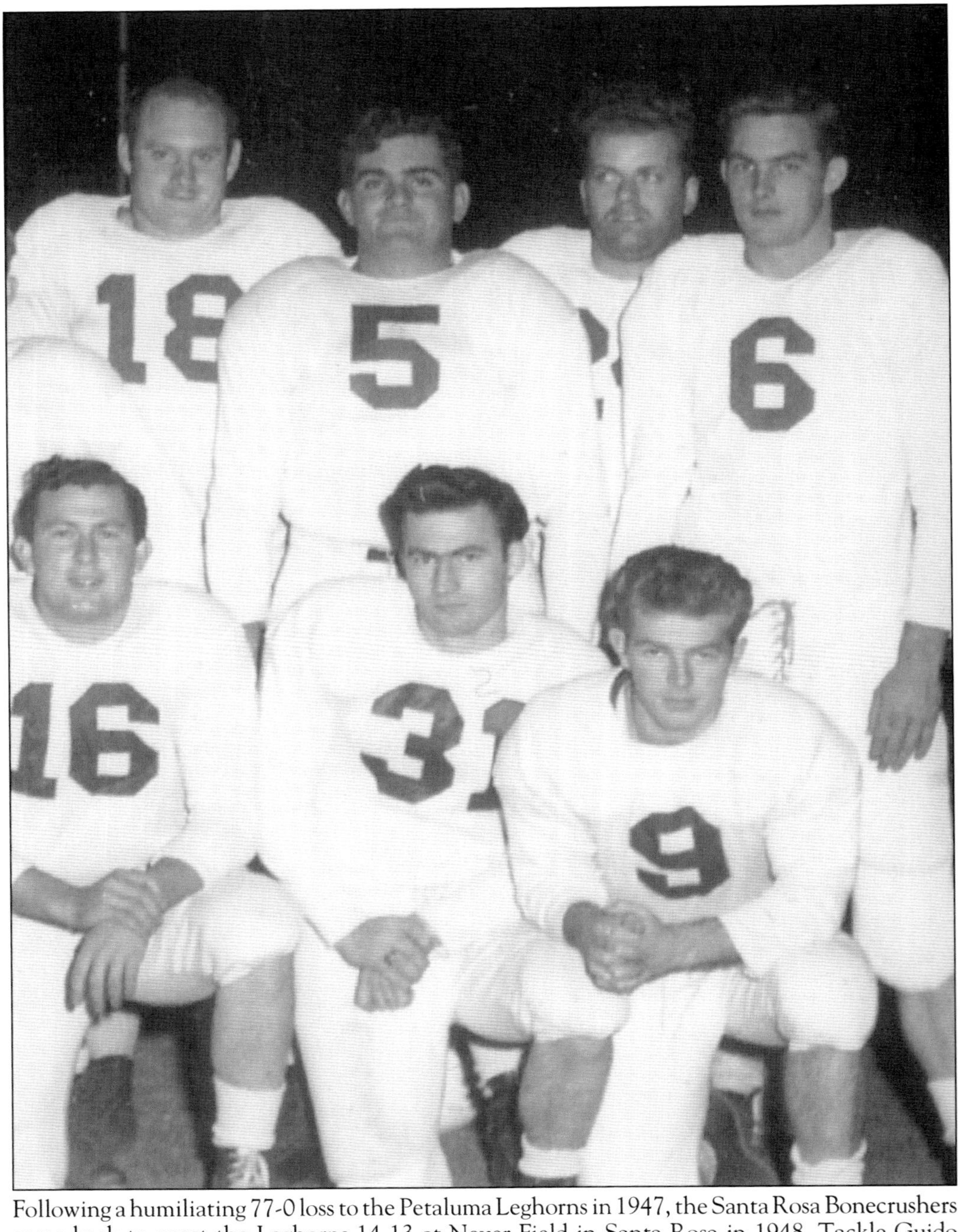

Following a humiliating 77-0 loss to the Petaluma Leghorns in 1947, the Santa Rosa Bonecrushers came back to upset the Leghorns 14-13 at Never Field in Santa Rosa in 1948. Tackle Guido Lorenzini kicked two extra points, which ultimately gave the Santa Rosans a one-point win. After the game, the Crushers were accused of wetting down the field, a controversy that raged for the next several years. Crushers on the "water bowl" team included, from left: (back row) John Fitzgerald, Lou Bertoli, "The Toe" Lorenzini, and an unknown player; (front row) Rod Barnett, Lou Bianchini, and scatback Wilbur Reine. Courtesy of the Guido Lorenzini collection.

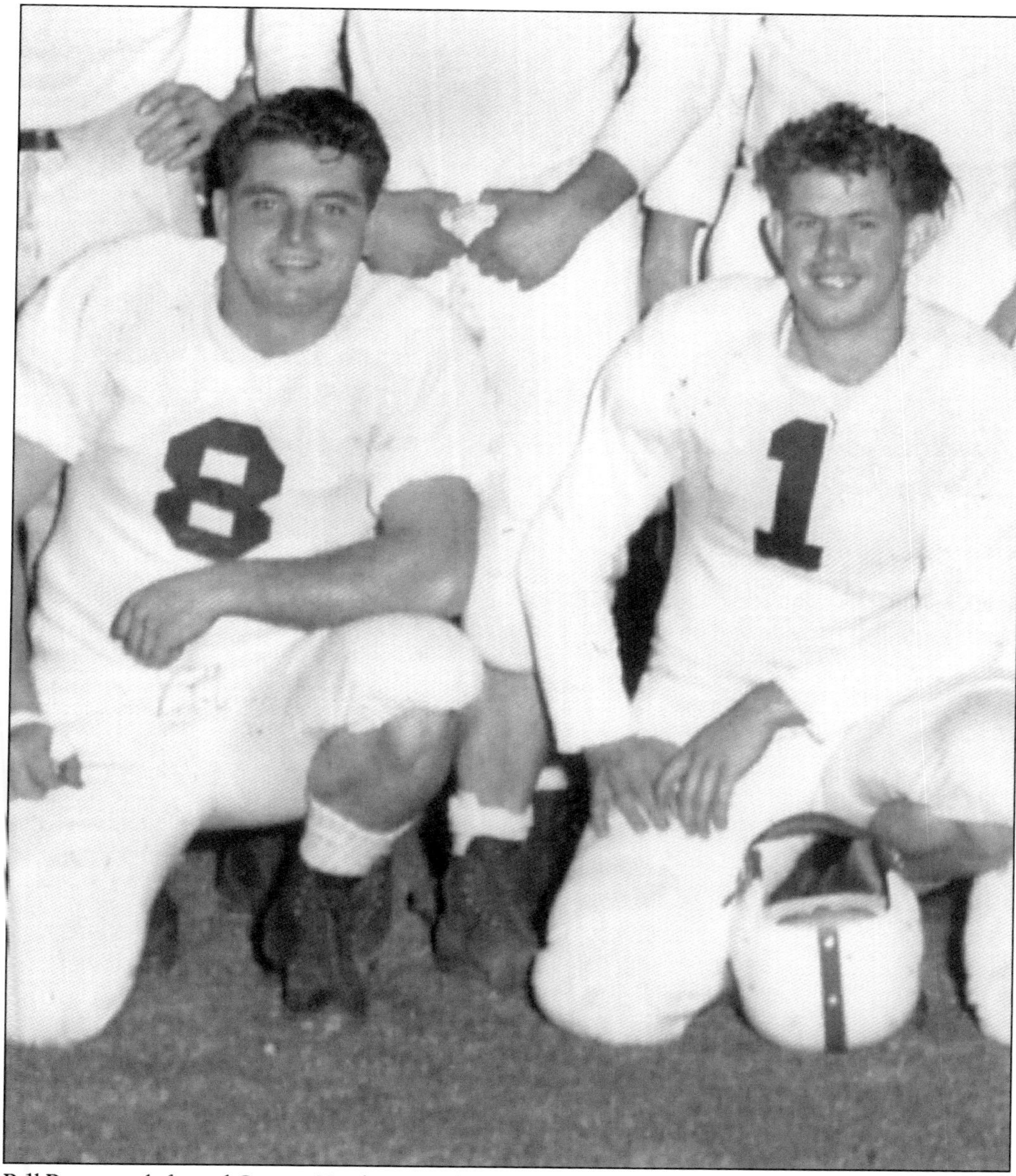

Bill Bottasso, left, and George Treder provided offensive punch for the Crushers in 1948. Bottasso caught one pass for a touchdown and scored another on a 60-yard run in the "water bowl" game. With Lorenzini's PATs, it was enough to upset Petaluma. Courtesy of the Lorenzini collection.

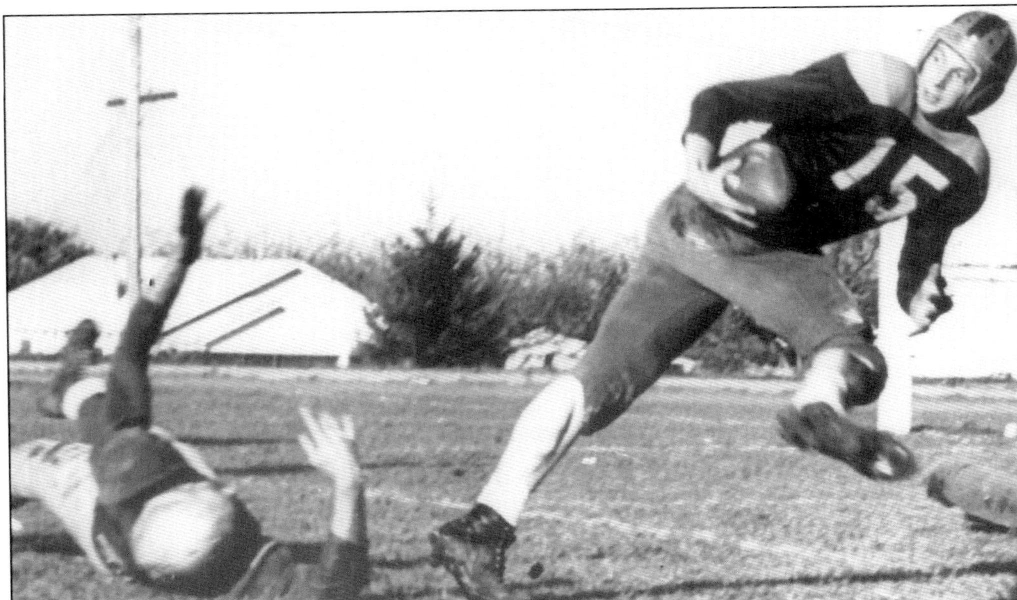

Leghorn end Ray Moneymaker made a big gain after snagging a pass and slipping out of the grasp of a defender. The Leghorns ran up a streak of 26 games without a loss, sponsored the Egg Bowl game, and drew capacity crowds at Durst Field in Petaluma. Courtesy of the Sonoma County Museum.

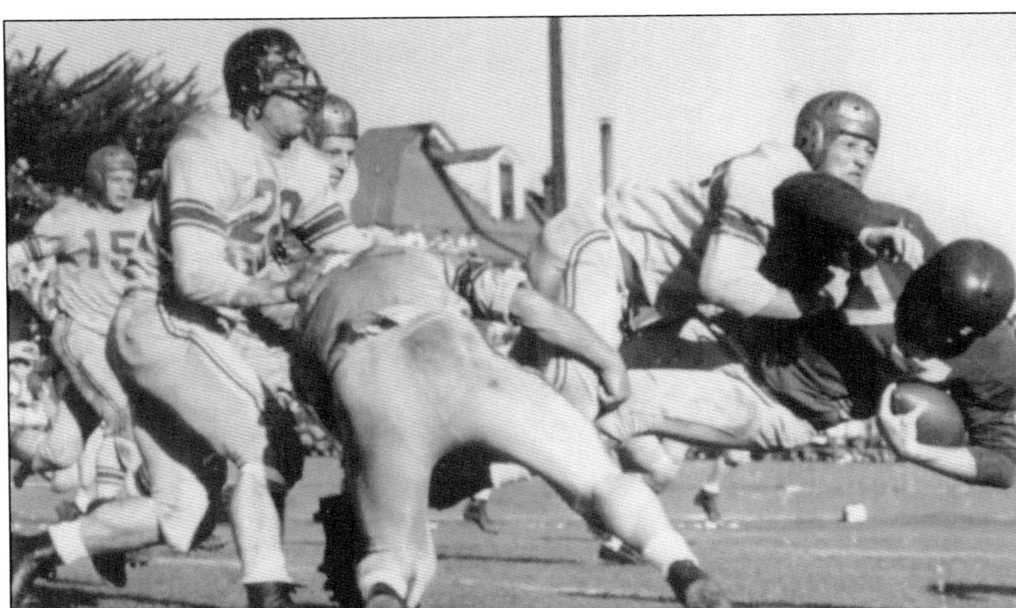

Leghorn defenders surrounded a runner during action at Durst Field in Petaluma. Halfback John Finney, formerly of University of San Francisco, made the tackle. Pat Henry, with the face mask, and Ken McNulty, helped out. Courtesy of the Sonoma County Museum.

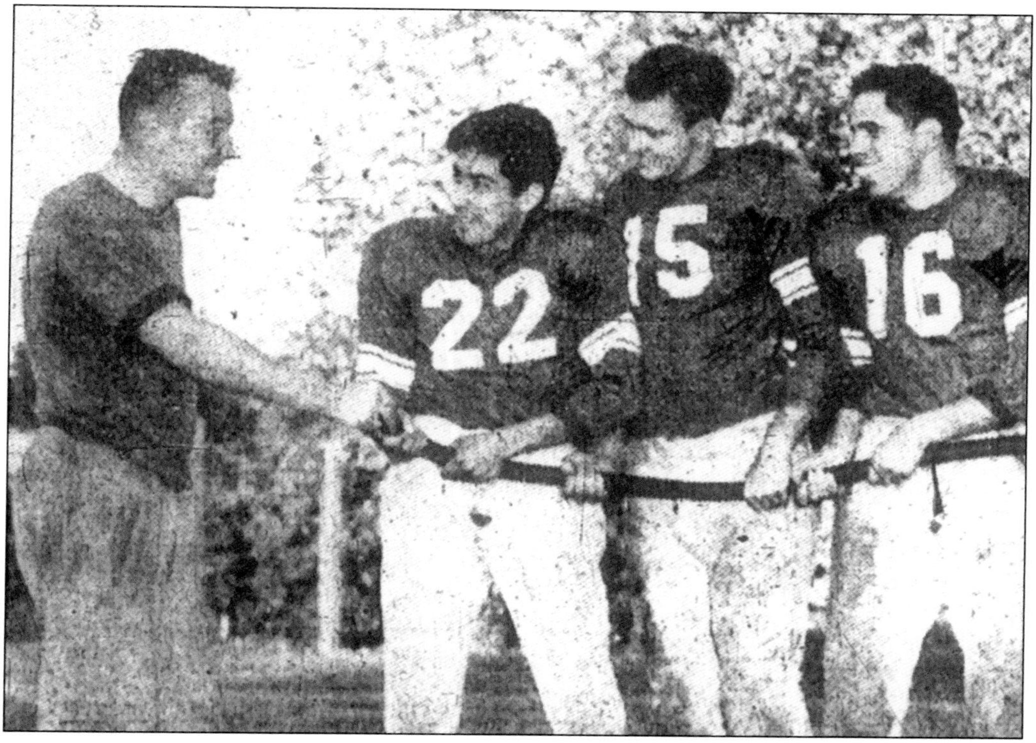

It may never be known whether the Bonecrushers intentionally watered down the field before their game with the hated Leghorns in 1948. Whatever the facts, the teams took advantage of the controversy to promote future games. In 1949, several Crushers posed in a canoe prior to the game with Petaluma. In 1950, Leghorn end Bud Chadwick (far left) tried to block several Crushers from hosing down the field. The Crusher players pictured here are, from the left, Rico Cruz, Bob Shestek, and Dick Gorman. Soaked or not, George Legorio and John Finney scored three touchdowns each as the Leghorns drowned SRAC 53-0 in 1950. Courtesy of the *Press Democrat*.

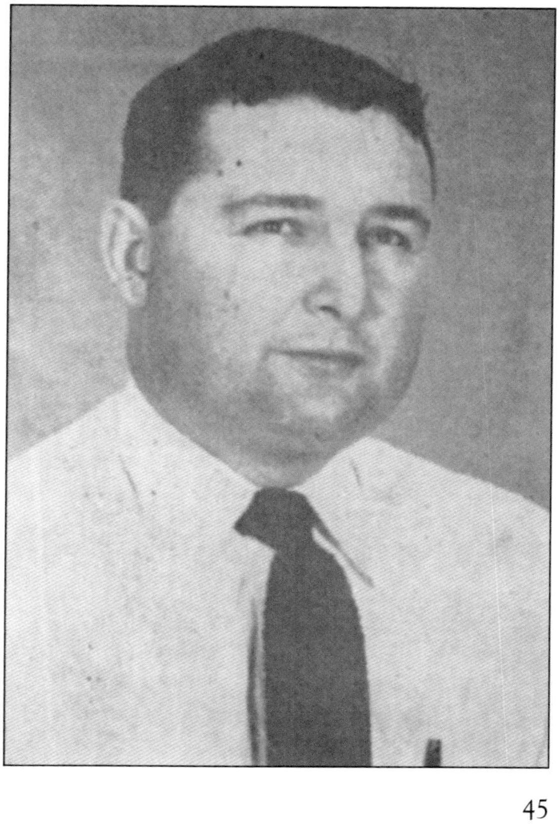

Gene Benedetti helped organize the Petaluma Leghorns for a special Armistice Day game in 1946. One teammate recalled, "He threw two touchdown passes, both for the other side." From there, Benedetti turned to coaching, winning 40, losing 6, and tying 2 over 4 seasons.

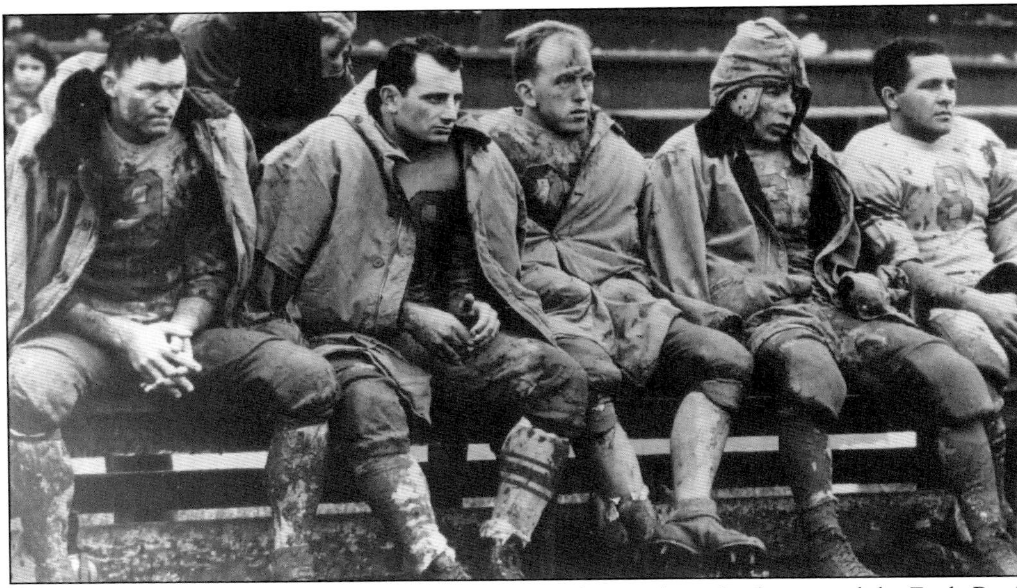

It was Egg Bowl 1951, a muddy battle raged between the Petaluma Leghorns and the Eagle Rock Athletic Club. Weary, worried, wet, and cold, Leghorns (from left) Ples Crews, Steve Mezzera, Gerv Hansen, Manny Braz, and Bill Hubbell watched the action. Overcoming miserable weather conditions, the Leghorns won 12-7. Courtesy of LeBaron Collection.

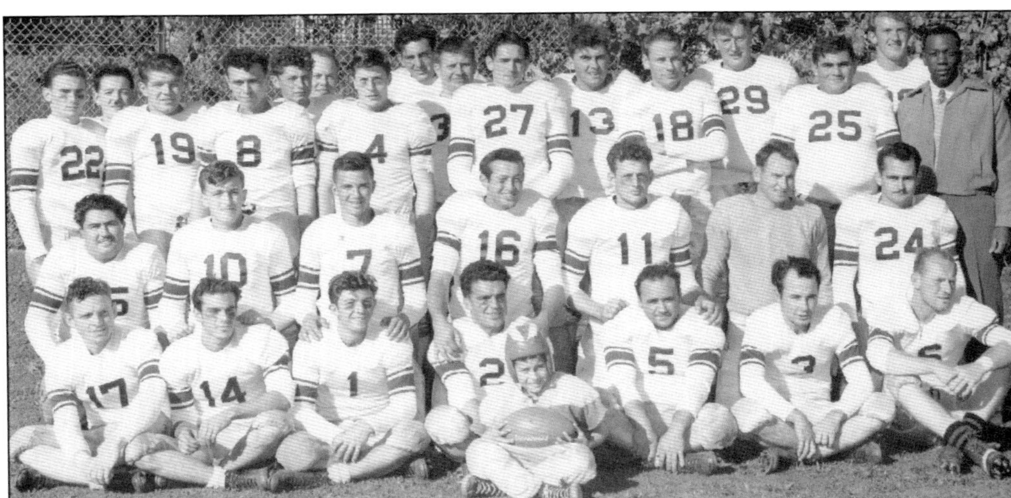

Smith Robinson, far right in back row and wearing a windbreaker, devoted hundreds of hours to coaching at Healdsburg High School, in spite of severe health problems. He put special energy into recruiting and coaching an alumni team that played an annual game against the high school Greyhounds. Robinson led a large squad into the 1947 game. Pictured, from left, are: (back row) Roy Danhausen, unidentified, unidentified, Dan Cardinotti, Gene Saini, unidentified, unidentified, unidentified, Art Ruonavaara, Ed Dean, Fred Jaggers, Fred Relyea, Red Mallon, Lou Bertoli, unidentified, and Robinson; (middle) John Bertozzi, Fred Haley, John Jacobsen, unidentified, Wood Wattles, Bob Van Winkle, and unidentified; (front) Bill Holst, Rabellino, Jack Zanzi, Bob Mascherini, Tony Pavoni, Louie Guibilo, and Buck Bennett. Courtesy of the Clarence Ruonavaara collection.

Three

BASEBALL

Sonoma County signed on early to the great American pastime. By 1900 there were numerous teams entertaining the local folks on Sundays and the Fourth of July. The names included individual talents like Nagle, Shader, Hansen, DeMaggio, Ruonavaara, Devoto, Ristau, Scheidecker, and Nishita. The teams occasionally changed names but monikers like the Prune Packers and Rosebuds tended to stick. The managers included Moch Lucchesi in Petaluma and Norm Maroni in Santa Rosa.

Walter "Lucky" Nagle was a turn-of-the-century baseball star, a pitcher, and captain of the Santa Rosa semi-pro team. Turning pro, he signed with the Los Angeles Angels in 1905 and was an immediate success, winning 14 straight games. He had a .625 record with the Pittsburgh Pirates and Boston Red Sox before being sidelined by an arm injury.

After his pro career, Nagle played with the hometown team and carved out a career as Chamber of Commerce manager and County Clerk.

It was Nagle's brainstorm to detour Thomas Edison, Harvey Firestone, and Henry Ford from the 1915 Panama-Pacific Exposition in San Francisco for a visit with Santa Rosa horticulturalist Luther Burbank.

Mickey Shader, a pitcher of limited talent, made his mark as a player and scout. One writer said Shader "threw a pretty good spitter, a fair swerver, and a nothing ball. But he had the noggin and the moxie."

Sid Hansen, a tall right-hander with hands that hung down almost to his knees, may have been the best raw talent to ever come out of Sonoma County.

When the lanky Petaluman tried out for the San Francisco Seals, one writer observed that he was "...the crudest rookie in camp (and) the best prospect...he has an arm of steel and plenty of stuff."

Shader made the most of his skills while Hansen spent much of his life fighting off the demons that kept him from reaching his potential.

In his best years, Shader went 15-8 in Utah and 14-3 in Arizona.

Hansen pitched in the San Francisco Seals system, winning 14 and losing 4 at Pocatello, Idaho. Sore arms and "misunderstandings" with management put him back on the Sonoma County circuit where he was a regular. He won 15 of his first 17 decisions with Ukiah in 1928. He played a few games with Joe DiMaggio (he spelled it DeMaggio in those days), a teenager about to start his pro career with the San Francisco Seals. Off the field, the writing of fictitious checks and a robbery conviction put him in San Quentin Prison for five years. He died at age 51, a great prospect whose chances went awry.

George (Serb) Devoto, slugging catcher for Santa Rosa High and the Rosebuds, was one of the toughest hitters in the North Bay in the 1940s. Healdsburg pitcher Clarence Ruonavaara said, "I threw him curve after curve after curve because he could really hit fastballs."

Devoto, a native Santa Rosan, won letters in three sports at Santa Rosa High School in the 1930s, and played baseball for the local semi-pros. Ruonavaara said Devoto kept the pressure on him when he got on base. In one game, the burly backstop scored a run by diving head first over another team's catcher.

The 1940s saw plenty of quality pitching. Clarence Ruonavaara worked his way through Healdsburg High, SRJC, and UC Berkeley.

As a youngster, Ruonavaara surprised hitters "because I was only a 140-pounder out there on the mound. I always kept (my fastball) moving around and mixed my curve ball in," he said.

After helping Cal's Golden Bears to a Western Division college baseball championship in 1942, Ruonavaara returned to Healdsburg and threw a string of one-hit and two-hit games. In 1947, he won 17 of his first 18 decisions, including a no-hitter over Crown Machine Works of Santa Rosa on July 4.

After a stint with the Coast League San Francisco Seals in 1937 and 1938, Mel "Lefty" Ristau returned to his grocery store in rural Cunningham. On Sundays, the slightly disheveled Ristau took off his apron, grabbed his glove, and frustrated batters with his left-handed knuckler. One foe said, "The batters went off mumbling to themselves but he never worked up a sweat." In the late 1940s, he pitched home games for the professional Santa Rosa Cats.

Petaluma's Mario "Moch" Lucchesi was one of the most respected managers around. Much of his life was spent performing a balancing act between his job as a barber and his work on the baseball diamond as coach and groundskeeper for one of the many teams he managed.

Lucchesi, one of Petaluma's best high school athletes of the 1920s, was known as Mr. Home Run. He led his team to a league title in 1923. He played semi-pro baseball until 1937 and then managed the Leghorns semi-pro baseball team in the 1940s, often raking the field and chalking the diamond the morning of a game. A large park and recreation facility in East Petaluma was named in his memory in the 1970s.

For many years in Santa Rosa, it was hard to find a baseball lineup that did not have one or more Maronis in it. There were at least five Maronis who played local baseball from the 1910s forward: George, Al, Pete, John, and Norm.

Norm, born in 1907, became a player, manager, and financial angel for Santa Rosa baseball. One friend said, "When times were lean—and they were for many years—Maroni would pay for uniforms, umpires, travel, and bats and balls out of his own pocket."

They played "Take Me Out to the Ball Game" at his funeral in 1993. Doyle Park baseball field, his home away from home, was also named after Maroni.

The professional Santa Rosa Pirates, Class D farm team of Pittsburgh Pirates of the National League, came to town in 1948. The team only lasted a year, but young Vern Law, who became the ace of the major league staff, made his debut with the Sonoma County team.

Baseball was a popular sport in high schools and at the junior college.

At Analy High, four-sports letterman Bill Scheidecker occasionally drew the ire of his mother for leaving too many uniforms hanging around the house. Sometimes he even dirtied two uniforms in one day. In 1950, the lanky pitcher hurled his Tigers to a 13-7 victory in Sebastopol. Then, with the sun setting, he hurried to Petaluma, donned his track uniform, and placed in the high and low hurdles. He had already won the North Bay League hurdle championships in 1948 and 1949.

A few years earlier, Ray Moneymaker played baseball one afternoon, then raced over to the track to pole vault, still wearing his baseball uniform.

Two Japanese Americans from Hawaii set the junior college baseball world on its ear in 1950. One was Bill Nishita, a 5-foot 11-inch, 160-pound pitcher with a variety of curve balls and excellent control. Behind the plate was his battery mate George Fujishige. Although he lost a game early in the year to the professional Yakima Bears, Nishita ran off a string of 15 wins, carrying the Bear Cubs to the state championship series.

With the Korean War on and a deadly flu bug sweeping the country in 1952, enrollment at Santa Rosa Junior College fell to less than 750 students. The school also lost its baseball coach, ex-Marine Cook Sypher, who was called back to duty. Basketball coach Bob Mastin became interim baseball coach but the man who ran the team, without a teaching credential, was Dolph Camilli, a former major league baseball star living in the Santa Rosa area. Camilli quickly shaped the Bear Cubs into a title contender.

One Saturday, the Bear Cubs visited San Quentin prison to meet a team that, not surprisingly, played only home games. The field at San Quentin in those days was one of the most peculiar in baseball. The fence in left field was only 150 feet from home plate. Any ball hit over that barrier into the jute mill behind the wall was a single. Center and right center fields were deep, but the right-field foul line ran up a wall, and was distinguished by a painted white line. Any ball hit to the left of the line was in play; anything hit to the right was foul.

Inmate fans rooted mainly for the visitors and made frequent threatening comments to the umpire. Cheered on by the inmates, the Bear Cubs pulled ahead 2-0 but the Cons rallied, putting a couple of guys on base. The next batter lofted a fly down the right field line that hit the wall in fair territory, bouncing back onto the field. The confused Santa Rosa right fielder, thinking the ball was foul, merely jogged after the ball. The inside-the-park homer gave the prison team a 3-2 victory.

That was the last major setback for the Bear Cubs in 1952. It won the Big Seven Conference title and, with ace pitcher George Read leading the way, the state championship in a playoff series.

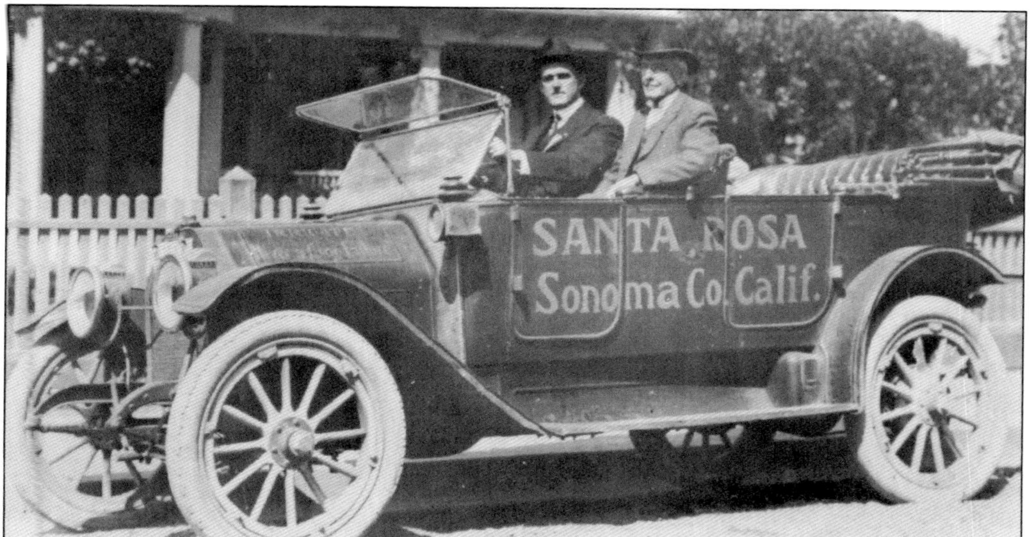

Pitcher Walter Nagle was one of the first big baseball stars to come out of Sonoma County. Retiring from pro ball with a sore arm, he returned home to serve a lengthy career as a political advisor, promoter, and County Clerk. Nagle (left) rode with Luther Burbank in the Chamber of Commerce car in 1915. Courtesy of the Sonoma County Museum.

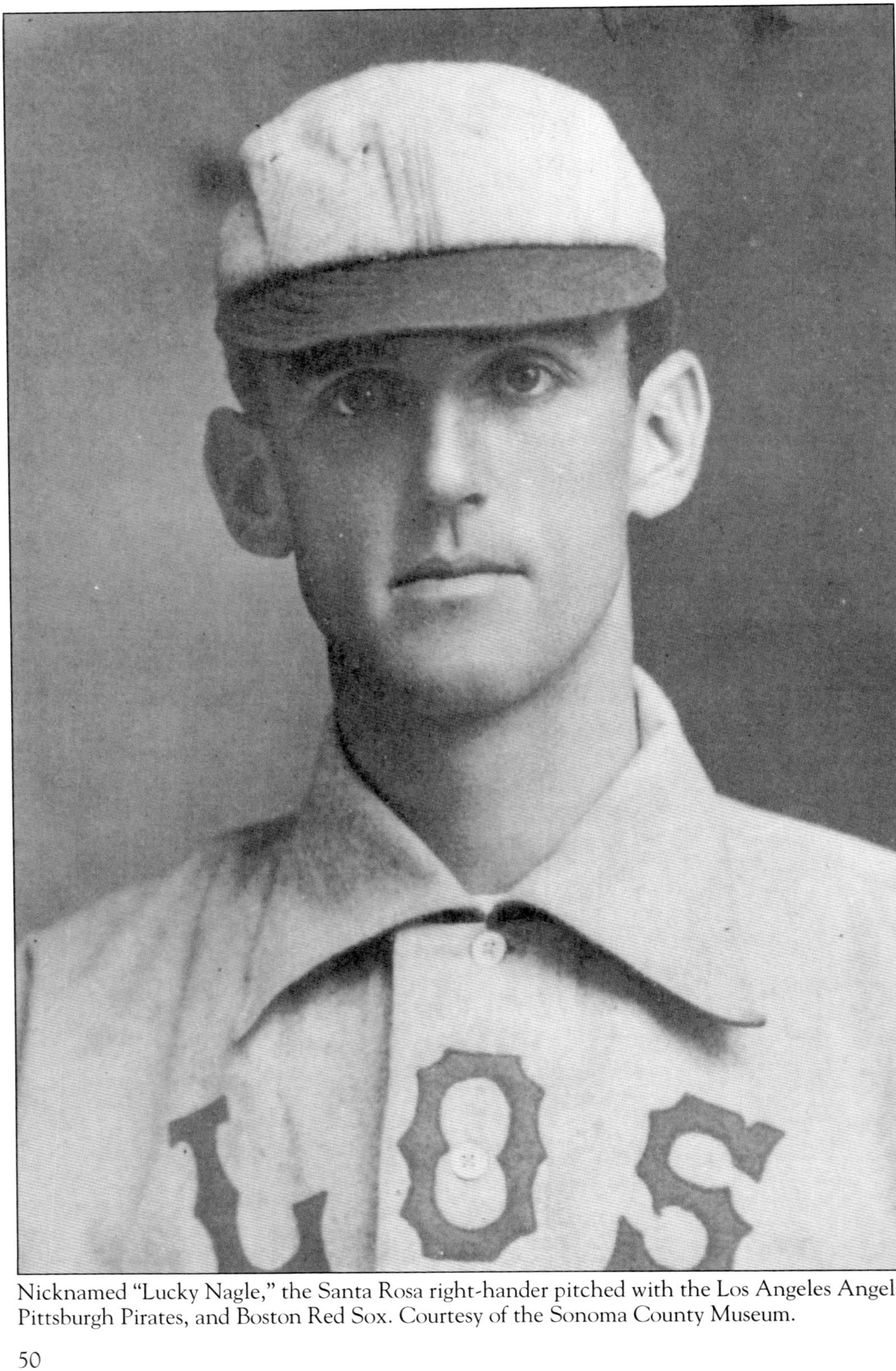

Nicknamed "Lucky Nagle," the Santa Rosa right-hander pitched with the Los Angeles Angels, Pittsburgh Pirates, and Boston Red Sox. Courtesy of the Sonoma County Museum.

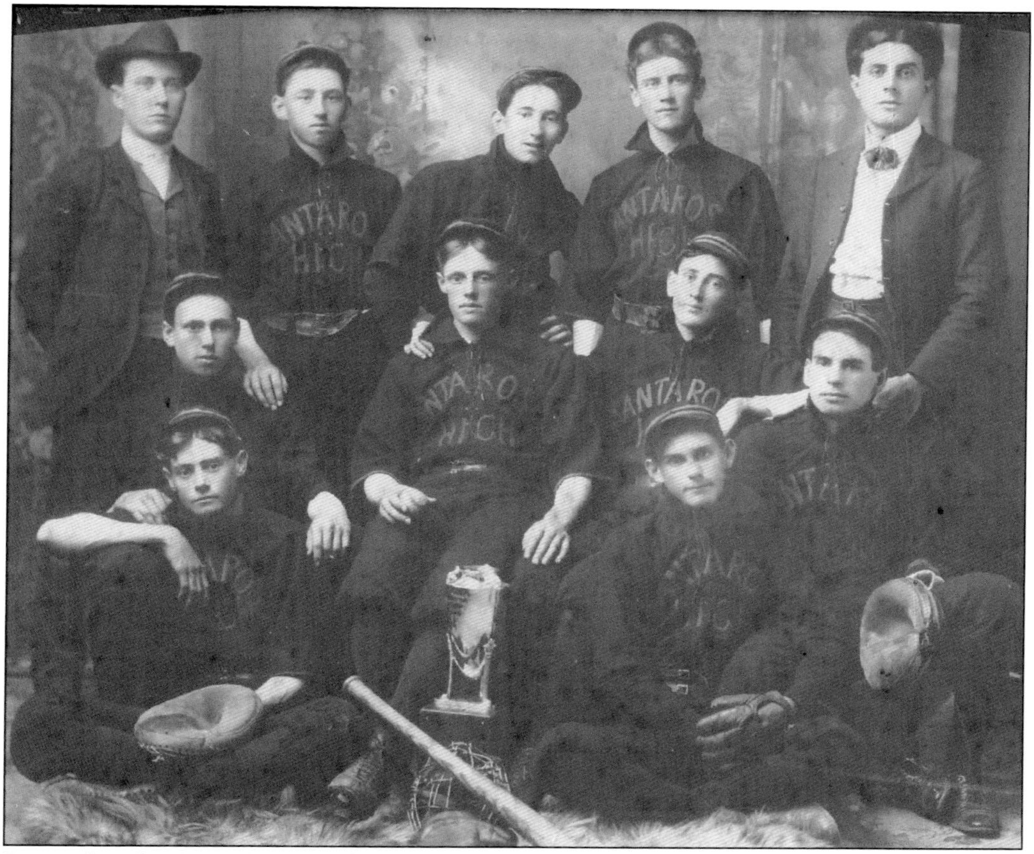

Pictured is the Santa Rosa High School baseball team, c. 1903. Players include: (back row) Ron Moody, second baseman Russell Smith, shortstop Bob Levy, right fielder Bill Williams, and Bruce Pamlin; (middle) centerfielder M. Youker, pitcher Claud Sanborn, and leftfielder C. Loughy; (front) catcher Jess Wright, and shortstop William Neurauter. The notation on the back of the photo indicated Russell Smith won the batting title "all by myself." Courtesy of the Sonoma County Museum.

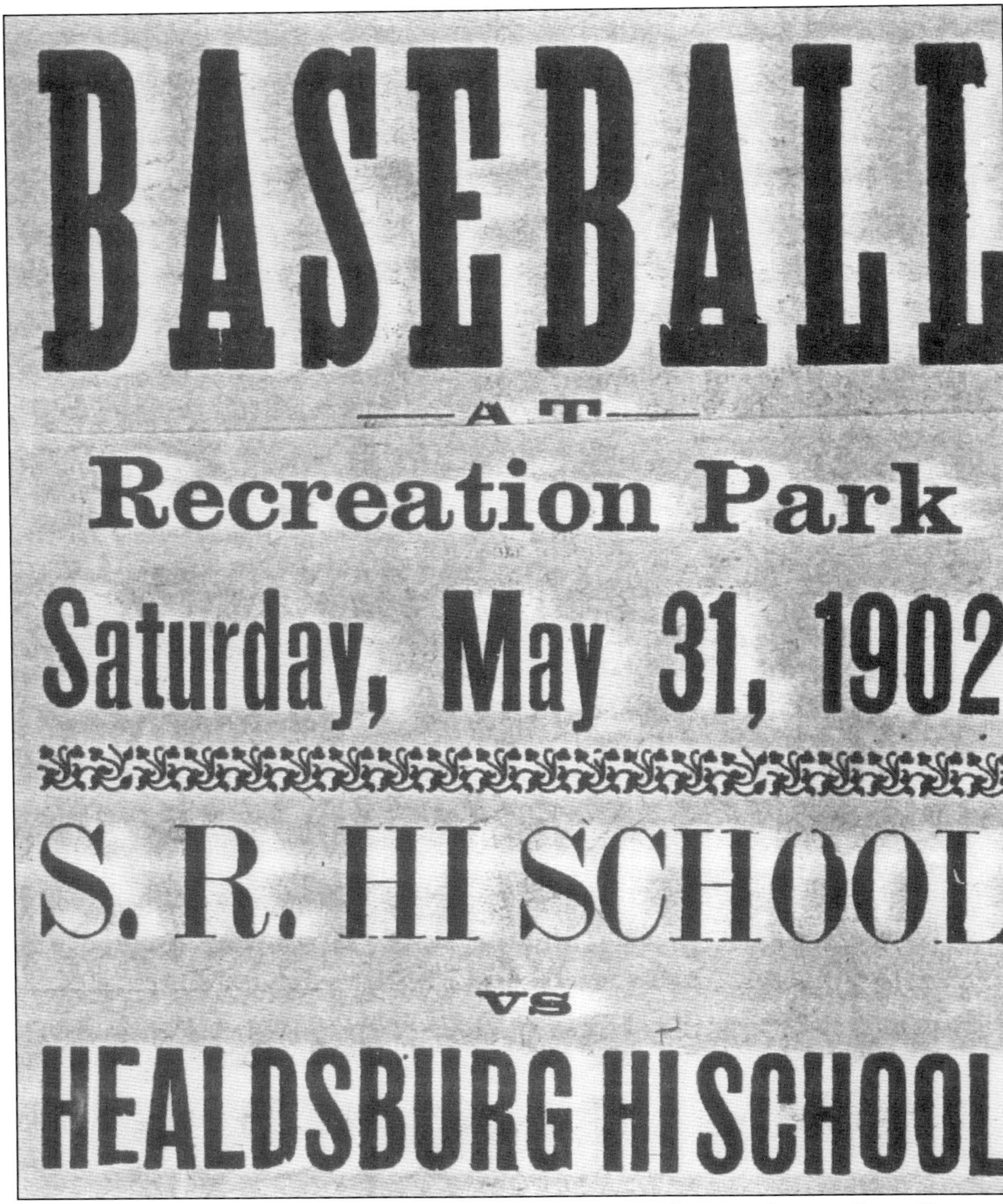

Baseball rivalries developed quickly in many communities in Sonoma County. Santa Rosa and Healdsburg high schools played May 31, 1902. Courtesy of the Sonoma County Museum.

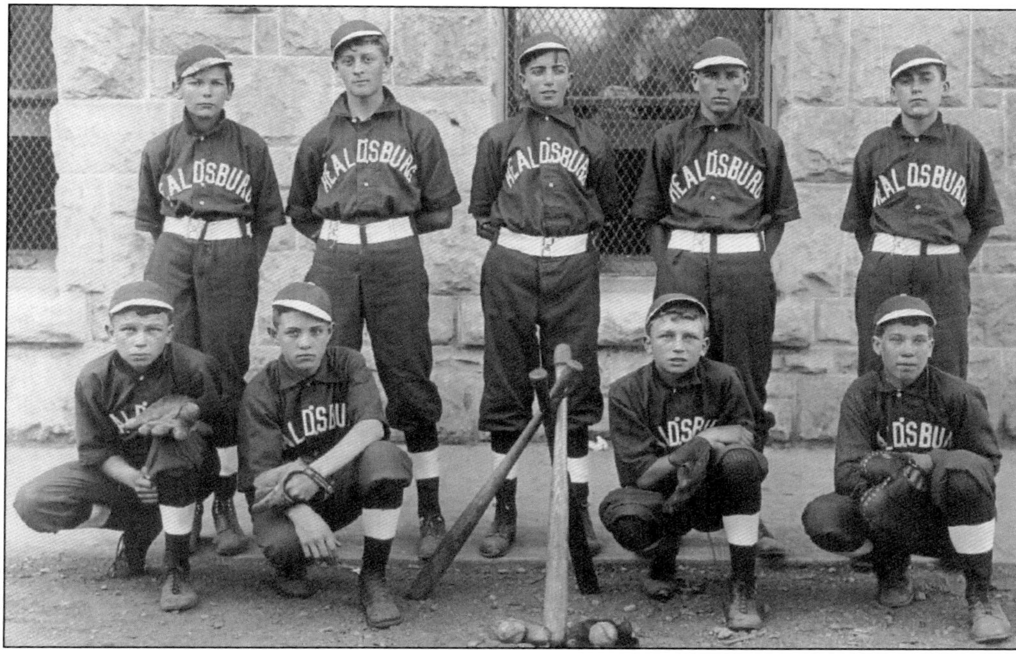

They trained their baseball players early in Healdsburg. The Healdsburg Grammar School fielded a dapper looking A team in 1911. Pictured are: (back row) Russel, Lloyd Hearing, Harold Laughlin, Howard Bledsoe, and Sewell Hilgerloh; (front) Gale Dewey, Charlie Hiatt, Glenn Dewey, and Ray Hoskinson. Courtesy of the Healdsburg Museum.

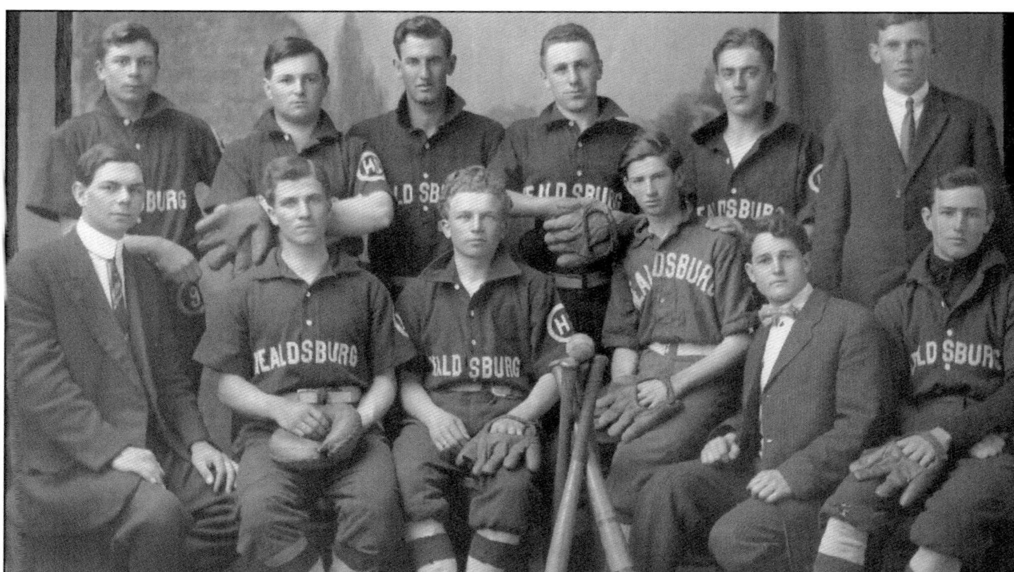

Healdsburg High School made it to the playoff semi-finals in 1914, losing to Santa Rosa 5-2. The next week, Analy won the championship as Ristau edged Frei 4-3. Pictured are the members of the Healdsburg team: (back row) Don Petray, Lou Rowland, Claude Burke, Teo Rosenberg, Sewell Hilgerloh, and Al Parker; (front) Ernest Frellson, Al Hoskinson, Glenn Dewey, Leslie Price, George Bovett, and Ward Grant. Courtesy of the Healdsburg Museum.

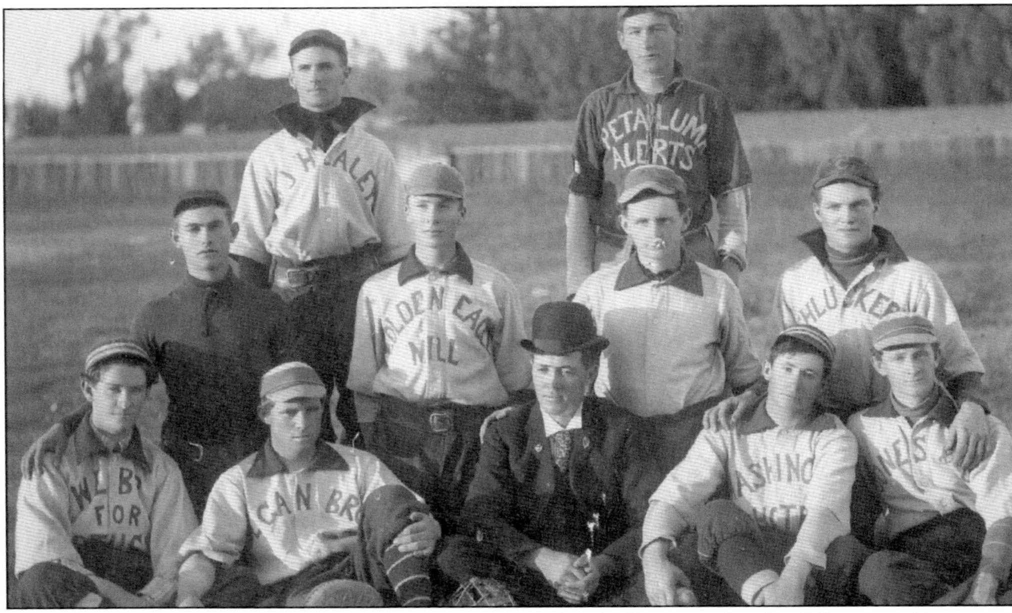

In 1904, Petaluma was represented on the semi-pro baseball circuit by the following: (front row) William Kennealy, L.V. Waymire, manager Bill Dunning, Bill Evart, and Toots Balderson; (middle) captain Clyde Beatty, Bob Ayers, Buck Howard, and Tom Caulfield; (back) unidentified. The 1904 nine had to live down a reputation built by the 1903 team that was labeled "a pack of hoodlums" after a bad weekend in Fresno. A Fresno writer claimed two members of the team took money to throw a game and that some players "smashed furniture and were drunk and disorderly in the streets." The game was cancelled to allow the offenders to leave as rapidly as possible. Courtesy of the Sonoma County Museum.

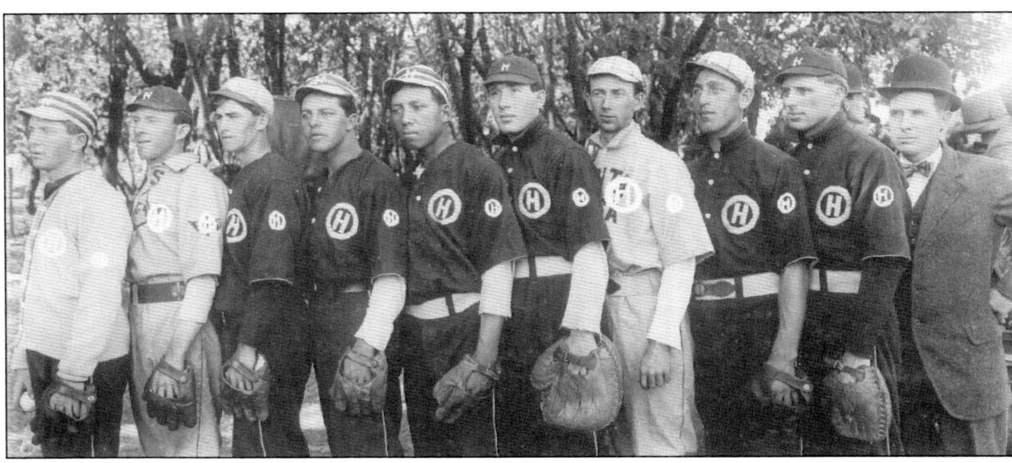

The catcher wore a mitt that almost covered his face and the team mascot was a wild pig named Clarice. The 1911 Healdsburg semi-pro nine took its Sunday afternoons seriously, however, winning the Sonoma County championship in a series of games with Petaluma. Catcher Jackson was the team's most feared slugger and pitcher. "Iron Man" Dolan once pitched two games in two days, beating Napa on a one-hitter on Sunday and following it up with a four-hit shutout over Petaluma on Labor Day. Other team members included Fraser, Esola, Laughery, Crowell, Guilfoy, Bennett, Scatena, and Martini. Courtesy of the M. Silberstein collection, Healdsburg Museum.

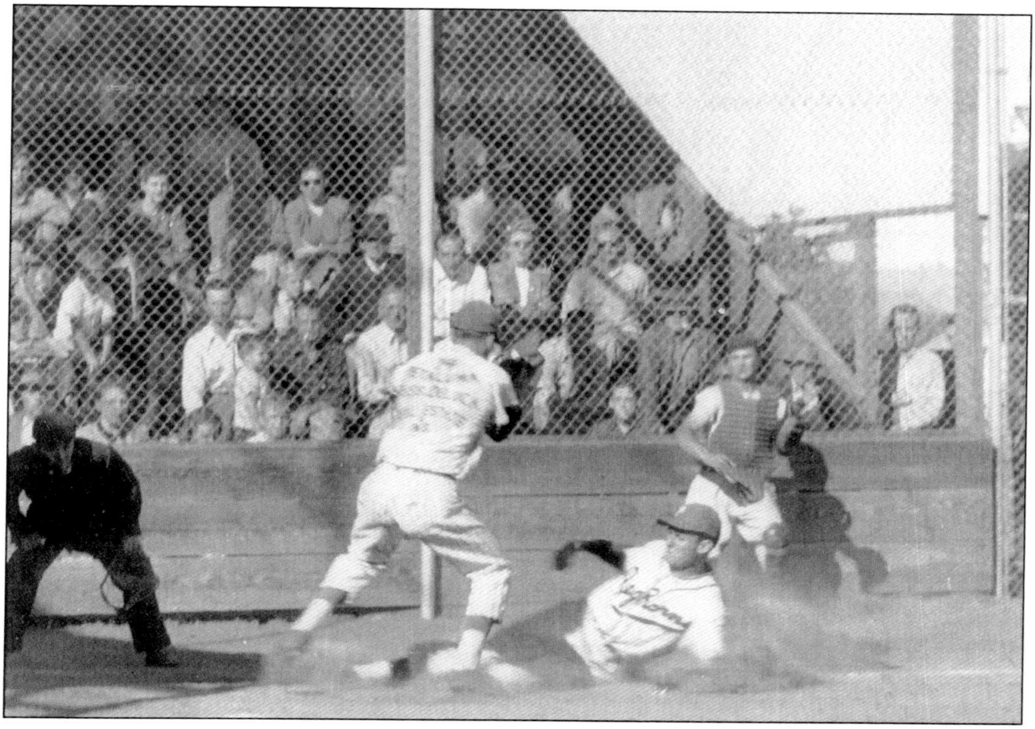

Teams fought it out for baseball supremacy on Sunday afternoons throughout Sonoma County. At McNear Park in Petaluma, a Leghorns runner slid in safe at home. A feature of the old Petaluma stadium was a ground to ceiling cyclone fence, which separated the players from the fans. Courtesy of the Petaluma Museum.

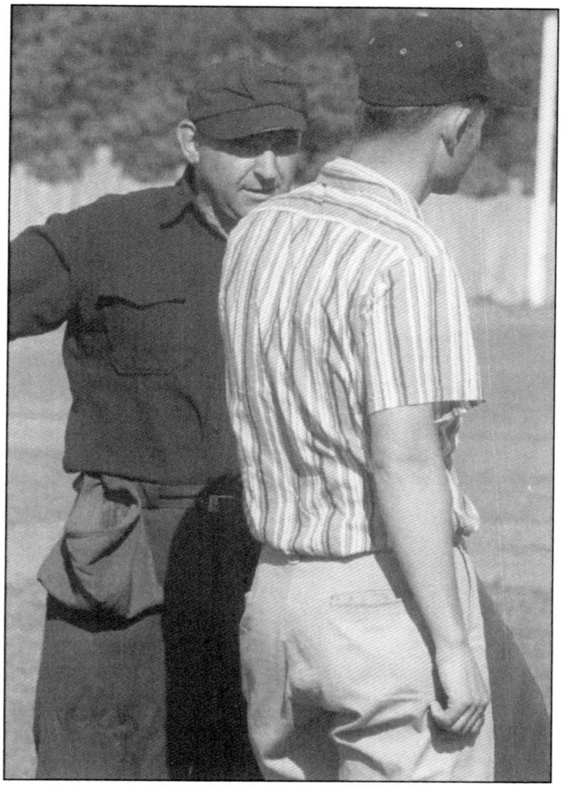

Willie Rossi of Santa Rosa made a name for himself as a player, manager, and umpire. As a player, Rossi was known as a "bad ball" hitter. One opposing pitcher said he swung at so many pitches out of the strike zone "I never threw him anything but strikes." As an umpire, he was cool, calm, and collected as he discussed the fine points of the game with Santa Rosa High School manager Wes Colgan. Courtesy of the Colgan collection.

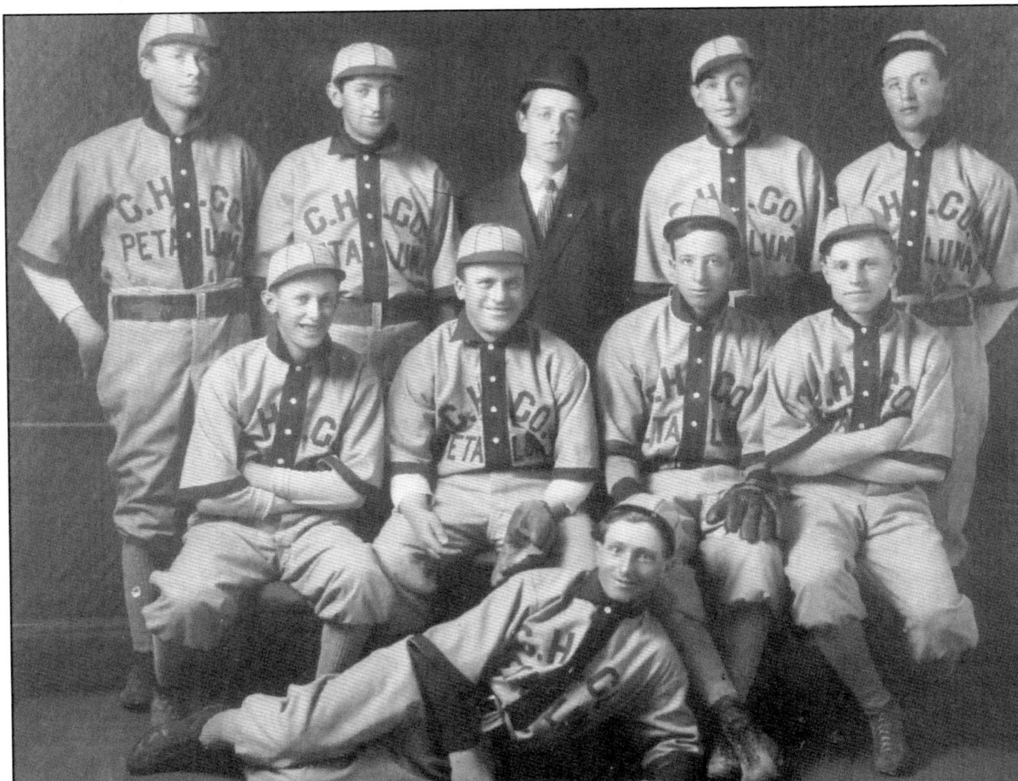

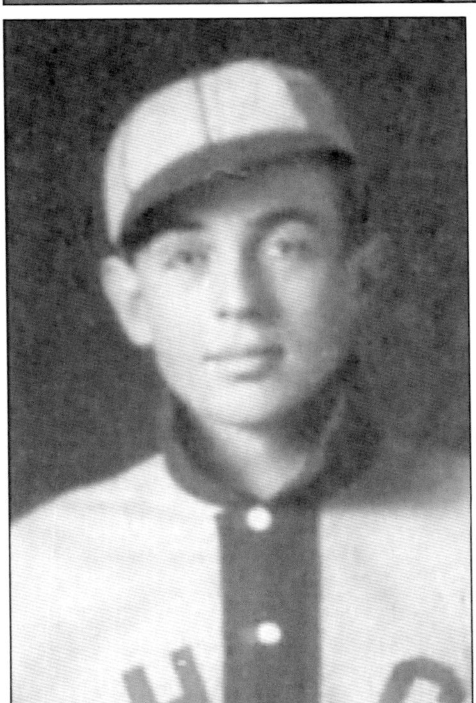

Mickey Shader, who went on to a long, nomadic career as a baseball pitcher and scout, got early training with the Petaluma Camm and Hedges team in 1911. The team won 11 of its first 15 games but lost the county championship to Healdsburg. The pictured players are: (back row) Bob Ayers, Ike McGovern, manager Bill Dunning, Mickey Shader, and Ed Evart; (middle) Fitz Boysen, Ernie Ayers, Scale Evart, and Robert Robertson; (front) Andy Mastrup, a left-handed second baseman. Courtesy of the Petaluma Museum.

One critic says Mickey Shader had "a pretty good spitter, a fair swerver, and a nothing ball" as well as "a good noggin and moxie." It was enough to carry him through a long career in baseball. Late in his career, it was noted he was "a man of many parts. Connoisseur of good bourbon, personification of the haberdasher's art, corrupter of the King's English. Shader is also one of the top scouts in baseball and one of the few colorful characters left in the national pastime hereabouts." Courtesy of the Petaluma Museum.

As a youngster in 1932 and 1933, "Dead Pan" Joe DiMaggio played baseball in Sonoma County. He spelled his name with an "e' (DeMaggio) and showed his talent early on. Playing with Sid Hansen, the teenage San Franciscan banged out three hits in his first game. At the pro level in 1933, he ran off a string of hits in 61 consecutive games, a league record. The Seals gave him a bonus check and a gold watch for his efforts. Courtesy of the Sonoma County Museum.

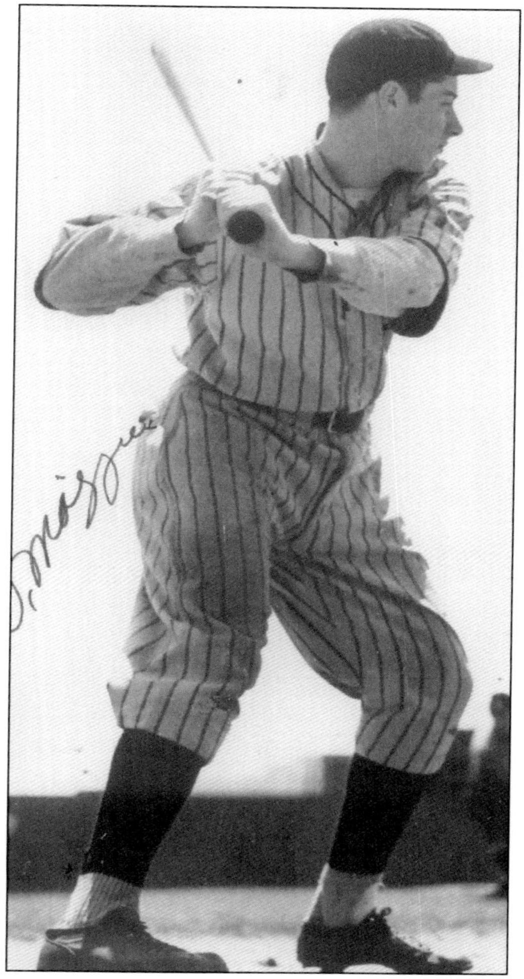

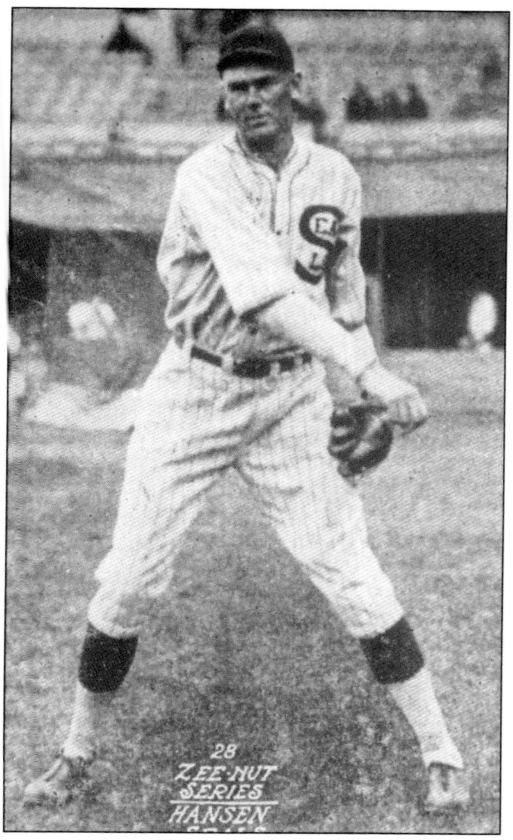

Sid Hansen of Petaluma was described by a writer in the 1920s as a "real busher" with "an arm of steel and plenty of stuff." Joe DiMaggio called him "one of the best I've ever seen." He got several tryouts with the San Francisco Seals and Missions of the Pacific Coast League, but ended up mostly baffling semi-pro batters in Sonoma County on Sunday afternoons. His personal problems finally led to a stretch in San Quentin Prison. Courtesy of the Sonoma County Museum.

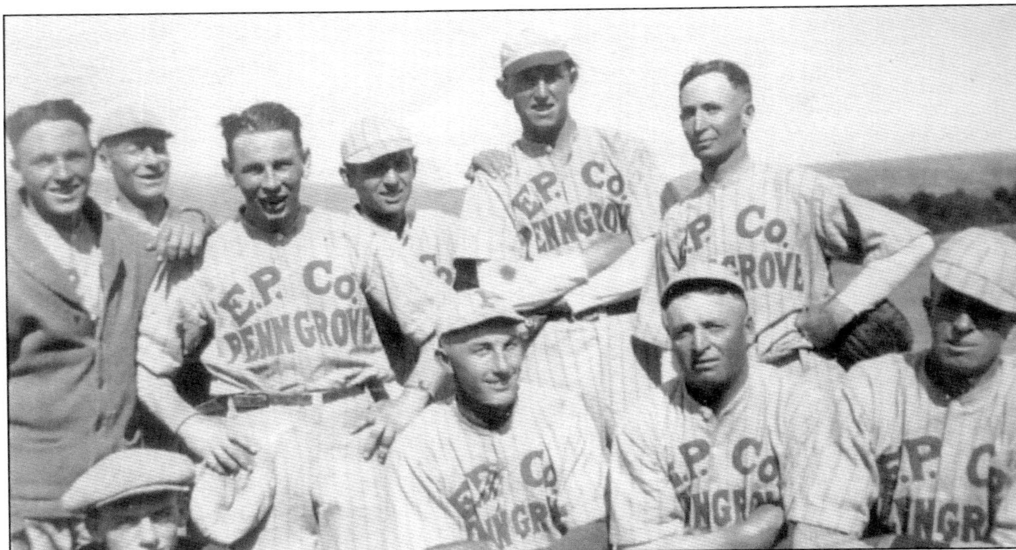

For many years, the Evart Produce semi-pro team in Penngrove consisted of mostly Evarts and a few other guys. Some of the team members are pictured here, c. 1920s: back row, third from left and hatless, Bob Ayers; fifth from left, Louie Flohr; far right, Bill Evart Jr.; front row, second from right, Ed Evart. Others on the team included pitcher Henry (Dutch) Evart, catcher Wilson, first baseman Fuller, second baseman Glynn, third baseman Hademann, and shortstop Scale Evart. In 1924, Dutch Evart was good enough to get called for a tryout with the San Francisco Seals of the old Pacific Coast League. Courtesy of the Petaluma Museum.

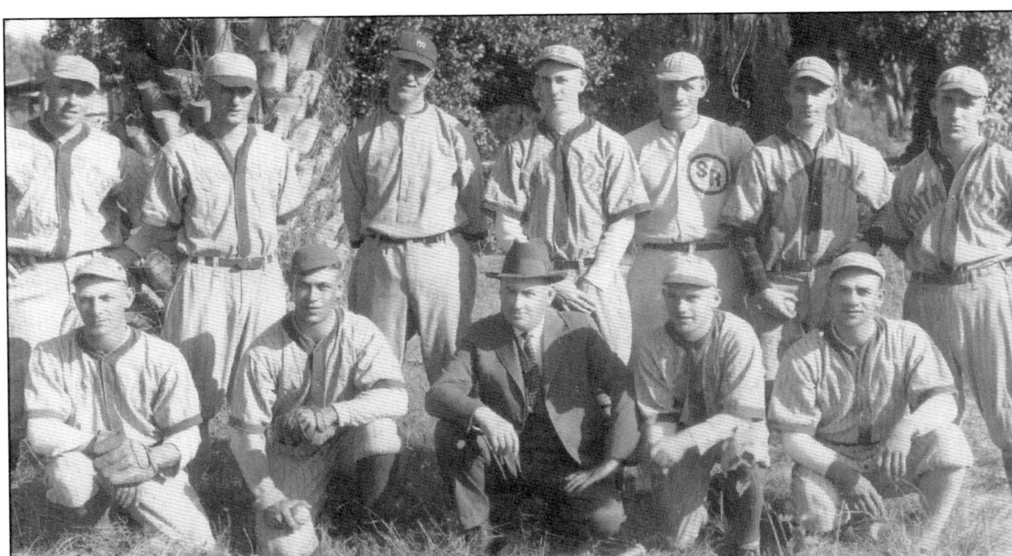

If Santa Rosa fielded a semi-pro baseball team, one or more of the Maroni brothers were usually in the lineup. John pitched and Pete played second base on Santa Rosa's town team in 1916 and George was getting in his licks by 1921. Norm Maroni, born in 1907, was a player, manager, and financial angel for Santa Rosa baseball. This Santa Rosa town team, c. 1928, included, back row and second from left, pitcher John Maroni, and catcher George Maroni, far right; front row, fourth from left, shortstop Pete Maroni. Courtesy of the Capitani collection.

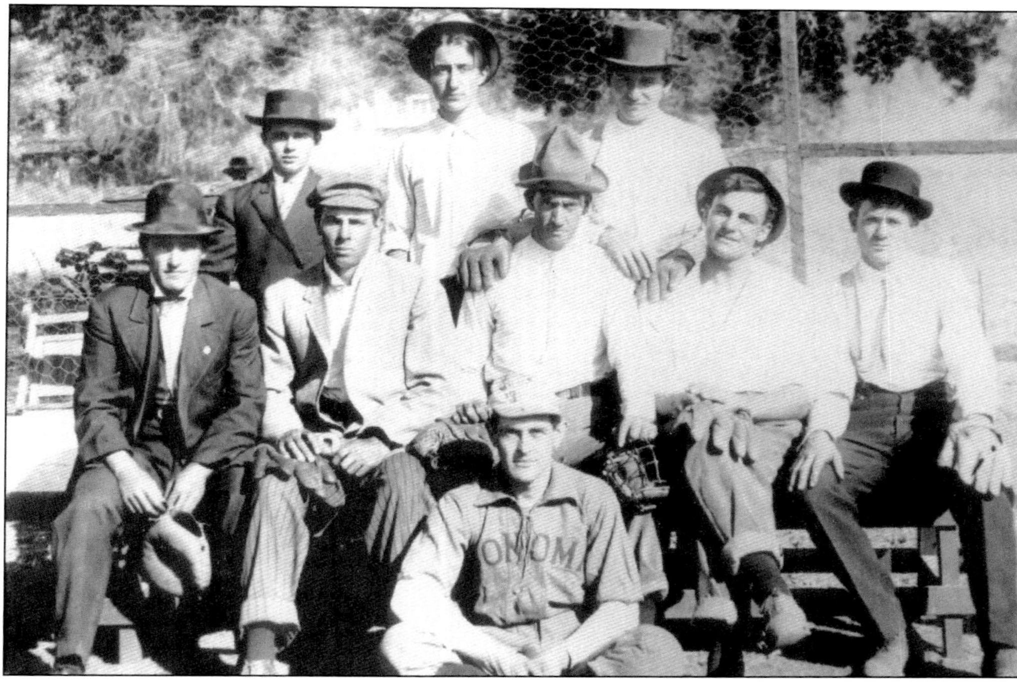

Even though there was little in the way of baseball uniforms, hats, or other equipment, the Sonoma town baseball team, pictured here *c.* 1920s, took time to proudly pose during a break in the action. It is unknown if any of the hats were sent to the Hall of Fame Museum in Cooperstown. Courtesy of the Sonoma Depot Park Museum.

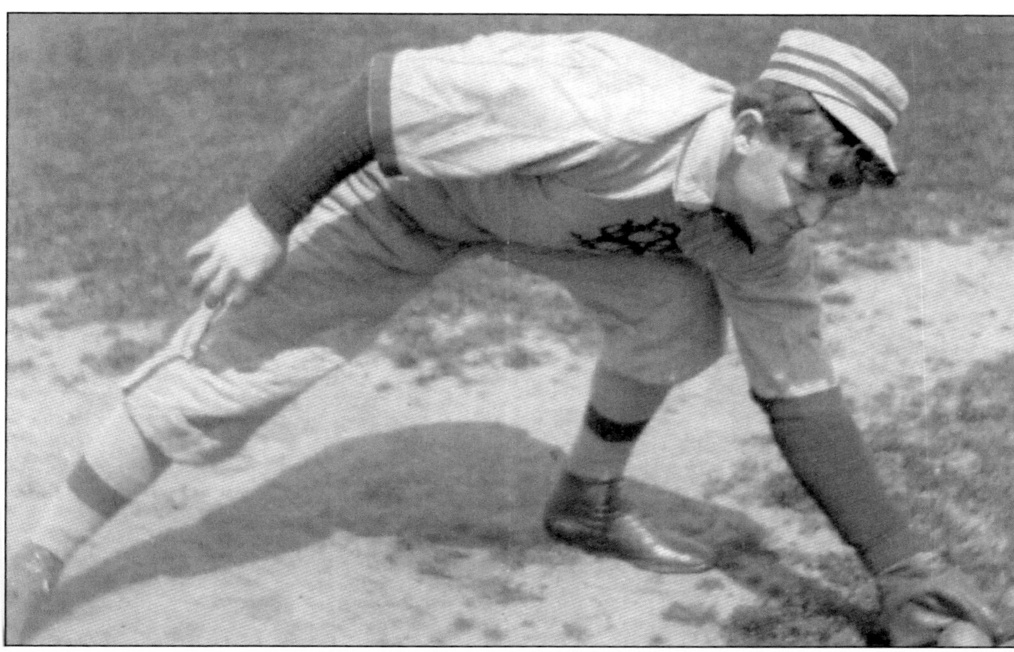

Cap at a jaunty angle, this early Santa Rosa infielder showed good form, stretching for a throw while keeping his foot on the bag. Courtesy of the Sonoma County Museum.

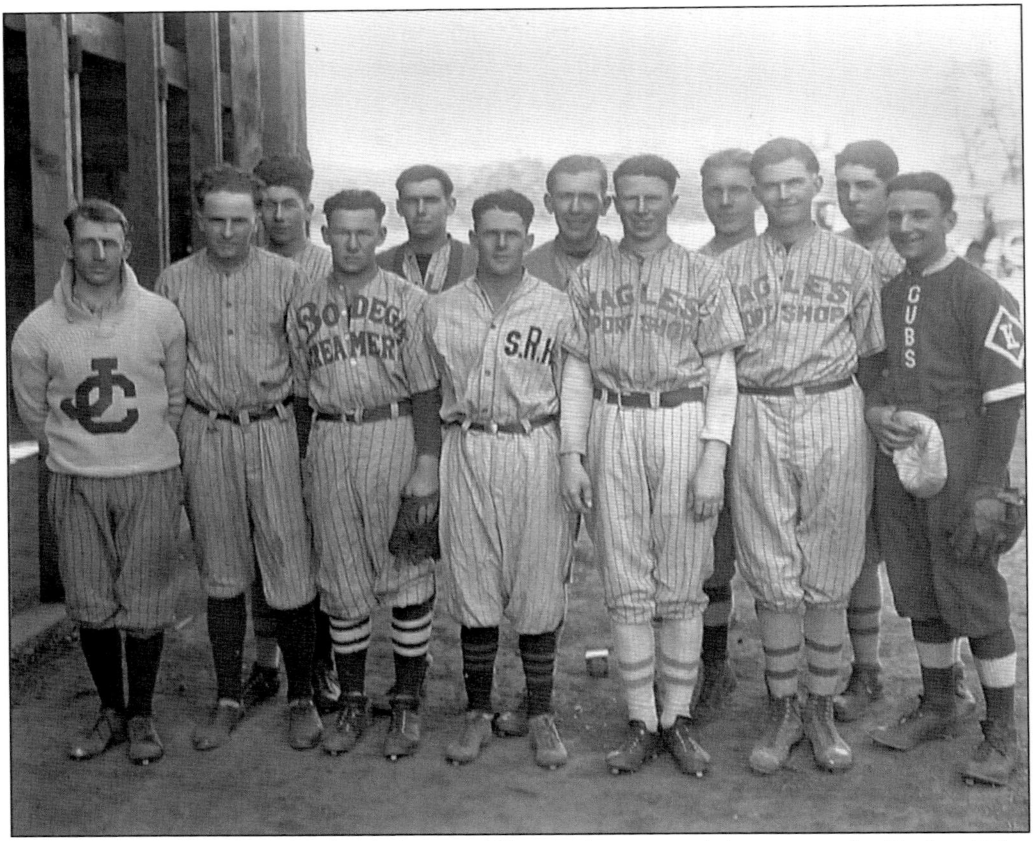

Ok, sports fans, it's time for the daily quiz: What is the name of this team—the Eagles, Cubs, Bodega Creamery, Santa Rosa High School, Santa Rosa Junior College, or Spacemen from Mars? Answer: It's the Santa Rosa Junior College Bear Cubs of 1924, back when the school was new, there were no paid coaches, and there was very little money for uniforms and equipment. Dean and future president Floyd Bailey coached this team while volunteer C.J. (Red) Tauzer handled basketball and football. Pitcher Bryant Forsyth won 6 of 8 games for coach Bailey, fanning 87 batters as the team won 7 of 11 games. The group included: (back row) Plover, Bryant Forsyth, Harvey Sullivan, Ken Shaffer, and Roy Waterman; (front) Howard Fry, Braun, Carl Witham, Stacy Lee, Rank, Wilson and captain Joe Cuneo. Courtesy of the SRJC collection.

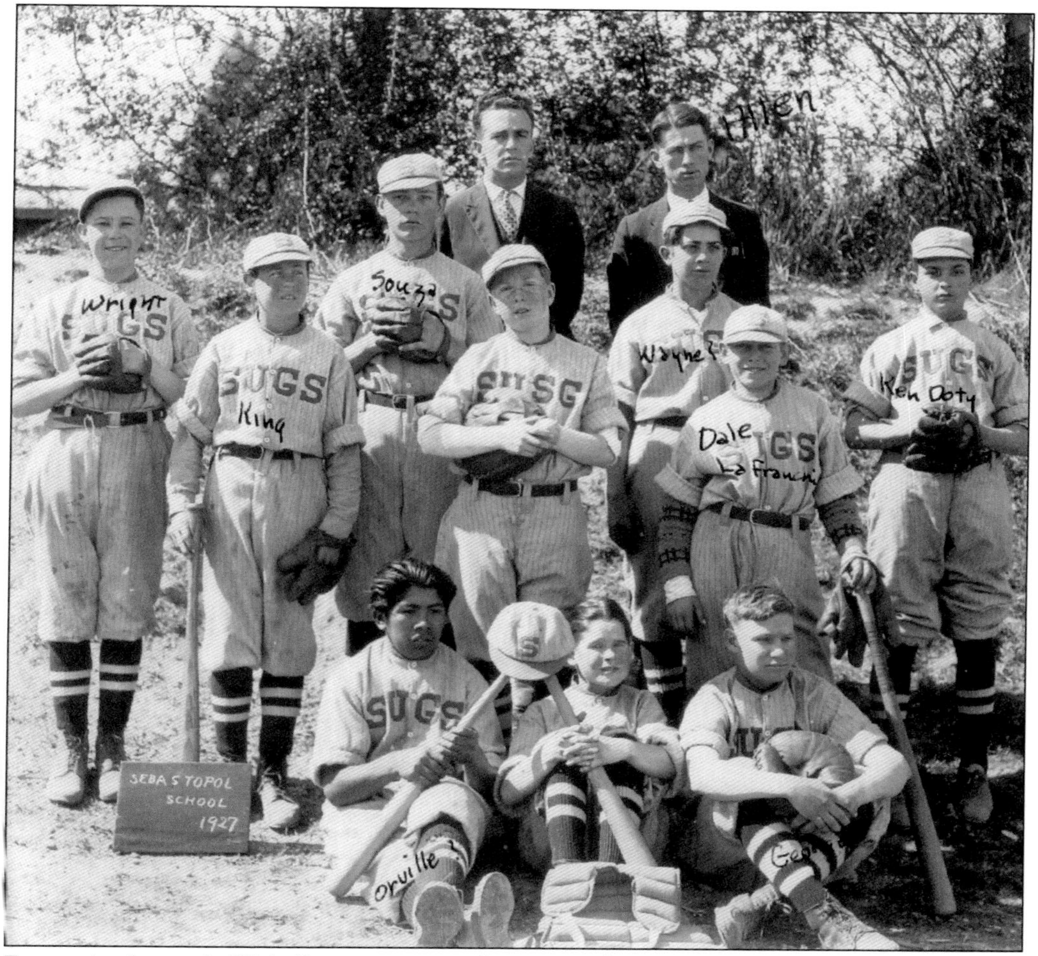

Future Analy coach Walt Foster got an early start on learning basic skills when he took the field for the Sebastopol grammar school hardball team in 1927. The team included: (front row) Orville, Joe Badger, and George; (middle) King, Walt Foster, and Dale La Franchi; (back) Wright, Souza, Wayne, and Ken Doty. Behind the players are coach George Lacey and an assistant. Courtesy of the Foster collection.

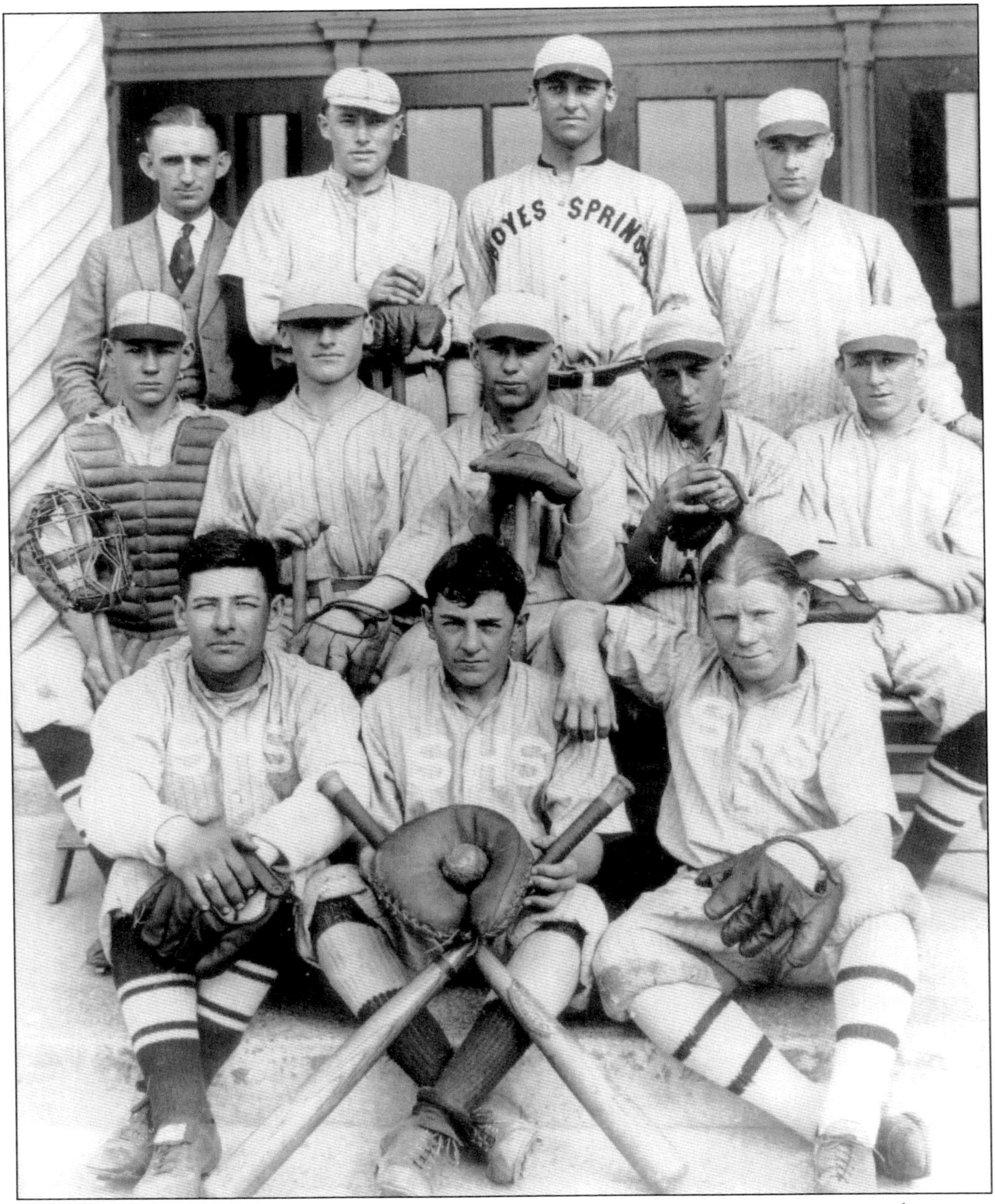

Sonoma High School put an impressive looking team on the field in 1925. Picture here are, from left: (back row) coach Lander Stenquist, first basemen Wallace Hall and Ernest Bosch, and shortstop Everett Murphy; (middle) catchers Chester Horn and William Duffen, pitcher Mike Kiser, center fielder Babe Mazza, and second baseman Vernon Douglas; (front) leftfielder Ray Tynan, third baseman Henry Martin, and rightfielder Watson Garoni. The Dragons fielded their first baseball team in 1914, losing their first game to Santa Rosa 5-0. Courtesy of the Sonoma Depot Park Museum

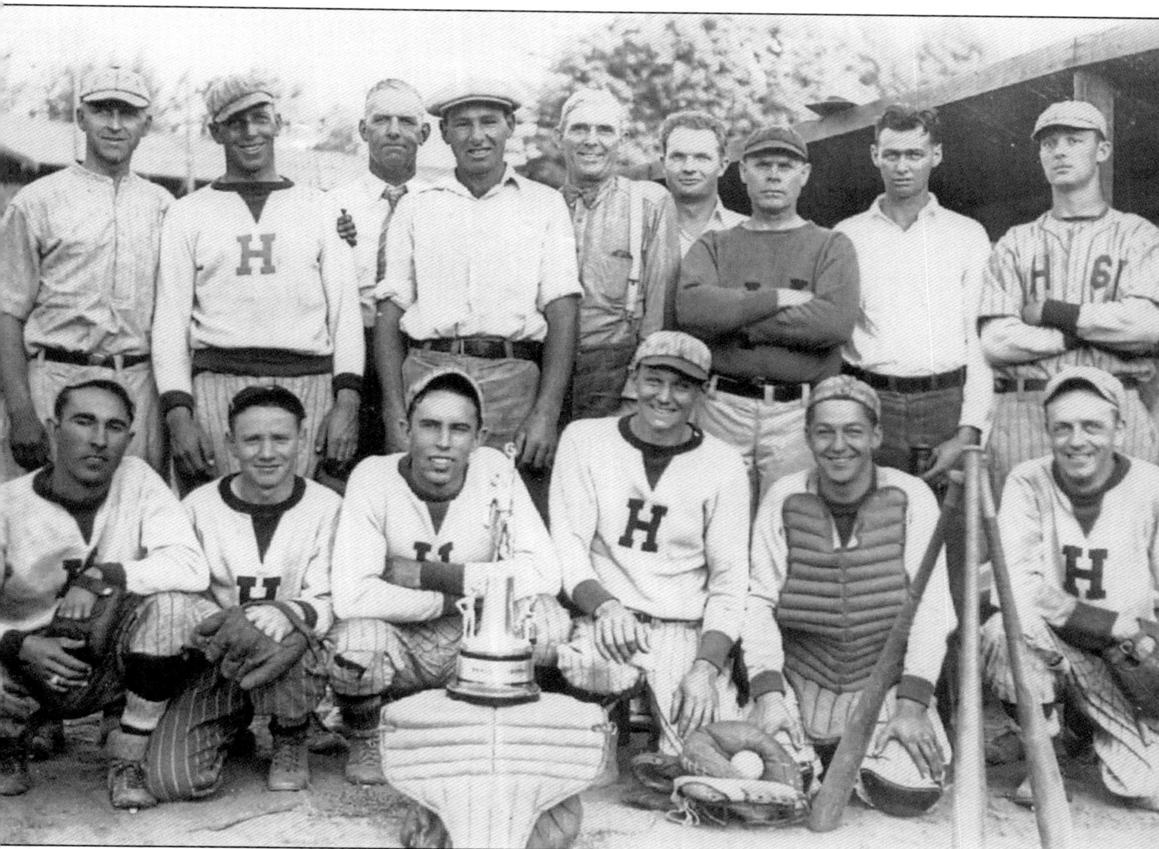

Healdsburg Odd Fellows baseball team beat Napa 3-2 to win the IOOF championship Oct. 1, 1933. Team members pictured here are, left to right: (back row) unidentified, rightfielder Walt Wright, Harvey Frost, leftfielder Frank Mott, third baseman Jake Tanner, unidentified, centerfielder Rollin McCord, utility man Neil Richardson, and unidentified; (front row) utility player Burnett Bidwell, unidentified, shortstop Homer (Duke) Bidwell, pitcher Waldo Iversen, catcher Ned Auradou, and first baseman Henry (Cotton) Williams. Courtesy of the Darla Budworth collection.

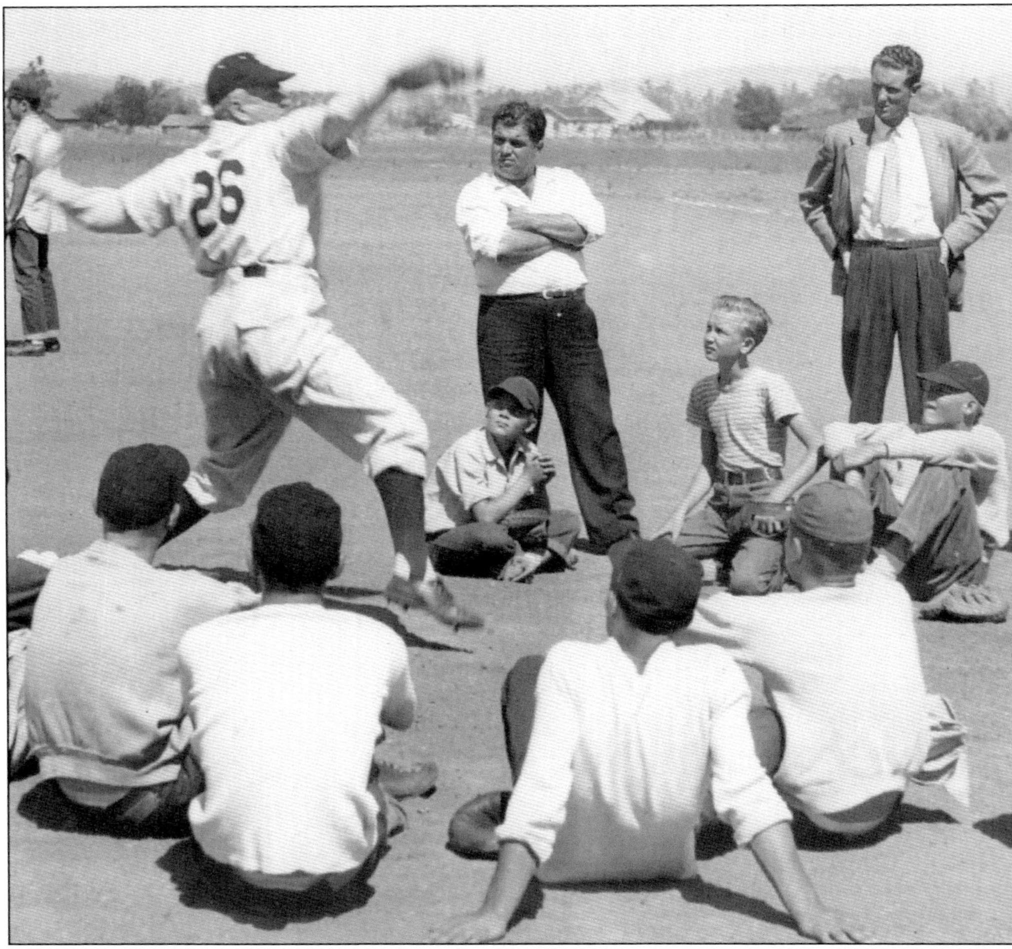

Awed youngsters watched as former major league lefthander Walter "The Great" Mails showed them proper pitching form at a baseball camp in Petaluma in the 1940s. Watching the demonstration, standing, were Leghorns semi-pro manager Moch Lucchesi and Leghorn pitcher Russ Lebeck; sitting, from left, Hank Soldati, Benny Walker, and unidentified. Frank Ricci photo.

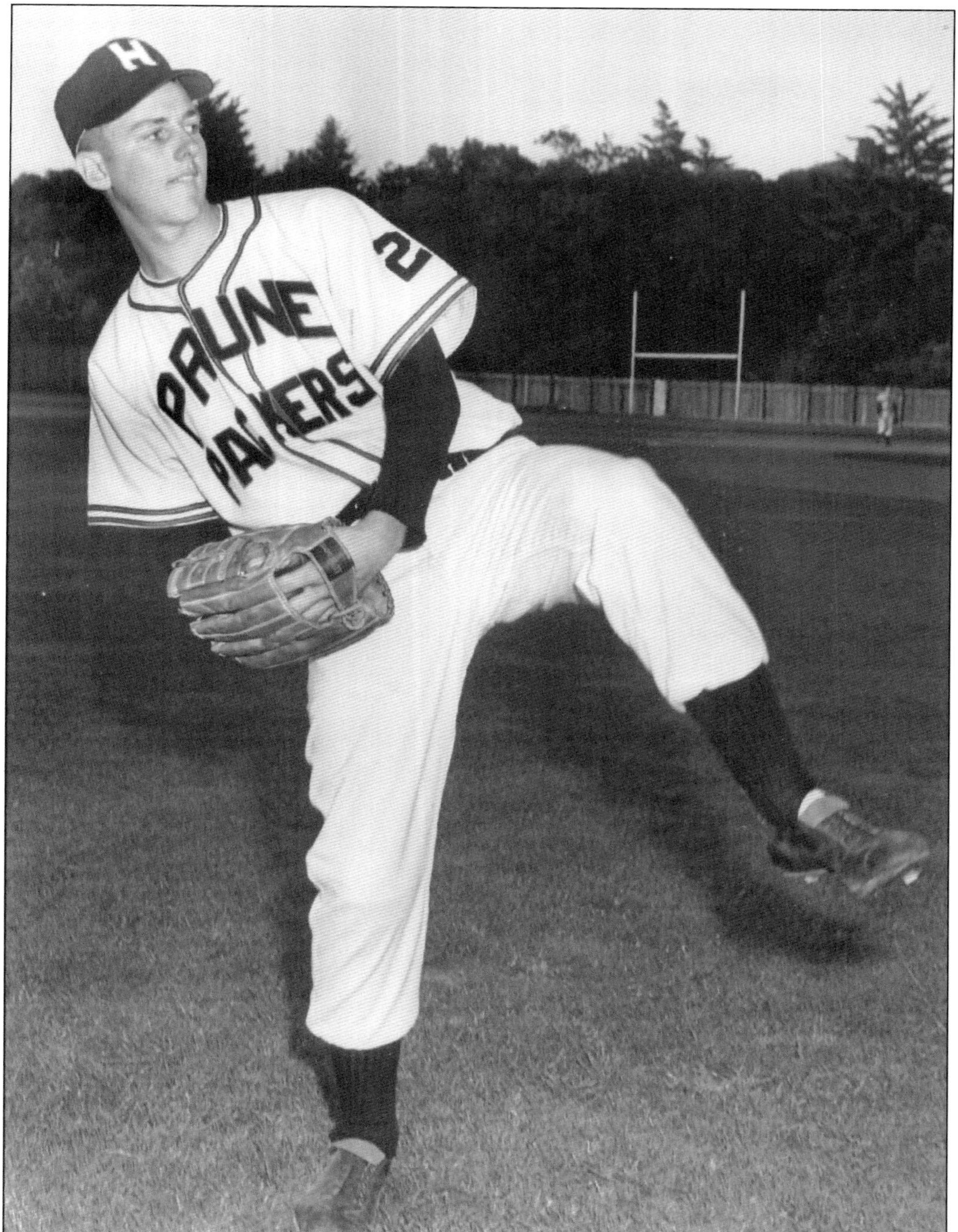

Lee Walker, a lanky pitcher from Sebastopol, played for Santa Rosa Jr. College, the Prune Packers, and other teams over a long career. In a 1951 game versus the San Francisco Seals, he earned a 4-3 win when the Prune Packers rallied for 3 runs in the late innings. A Sebastopol apple rancher, he was still pitching at age 45. Courtesy of the Ruonavaara collection.

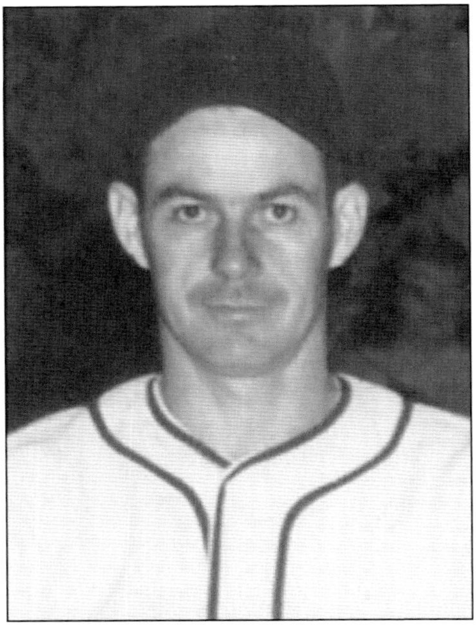

Clarence Ruonavaara was a coach, teacher, administrator, and weekend pitcher for Healdsburg semi-pro teams. He hit his peak as he pitched the Healdsburg IOOF to the county title in 1947, beating Lefty Ristau and Santa Rosa in a best-of-three series. He saw limited pitching action after hurting his arm installing light poles at Recreation Park in 1948. Courtesy of the Ruonavaara collection.

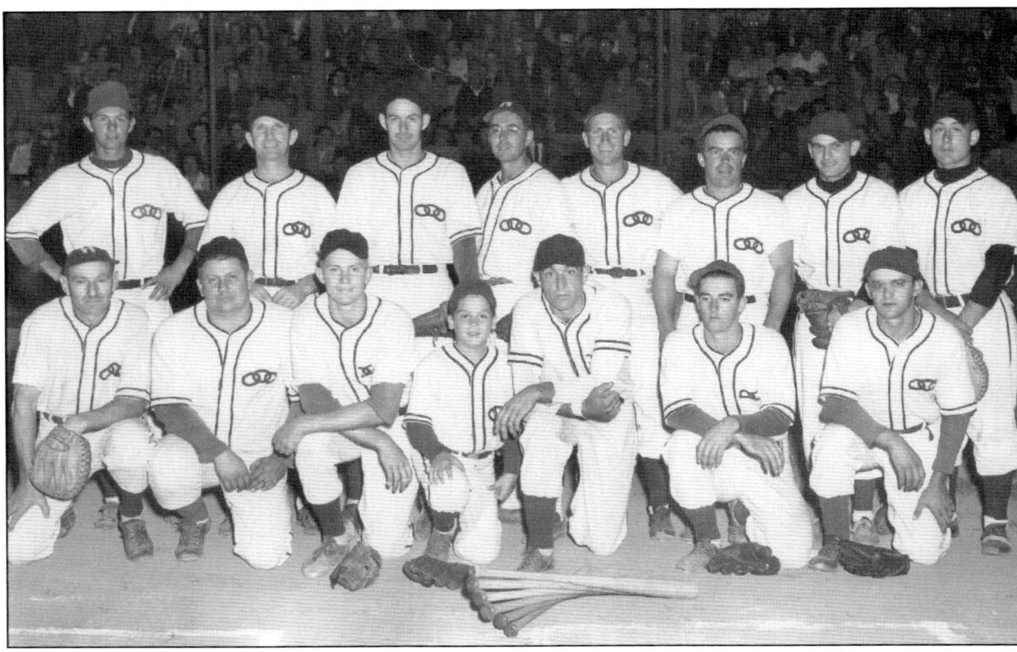

The 1949 Healdsburg IOOF nine, the first team to play under the new lights at Recreation Park, responded by winning the Sonoma County League title. Keith Walker, a surprise starter from the high school, pitched a 12-2 win over Crown Machine Shop of Santa Rosa to cinch first place. Morris Ruby's four hits led the attack. The IOOF team is pictured as follows, from left: (back row) Bill Wight, Dan Modena, Clarence Ruonavaara, Doug Badger, Morris Ruby, Bob Mascherini, Russ Coffman, and Bob Luzzi; (front) Frank Mott, Art Ruonavaara, Keith Walker, batboy Tom Passalaqua, Fred Figone, Pete Shreiber, and Elmo Barbieri. Courtesy of the Ruonavaara collection.

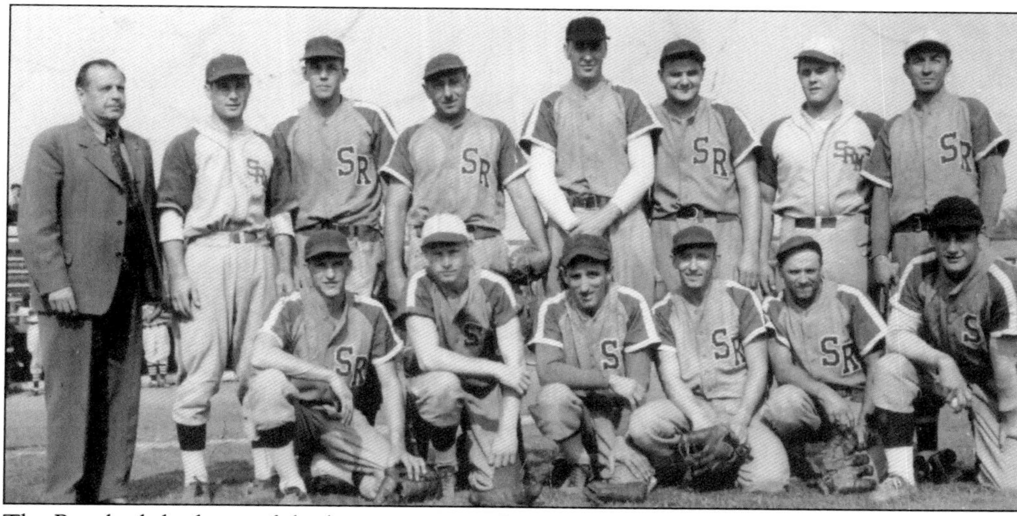

The Rosebuds had one of the better teams in Sonoma County from the 1920s on. This edition probably played around the end of World War II. Pictured are: (back row) public relations man Bill Claus, unidentified, John Smith, Frank Mott, Gordon Mann, John (Lefty) Wetch, Don Noriel, and manager Denny Moore; (front) Len Williams, Dick Read, Joe Dosal, and three unidentified. Courtesy of the Sonoma County Museum.

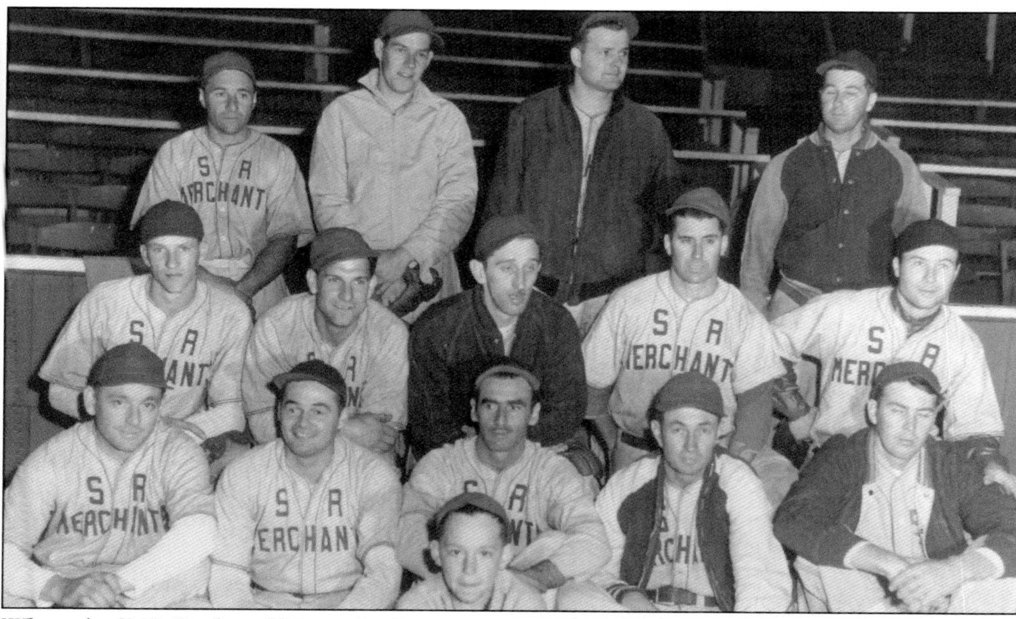

When the E.C. Kraft and Moose Lodge teams merged in the late 1930s, they called themselves the Santa Rosa Merchants. Later, the team changed its name to the Rosebuds. This Merchants team included: (back row) third baseman and outfielder Delmo Poli, unidentified, first baseman John (Lefty) Wetch, and second baseman and manager Norm Maroni; (middle) second baseman Len Williams, catcher George (Serb) Devoto, player-manager Joe Dosal, centerfielder Johnny Romero, shortstop Hal Eckhart; (bottom) catcher Pete Lencioni, pitcher Mel (Lefty) Ristau, unidentified, player-manager Denny Moore, and pitcher Gordon Mann. The batboy is unidentified. Courtesy of the Sonoma County Museum.

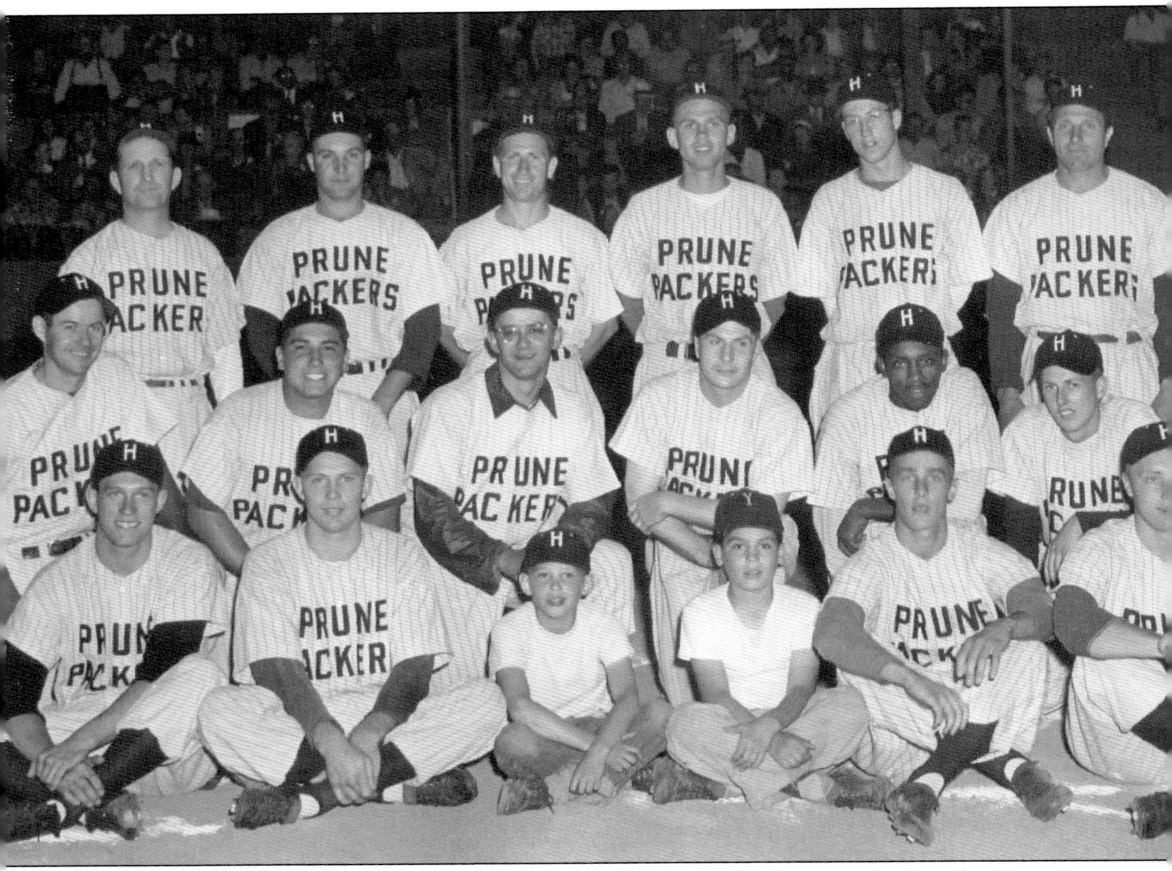

Healdsburg had another potent Prune Packer team in 1951, beating the Pacific Coast League San Francisco Seals in an exhibition game. In a battle of ex-major leaguers, Healdsburg manager Dolph Camilli outslugged Seals mentor Lefty O'Doul in a home-run hitting contest. The team is pictured here as follows: (back row) Dan Modena, Ed Seghesio, Morris Ruby, John McClellan, Dick Ament, and Dolph Camilli; (middle) Clarence Ruonavaara, Lou Lucas, Elmo Barbieri, Bob Lebsack, Marion Sims, and Lee Walker; (bottom) unidentified, Keith Walker, batboys Lonnie Hayworth Jr. and Tom Passalacqua, Gus Suhr, and Dick Camilli. Courtesy of the Darla Budworth collection.

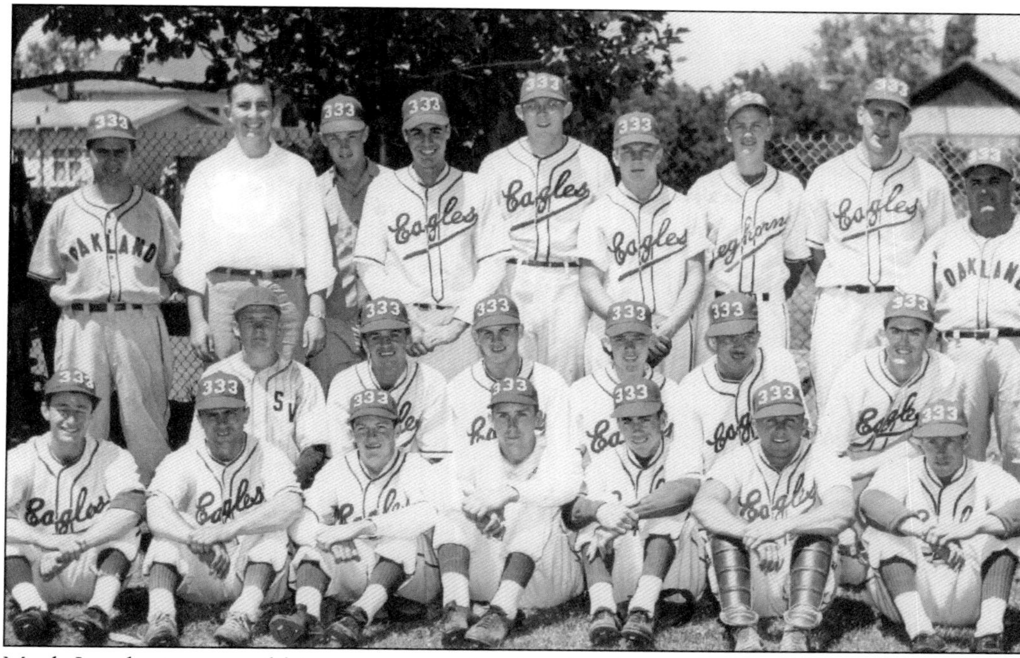

Moch Lucchesi managed his own son, pitcher Ron Lucchesi, and other young players on the Petaluma Eagles team in 1950. Players pictured here, on the squad, are: (back row) Roger Dempsey, writer Lee Torliatt, unidentified, Ron Lucchesi, unidentified, Dick Treadwell, Benny Walker, Walt Miller, and manager Lucchesi; (middle) Hank Soldati, Nardi Woodson, Jack Cameron, unidentified, Hank Simoni, and Allan Gilmore; (front) Norm Harris, Jack Segerman, Brad Evart, Ron Crandall, Darrell Gilmore, Harvey Jerome, and unidentified. Frank Ricci photo.

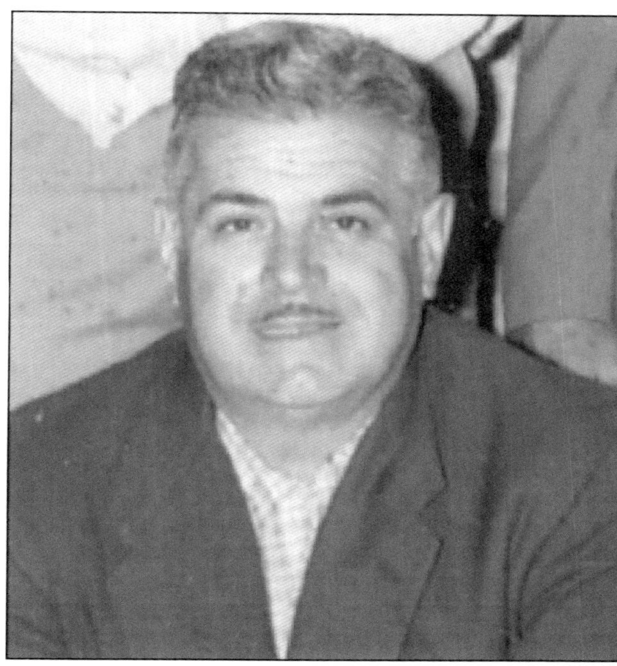

Moch Lucchesi was a power-hitting third baseman at Petaluma High School in the 1920s. He spent much of the rest of his life "paying back" to the community by managing teams and teaching young people to enjoy baseball. After World War II, he organized the Optimist Club father and son bean feed.

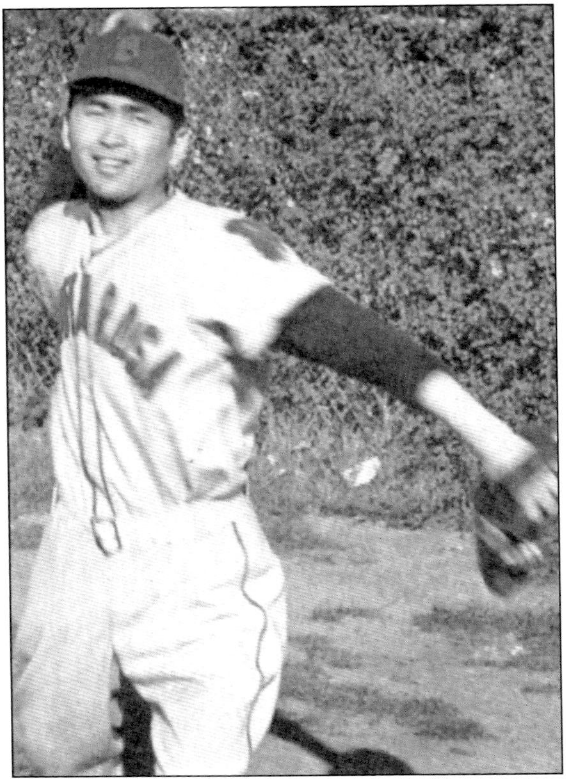

Bill Nishita, a clever right-hander from the Hawaiian Islands, was the ace of the Santa Rosa Junior College pitching staff, winning 15 games in a championship season in 1950. He boasted a 1.60 earned run average and helped himself at the plate with a .450 batting average. The Cubs went to the state playoffs but Nishita was only able to pitch once and the team lost the other two games. Courtesy of the 1950 *Patrin* yearbook.

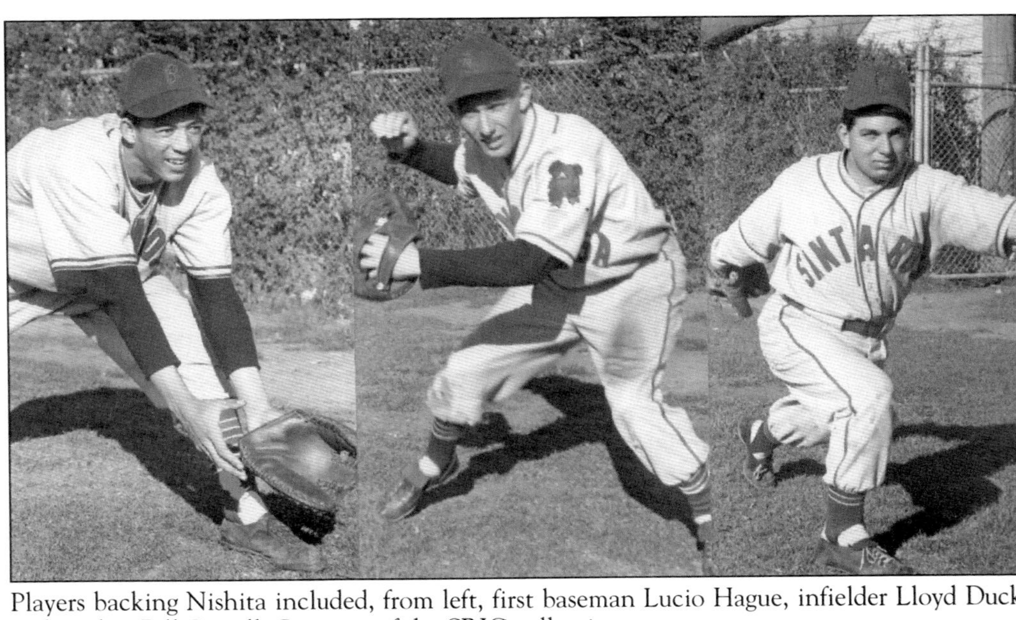

Players backing Nishita included, from left, first baseman Lucio Hague, infielder Lloyd Duck, and pitcher Bill Castell. Courtesy of the SRJC collection.

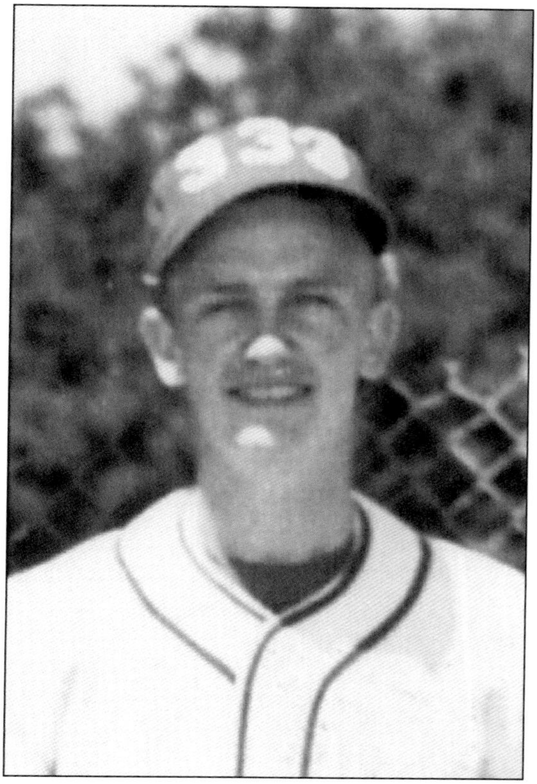

A lean right-hander with a sweeping curve ball, Benny Walker made good at Petaluma High and Santa Rosa Junior College in 1952. With backup from hitters such as captain Johnny Walker, Howard Herman, Larry Weller, and Bob Armstrong, pitchers Walker, George Read, and John Lynch breezed through the Big 7 Conference season with only one loss and beat Santa Ana for the state championship. Courtesy of the Petaluma Museum.

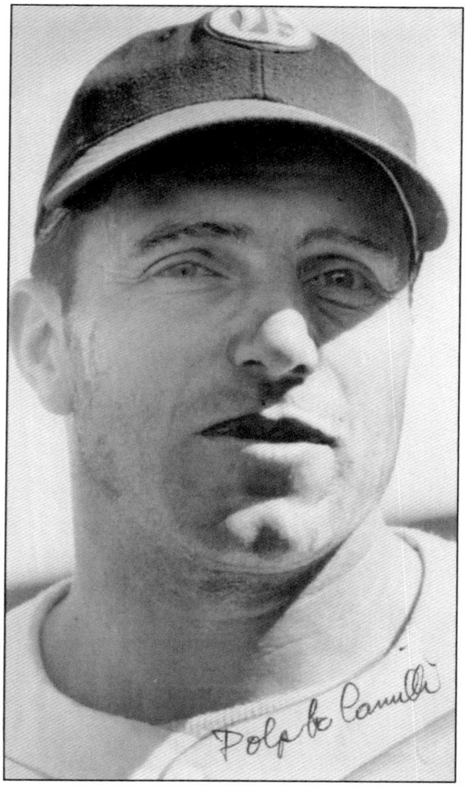

Dolph Camilli, the National League's Most Valuable player in 1941, was tapped to join the SRJC baseball staff in 1952 when coach Cook Sypher was called to serve in the Korean War. The former major league MVP masterminded the team to a state championship. Courtesy of the Sonoma County Museum.

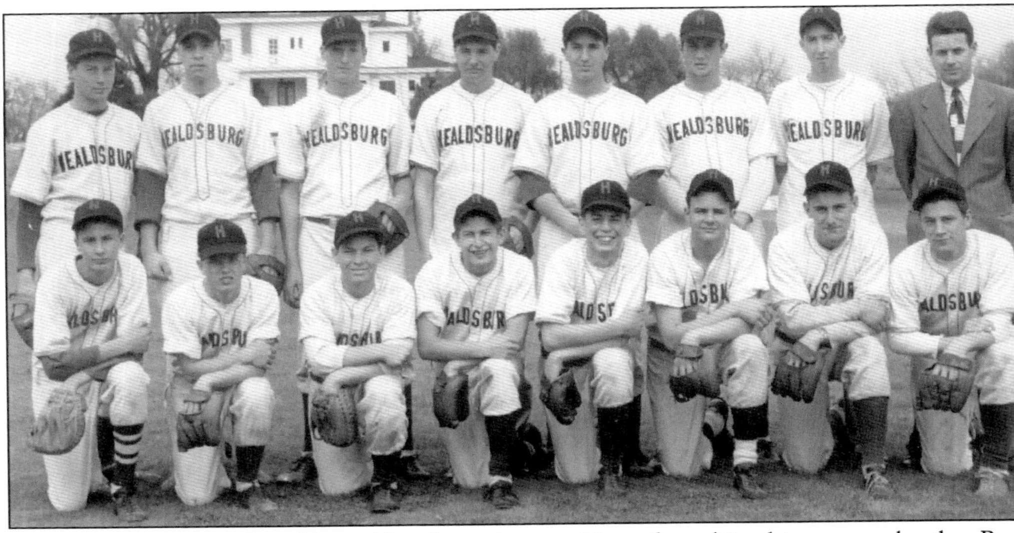

Clarence Ruonavaara found himself in the unique position of coaching his younger brother Russ on the Healdsburg High School Greyhounds team in 1949. The team played to a dead heat against Geyserville, which featured a future pro pitcher in hard-throwing Ernie Domenichelli. The Healdsburg team players are pictured here as follows, from the left: (back row) Roman LaRue, Dave Manley, Bob Lelouarn, Bill Rich, Dan Modena, John Gromo, Dick Patteson, and coach Ruonavaara; (front) Joe Farris, Bob Fisher, Don Potts, Geno DeRicco, Russ Ruonavaara, Darrell Chapman, Joe Rochioli and Gene Fletcher. Courtesy of the C. Ruonavaara collection.

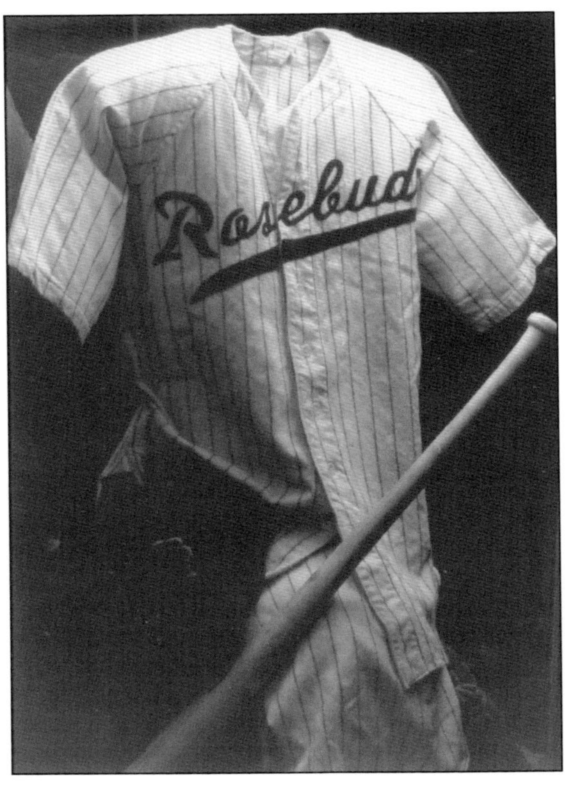

This is what the well-dressed Santa Rosa baseball player wore with pride on Sunday afternoons in the summer. This uniform belonged to Rosebud player-manager Denny Moore. Courtesy of the Sonoma County Museum.

Four

SOFTBALL

Numerous towns in Sonoma County built softball rivalries in the early 1930s, creating town leagues and playoffs for the county championship. Unlike hardball, the games went 7 innings and there were 10 players per team, including a roving shortstop. An active schedule filled grandstands in many parts of the county.

In 1937, with "Hap" Bridges pitching, Cook Sypher catching, and one of the famed Maroni brothers at second base, the Santa Rosa Elks won Santa Rosa's Twilight League title and went on to win the county crown as well. Bridges worked with the phone company during the day and Sypher coached night and day (football, rugby, ice hockey, and baseball) for Santa Rosa Junior College.

The Elks made the county finals against the unbeaten Mitchell's Jewelers of Healdsburg. In the showdown game, Bridges edged Americo Rafanelli 4-2 to end Healdsburg's win streak. Bridges reached his personal peak in the Santa Rosa League in June 1939, when he pitched a no-hitter, beating the post office team 4-0.

The Sebastopol National Bank won the label "Yankees of Sonoma County" in 1939, capitalizing on the slugging of John (Lefty) Wetch and the powerful pitching of Nick Wetch and George Wetch. Playing for the Gravenstein League title, the Wetch brothers made quick work of Mitchell Jewelers with a two-game sweep.

By the 1940s, a migrant from Ireland named Dick Gray impressed the world with his million-dollar arm. He continued to pitch into the 1970s while building a multi-million dollar dairy business in Petaluma.

Gray, a quick learner, was nine years old when his family emigrated from Ireland in 1928. Six years later, as a sophomore at Santa Rosa High School, he had developed into a national champion future farmer. As a senior he was student body president.

Called Dick "The Wheel," he developed his skills during World War II pitching for a team at Mare Island Naval Base. After the war, Gray hooked up with the Petaluma Merchants. In 1947, the Merchants won 32 of 34 games and in 1948 they were almost as good at 33 and 5. Gray pitched Petaluma teams to the semi-finals of the state tournament on several occasions and was known as one of the dominant hurlers of his time. He shared pitching duties in the late 1940s with Don Higgins, a rubber-armed right-hander from Sebastopol, who was known to toss a 7-inning game in Sebastopol, hop in his car for the 15-mile drive to Petaluma, and pitch another game the same night.

Some observers say Gray was not above using a little trickery to get a psychological edge over a batter. He was known to pull out his comb at a crucial moment and stop the action while he ran it through his locks, causing impatient batters to wait frustrated in the batter's box.

The talented Gray handled the matter of making a living as well as he pitched. A farmer at heart, he rented a dairy ranch on the outskirts of Petaluma in the early 1940s for $45 a month and sold Jersey milk in glass bottles. Over the years, he built a multi-million dollar empire that included 8 ranches and more than 1,300 acres.

Herb Dower, reflecting on his days as a softball pitcher in Sebastopol, says, "Sebastopol's softball field was located in those days on the playing field of the present Park Side Elementary

School...Down the right-field line were some tall trees, and I still remember John "Lefty" Wetch clearing them with a tape-measure blast.

"Sebastopol was the breeding ground for outstanding pitchers...How could anyone forget those great pitching battles that took place whenever pitchers like Don Higgins, Calvin Johnston, Jim Johnston, fire-balling Frank Frediani (the pride of the Graton Merchants), 'Red' Baker, or brothers Ken and Willie Johnson faced each other?

"How could anyone forget the 'swan-dive' catches of Jim Nagy, that 'Red' Baker always pitched without wearing a baseball glove, and that Petaluma's Dick Gray would gall Sebastopol fans by taking out his comb and combing his hair on the pitcher's mound."

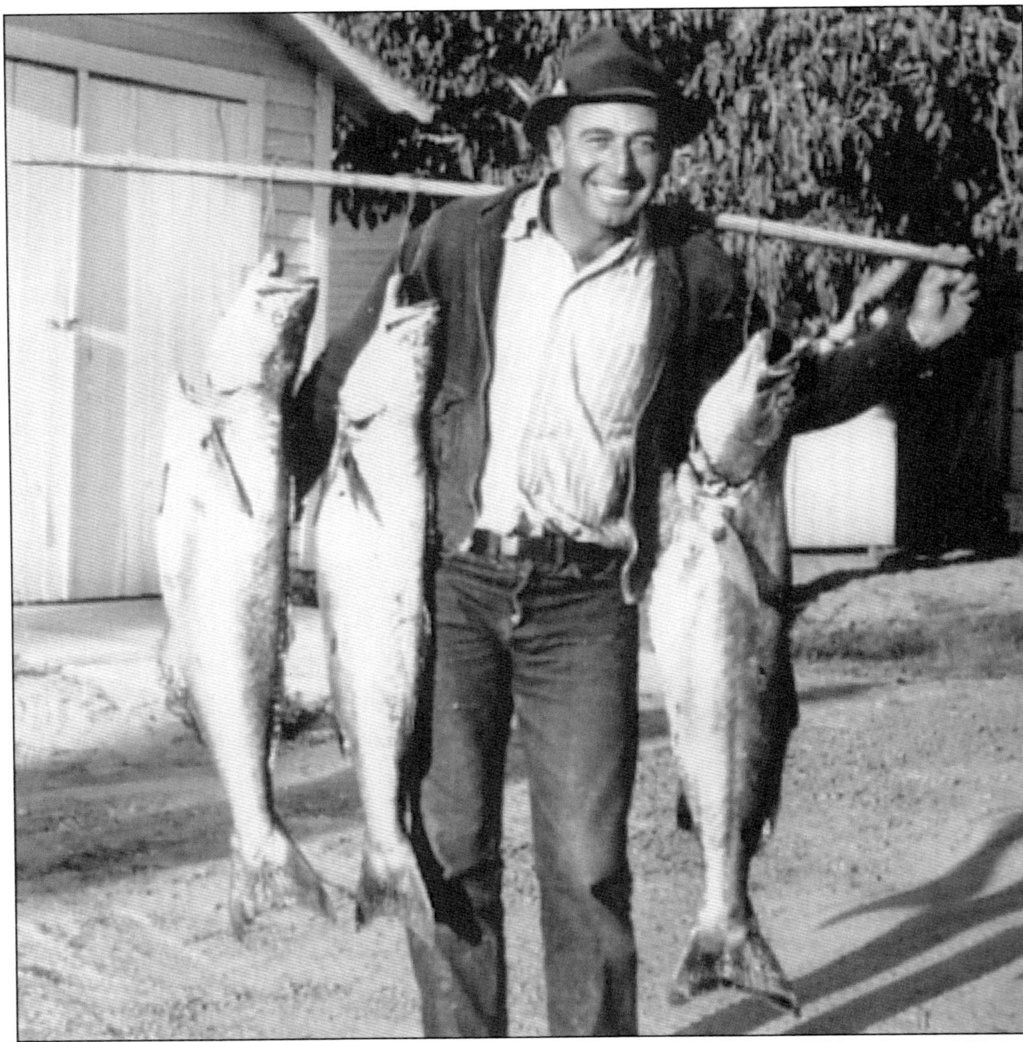

Charles (Hap) Bridges went fishing for the big ones on weekends but on Tuesday and Friday nights in the 1930s he threw a wicked fast ball and deceptive change-up to batters in the Santa Rosa Twilight Softball League. One of the best hurlers in the area, Bridges led his team to a county title in 1937 and a league title in 1938. In 1939, he shut down the post office team with a no-hitter. Fishing and pitching didn't interfere with his long career with the Pacific Telephone and Telegraph Co. Courtesy of the Laskelle collection.

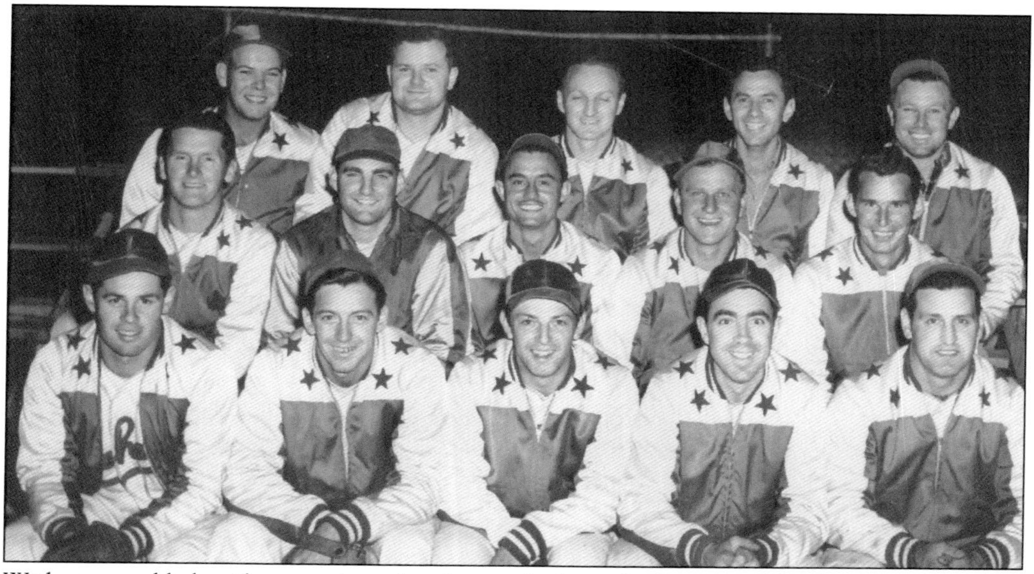

With star-studded uniforms and an abundance of talent, the Petaluma Merchants softball team was established in 1947 and stayed together for seven years. The Merchants won 32 of 34 games in 1947 and went 33 and 5 in 1948. The 1949 team is pictured as follows: (back row) Bill Jackson, John (Lefty) Wetch, Jack Cline, manager Lou Kaiser, and Gig Shoemaker; (middle) Dick Gray, Dick Michaels, Guido Cazazza, Merle Taylor, and Don Higgins; (front) Ed Noriel, Gil Winslow, Don Adams, Cecil Clippinger, and Bill Spaletta. Frank Ricci photo.

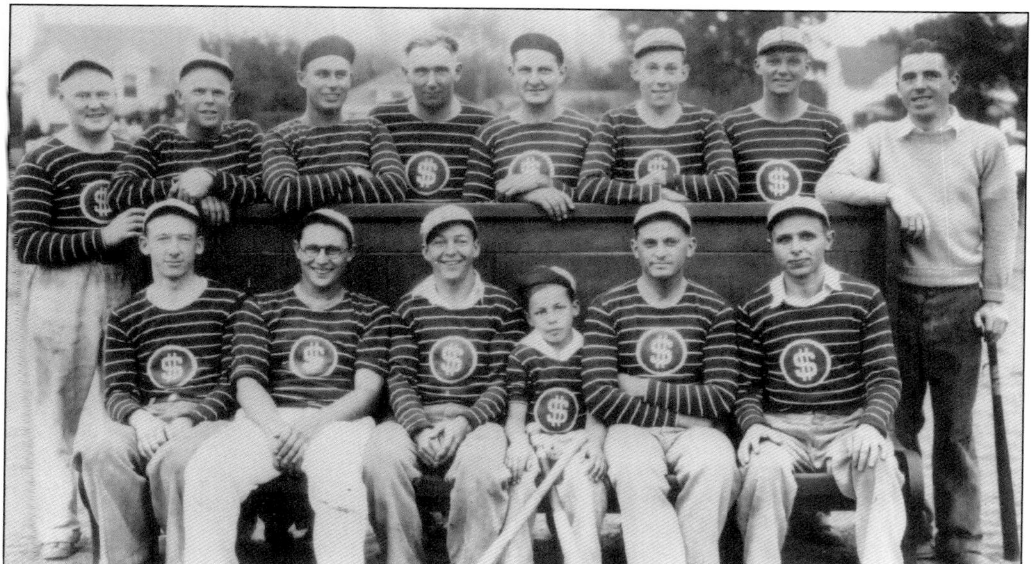

Dollar signs everywhere, they claimed they never shortchanged the opposition but they did know how to keep the crowd's interest. We're in debt to officials of the Healdsburg Bank of America team of 1931 for passing on team identifications. Pictured here are: (back row) Wilburn, Dick Cadd, Malone, Charles McCutchan, Leo Demostene, Everett Iversen, Waldo Iversen, and manager August Wagele; (front) Howard Pohley, Fred Comstock, Ned Auradou, Pat Dennes Jr., Ernie Demostene, and Frank Sillano. Courtesy of the Healdsburg Museum.

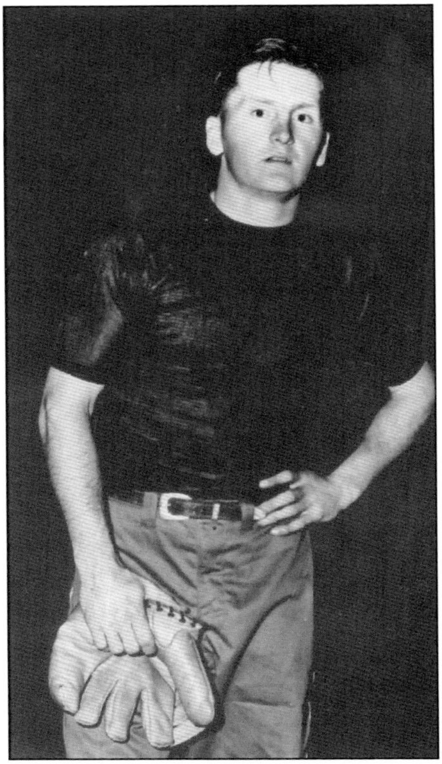

Dick Gray, who arrived in America from Ireland at age nine, carved out a business career as a dairyman and a sports career as a softball pitcher. Gray, who started pitching in the 1930s, was a regular on the mound for 34 years. Courtesy of the Gray family collection.

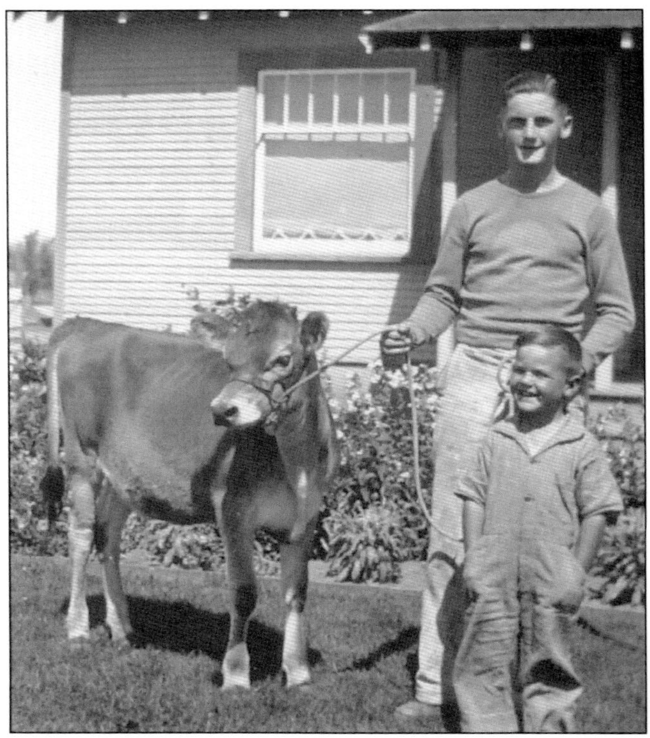

Future Farmer and future pitching ace Dick Gray, a student at Santa Rosa High School, showed his calf Wondalette at age six months in 1935. The cow was shown at the State Fair the following year. The small boy in the photo is unidentified. Courtesy of the Gray family collection.

Five

TRACK

The four teams of the Sonoma-Mendocino Athletic League—Ukiah, Santa Rosa, Petaluma, and Healdsburg—gathered in April 1900 in Ukiah and watched the host team win an easy victory. Healdsburg finished last but a young giant named Ralph Rose earned the team's only blue ribbon by tossing the shot 42 feet, 8 inches.

When Healdsburg sent three men to a field day at Berkeley in October 1900, Rose got all the attention, drawing guffaws from the crowd when he came on the field draped in a white woolen blanket. Some fans tagged him with the derisive nickname Hiawatha and continued chortling when he displayed his unorthodox style in the shot put. The awkward young man, with virtually no coaching, used a peculiar style, taking two short steps and then making a violent swing of his large body—215 pounds on a 6-foot, 5-inch frame. He silenced his critics by finishing second in both the shot put and the hammer throw. A couple of years later, still in high school, Rose broke the world's amateur shot put record with a toss of 49 feet 6 inches.

Rose showed up at the University of Michigan, and "without any preparation and in his street clothes," tossed the shot well over 40 feet. Soon he was routinely breaking world records in national and international events. He won gold medals at the Olympics of 1904, 1908, and 1912.

At Healdsburg High, Rose gave encouragement to Ed Beeson, a high jumper with potential. Beeson broke records at Healdsburg High, UC Berkeley, and the San Francisco Olympic Club.

Rose urged Beeson to use a left-footed takeoff from the left side of the bar in the high jump. Beeson liked the approach, and improved his numbers at Healdsburg and then at University of California with a version of what came to be known as the "western roll."

Beeson's main nemesis was George Horine, the high jump record holder at 6 feet, 7 inches. Beeson drew a crossbar on the wall of his room at 6-8, studied the mark morning and night and promised himself he would beat Horine. On May 2, 1914, he set a world's record of 6 feet, 7 5/16 inches, a mark that stood for 10 years.

Rose became a lawyer, joining a law practice in San Francisco. In 1913, the Healdsburg giant, often described as "the perfect man," was stricken with typhoid fever. After a brief illness, he died at the age of 29.

Beeson served in the U.S. Army Dental Corps during World War I and later divided his time between dentistry and coaching.

Aside from the Healdsburg superstars, track was one of the most popular sports early in the 20th century. Roy Evans, a prominent Petaluma real estate man, told the story of how the Petaluma High School track team took a water route to take on the Vallejo team in 1905. Fifteen Petaluma athletes boarded the Steamer Gold in Petaluma and braved rough waters before transferring to another ship in San Pablo Bay near the present San Rafael-Richmond Bridge.

Jim Anderson, later known affectionately as "Dr. Jim" to his hometown patients, led the Egg City team to a convincing victory. The future M.D. won four events and in one race reportedly pushed another runner across the finish line first.

Track competition in 1910 included teams in Santa Rosa, Benicia, Napa, Vallejo, Analy, and St. Helena. That same year, Healdsburg had a distinguished group of alumni, some in top shape and some less so, who took on the high school team on the new school track. Rose, Beeson, sprinter Mervyn

Silberstein, and many other "relics of the graveyard" showed up "in 57 varieties of conditions." When the smoke had cleared the high school and alums ended up tied at 65 points each.

At Santa Rosa in 1911, I.D. Steele, vice-principal and teacher of History and Civics, coached the track team, which was, according to the yearbook staff, "practically the victor of all the North Bay schools."

The school's governing board authorized tickets for the track team to travel to Stanford and Benicia; the track captain was authorized to spend $1.60 to send the vaulting pole to and from Palo Alto.

Eight teams went to Ukiah for the field day involving representatives from Sonoma, Mendocino, and Marin counties in 1915. A 14-car train carried fans from Healdsburg and Santa Rosa to the meet.

The Santa Rosa band "gave the merry students many selections, playing at every stop along the road." The students, headed by the band, paraded from the depot to the plaza at Ukiah. Santa Rosa's team captain, Russell, led his team to a first place finish.

At Santa Rosa Junior College, an interclass track meet was held for the first time in 1924. A coachless team of eight men placed in a conference meet for the first time in 1926. Greater recognition came when the B team won the division conference crown in 1937. In 1941, a lad named Ben Steele did triple duty as a javelin, shot, and discus thrower.

In the late 1920s, Sonoma County found itself part of the marathon to end all marathons: a 480-mile chase from San Francisco to Grants Pass, Oregon. Native Americans, armed with ragged running shoes and strong hearts, competed in the grueling run in 1927 and 1928.

The race was the brainstorm of Charlie "Cash and Carry" Pyle of Santa Rosa, who was hired by the Redwood Empire Association to promote travel on Redwood Highway 101.

Eight Karook Indians from Happy Camp near the California-Oregon border and three Zuni from the Gallup, New Mexico area, started the 1927 race. Mad Bull, alias John Southard, won the race and the $1,000 grand prize, completing the course in 7 days, 12 hours and 34 minutes.

With his winnings, Mad Bull bought a "brilliantly-painted" sedan and ordered the name "Mad Bull" painted on the side in gilt lettering.

In 1928, 29 starters competed for the first place money of $5,000. Henry Thomas, racing as Flying Cloud, took the lead in Marin County and finished the course in 7 days. Ten miles behind in 1927, he won by 17 miles in 1928.

The Petaluma Spartans organized the first full-fledged marathon run west of the Mississippi in 1934 as runners huffed and puffed 26 miles, 385 yards from Petaluma to Sebastopol, Santa Rosa, Penngrove, and back to Petaluma. Later, the course was laid out in and near Petaluma only.

Spartan Leland "Clipper" Smith set the record for the event, coming in just over 2 hours and 47 minutes. The marathon was run for the 18th time in 1952, under the guidance of Petaluma runner, banker, and historian Ed Fratini.

The Spartans competed in numerous AAU-sanctioned events. In 1943, their best year, the team took 7 of 11 events they entered. The Spartans were also frequent winners in the rugged Dipsea run in Marin County.

When the club was formed in the 1920s, the runners covered shorter distances. In August 1929, for instance, Art Spolini of the Spartans raced 5.7 miles from Penngrove to Petaluma in 34 minutes. One runner was disqualified for hitching a ride on the running board of a car.

Bert Kerrigan, who came to Petaluma after World War I and put the town on the map as the "World's Egg Basket," was an outstanding high jumper, even though he was only 5 feet, 5 1/4 inches tall. The bouncing Kerrigan, who would later impress people with his promotional skills, electrified track fans in Portland, Oregon in an 1897 meet with "the greatest high jump ever recorded." Cartoonist Robert Edgren said that Kerrigan, jumping for the Multnomah A.C. of Portland, cleared the bar at 6 feet, 4 1/2 inches, 11 1/4 inches above his own head. He later competed for the U.S. in the Olympic Games.

To put Petaluma on the map, Kerrigan created a wide range of Egg Day activities, including a "human rooster," parade, an Egg Day wedding, and Egg Day queen contests.

Kerrigan helped organize the Spartan Athletic Club and, to celebrate his 52nd birthday, took several witnesses to a ranch outside Petaluma where he calmly high jumped over a 5-foot high horse. Returning to his office, the feisty Kerrigan "made a neat jump over a 4-foot mail box on the side walk before going to his office to settle down for a hard day's work."

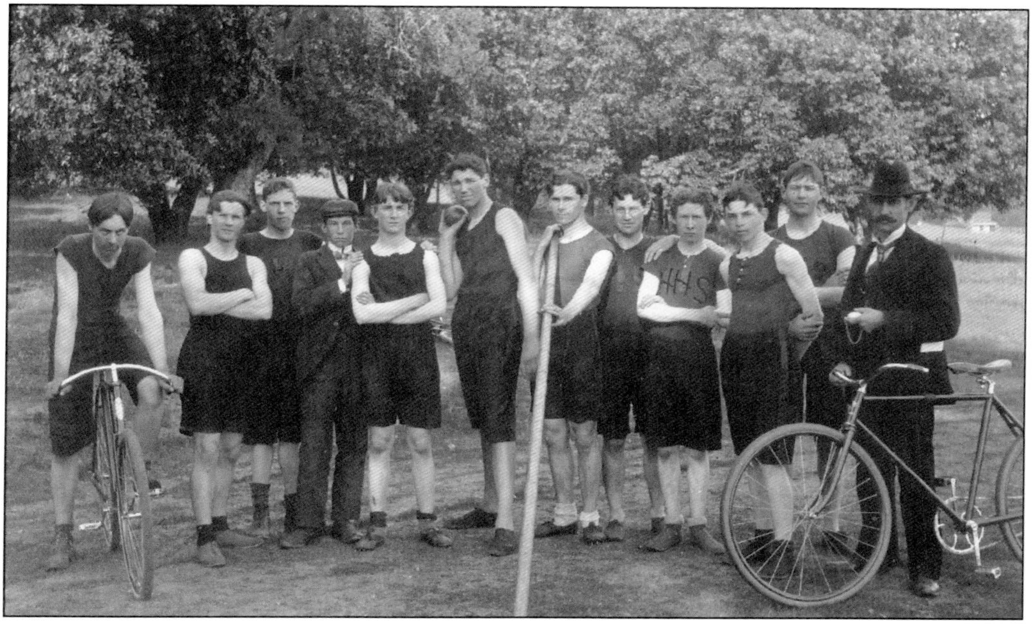

There was this big guy named Ralph and a lot of littler guys with desire. That was enough to make Healdsburg competitive in high school track in 1901. Pictured, from left, are: Russell Galloway, unidentified, Harvey Frost, Ed Jackson, unidentified, weightman and future Olympic champion Ralph Rose, pole vaulter Harry Bell, Guy Jackson, unidentified, Mervin Silverstein, Wagers, Derral, and "Dad" E.B. Snook. Courtesy of the Healdsburg Museum.

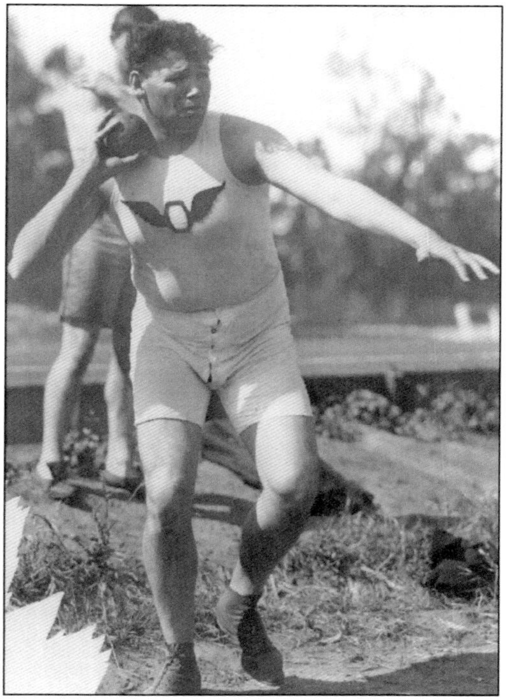

Ralph Rose won the 16-pound shot put event in the 1904 St. Louis Olympics. In Sweden in 1912 with the U.S. team, he set a world record of 51 feet, 7 1/2 inches for the shot put. A product of Healdsburg schools, the powerful Rose won the national AAU shot put title four years in a row. He won the discus title twice and the javelin once. Stricken with typhoid fever, he died in 1913 just short of his 30th birthday. Courtesy of the Sonoma County Museum.

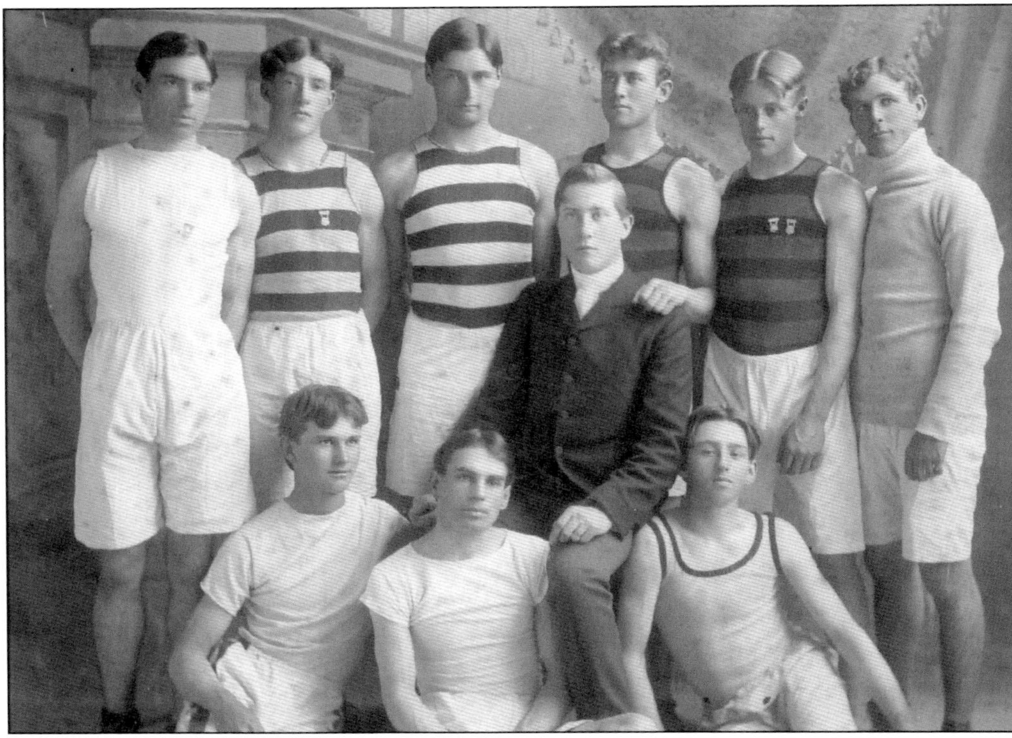

Santa Rosa High School didn't have a Ralph Rose but it did have a strong track team in 1901. Manager Ross Moody is in the center and Claud Sanborn is fifth from the right in the top row. Team members (not in order) included Alfred Howe, Ed Harris, Louis Frei, Bill Kullian, Sanborn, Mulgrew, Mallory, Lenard Davis, Jeffrey Wright, Albert Howe, and Russell Smith. The relay team of Mulgrew, Mallory, Howe, and Sanborn set a record for the event as the team placed second in the field day at Ukiah behind the host team. Courtesy of the Sonoma County Museum.

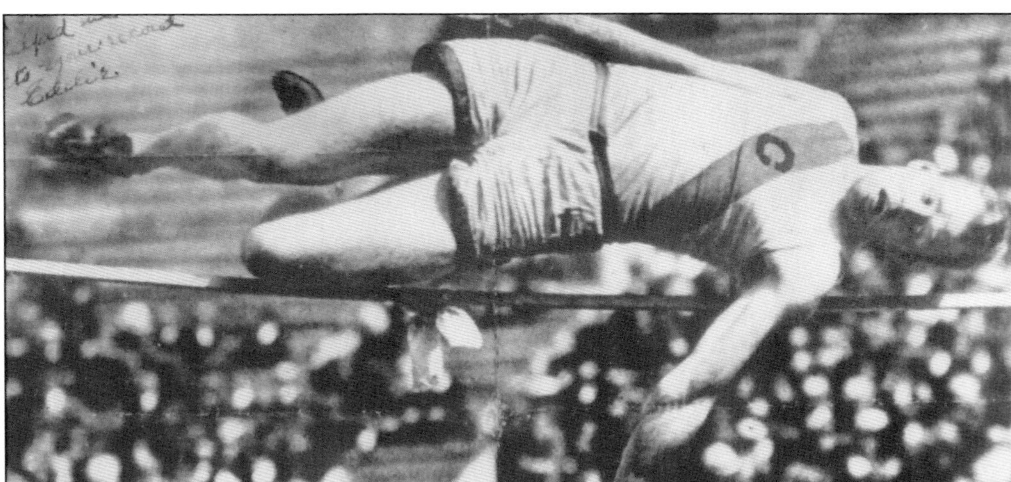

Ed Beeson of Healdsburg's class of 1909 developed a version of the "western roll" that served him well in the high jump. Beeson, called "the man on springs," broke the world record in 1914, clearing the bar at 6 feet, 7 and 5/6 inches. Courtesy of the Sonoma County Museum.

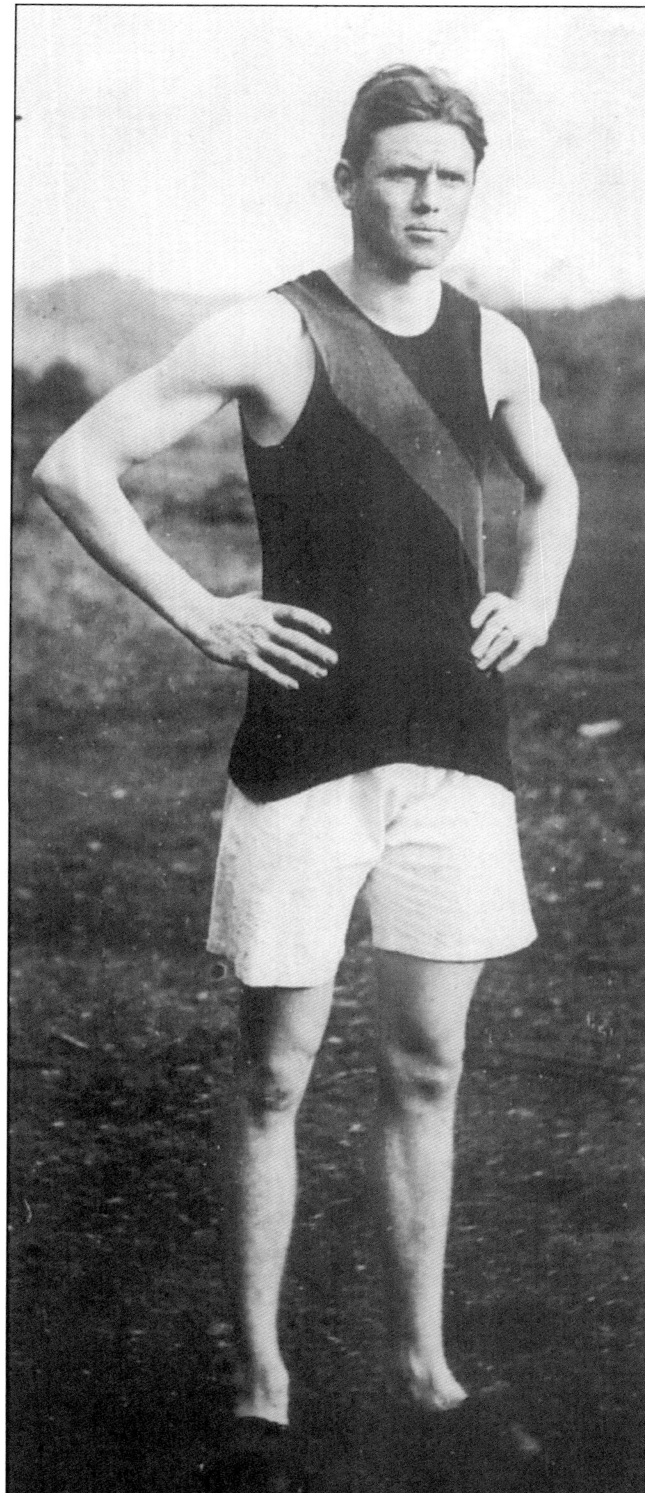

Ed Beeson followed in the footsteps of the legendary Ralph Rose, becoming one of the great track athletes in Sonoma County. Courtesy of the Healdsburg Museum.

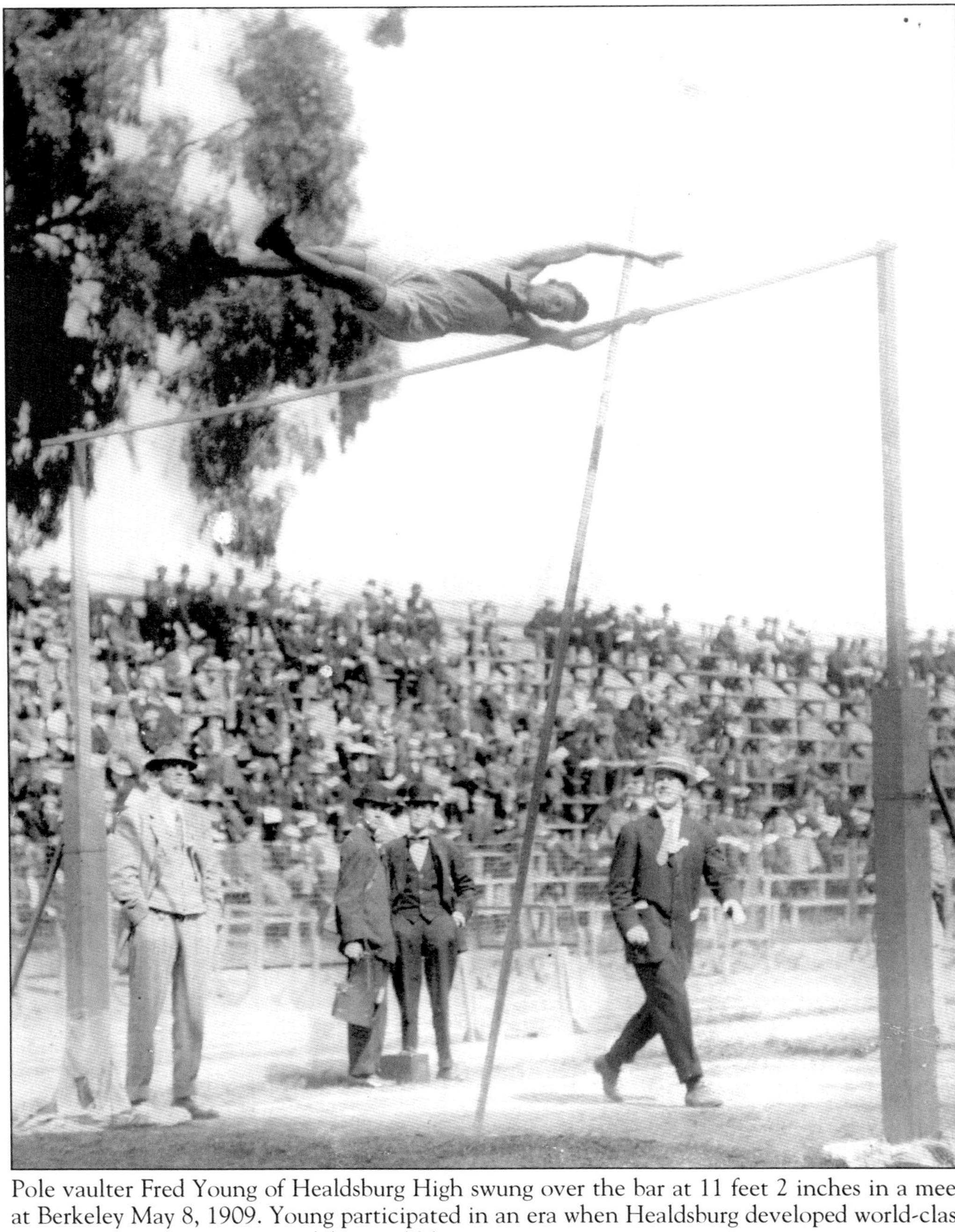

Pole vaulter Fred Young of Healdsburg High swung over the bar at 11 feet 2 inches in a meet at Berkeley May 8, 1909. Young participated in an era when Healdsburg developed world-class track competitors. Courtesy of the Healdsburg Museum.

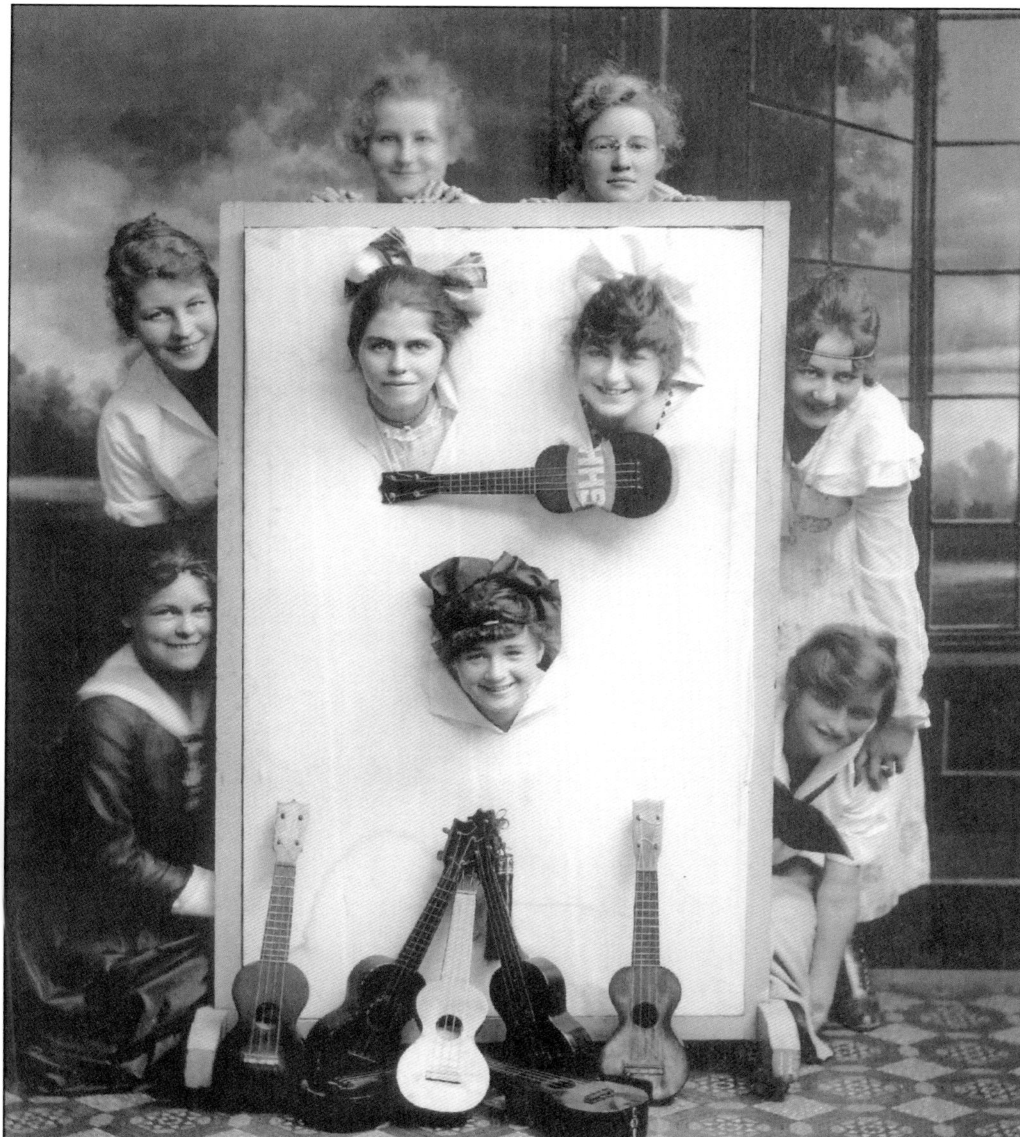

Let's hear it for good old school spirit. When teams began to compete in sports, rooters poured out to cheer their favorites to victory. There were rallies, parades, bands, pom-pom girls, cheerleaders, and lots of noise. Healdsburg High School gave it a melodic twist with their hard-playing and loud-cheering ukulele girls who came out in 1916 to root their Greyhounds to victory. The group also did a recital, featuring "old plantation songs and popular Hawaiian airs." The group, pictured here from left: (top row) Marguerite Snook Rowland and Cleone Snook Stevens/Tilley; (middle) Rossaline Mason Maher, Laura Jones, unidentified, and Marie Wagers Phillips; (front) Margaret Wrenn and two unidentified. Courtesy of the Healdsburg Museum.

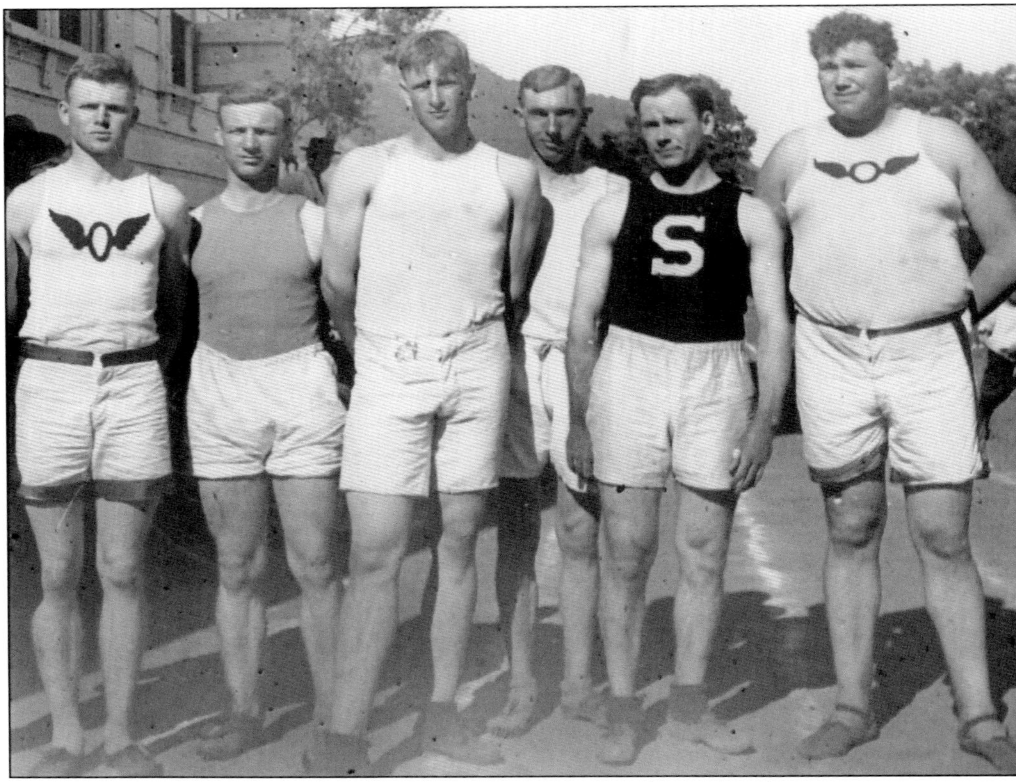

Gathering at the Healdsburg alumni meet in 1910 were former trackmen in "various stages of conditioning." Pictured here are, from the left, Ed Beeson, Floyd Bailey, Charles Widlund, Henry Coffman, Harry Bell, and Ralph Rose. Courtesy of the Healdsburg Museum.

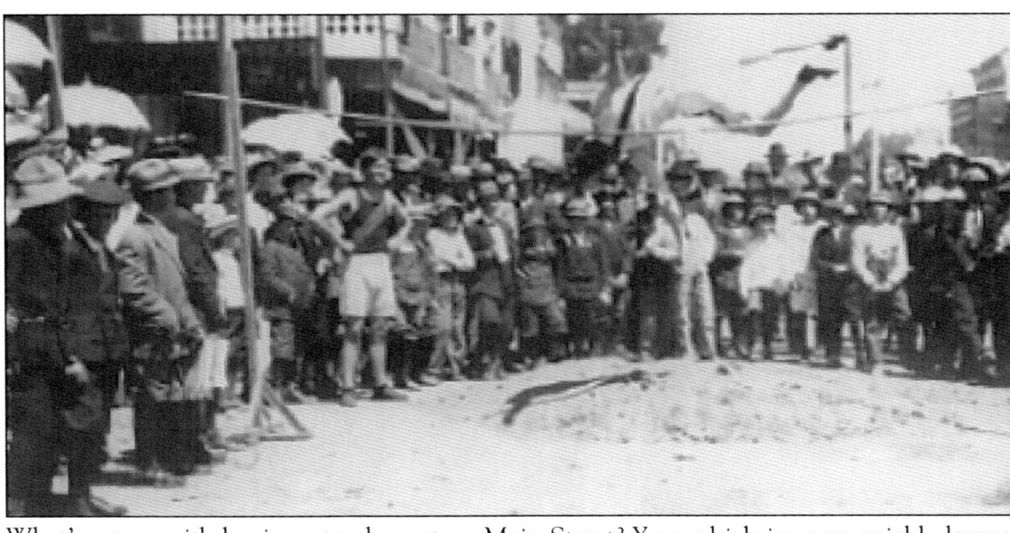

What's wrong with having a track meet on Main Street? Young high jumpers quickly learned what it was like to take a hard fall into a makeshift pit in the middle of the street in Healdsburg. Undaunted by the prospect of a rough landing, high jumper Ed Beeson soared over the bar. Courtesy of the Sonoma County Museum.

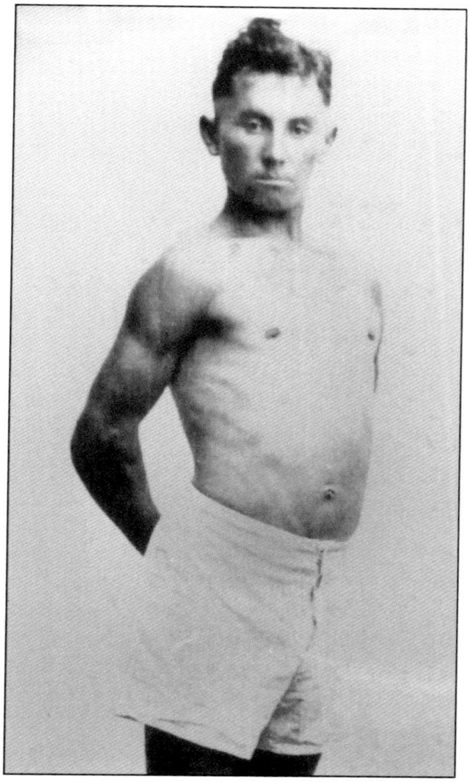 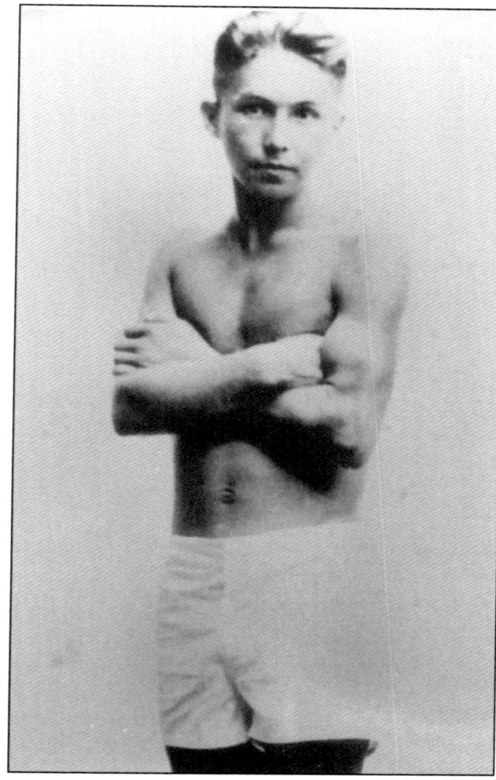

It was the equivalent of running 18 marathons. The Indian ultra-marathon, a 480-mile chase from San Francisco to Grants Pass, Oregon, held in 1927 and 1928, featured Karook runners from the Klamath River area in northern California and Zuni Indians from New Mexico. Mad Bull (left) a name given to John Southard by an inventive public relations man for the Redwood Empire Association, was the first winner in 1927; other runners included (right) his brother Rushing Water (Gorham Southard). Gorham died shortly after the race. Henry Thomas, also known as Flying Cloud, ran the course in 7 days in 1928, winning $5,000. Courtesy of the Sonoma County Museum.

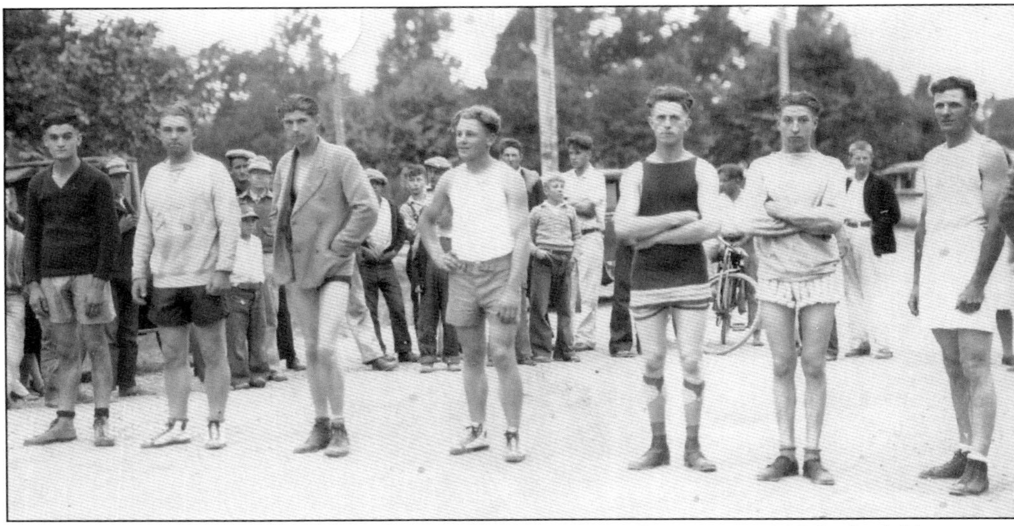

Compared to the run to Grants Pass, events in Sonoma County in 1928 looked like sprints. There was a 15-mile run in Cloverdale in late June followed by a 10-miler in Cotati in July. The Cotati runners, although a bit short on sartorial splendor, showed plenty of enthusiasm. Pictured here are, from the left, Jim Veronda, Petersen, William Sarlin, Joe Roberts, Ray Starks, and R. Scilling. Courtesy of the Petaluma Museum.

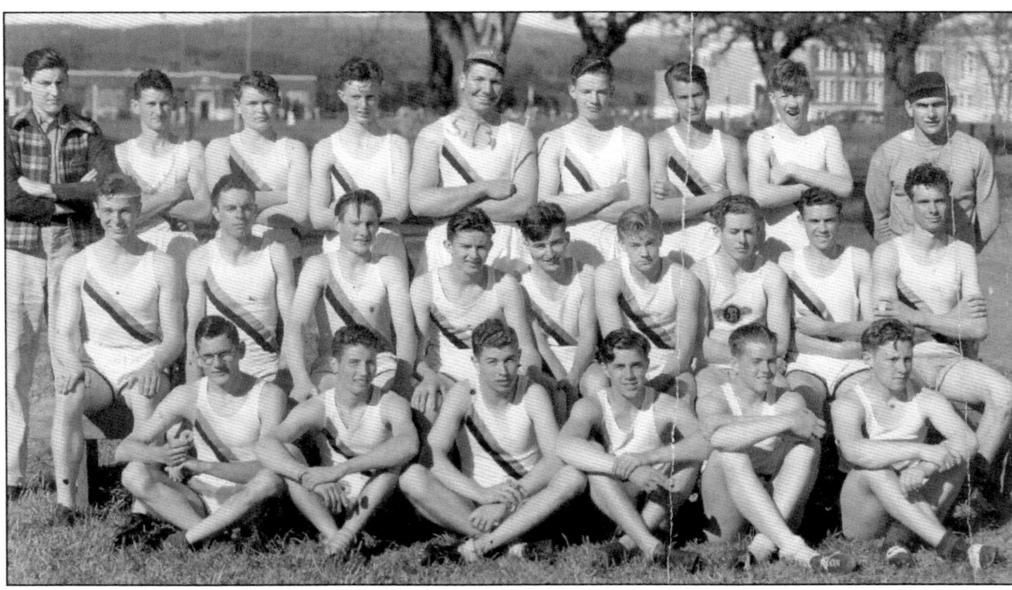

The 1936 Santa Rosa High School track team included giant weightman Sterling Bussman (fifth from the left in the back row) who held major discus records for many years. Other team members included Pete Cambra, second row, third from right; Doug Whited, front row, far left; and Bob Call, third from left, front row. Courtesy of the Bussman family collection.

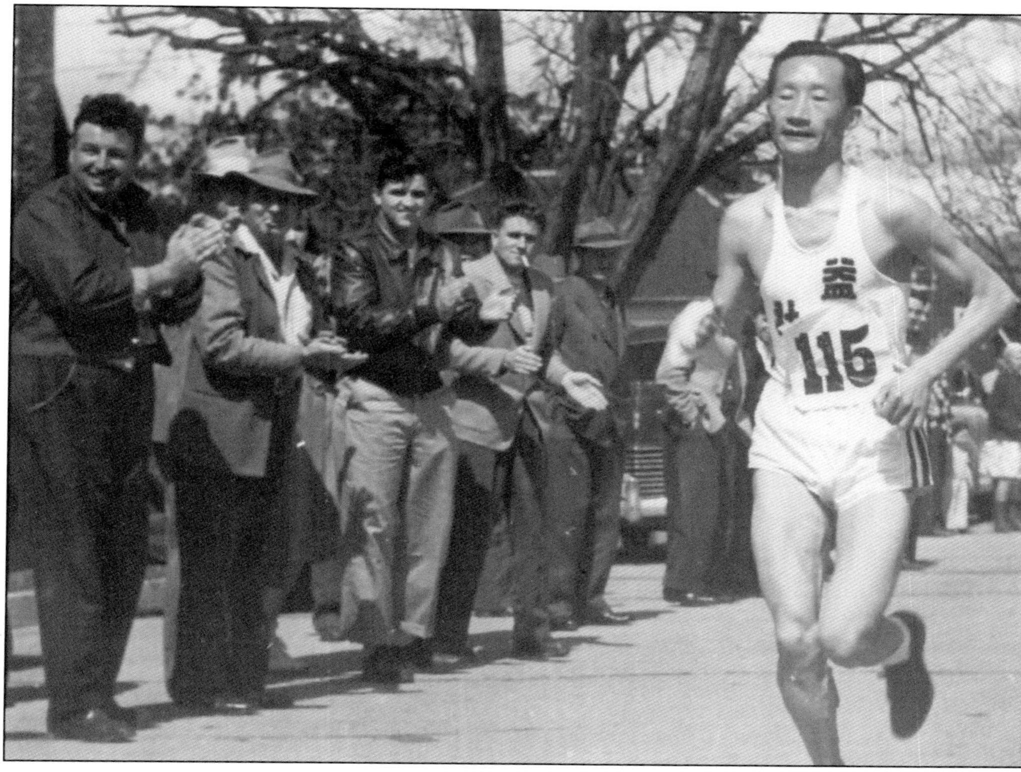

Wang Chang Ling of China won the 1948 Petaluma Spartans marathon in 2 hours, 48 minutes, 18 seconds—about a minute shy of the record set by Clipper Smith of the Spartans in 1943. Ling came back to win again in 1951 in just under 3 hours. Courtesy of the Petaluma Museum.

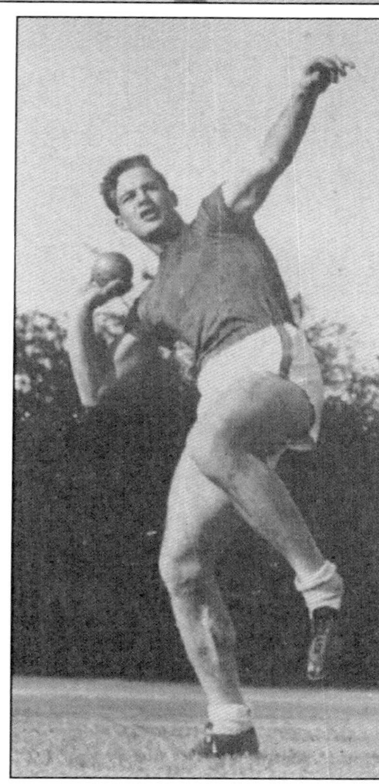

Big Ben Steele, a versatile weightman, gave a "lift" to the Santa Rosa Junior College track team in 1941, coming up with his best performance in the "Big Meet" against Marin. Steele set meet and conference records in the shot put, discus, and javelin, and added a second in the 120 high hurdles.

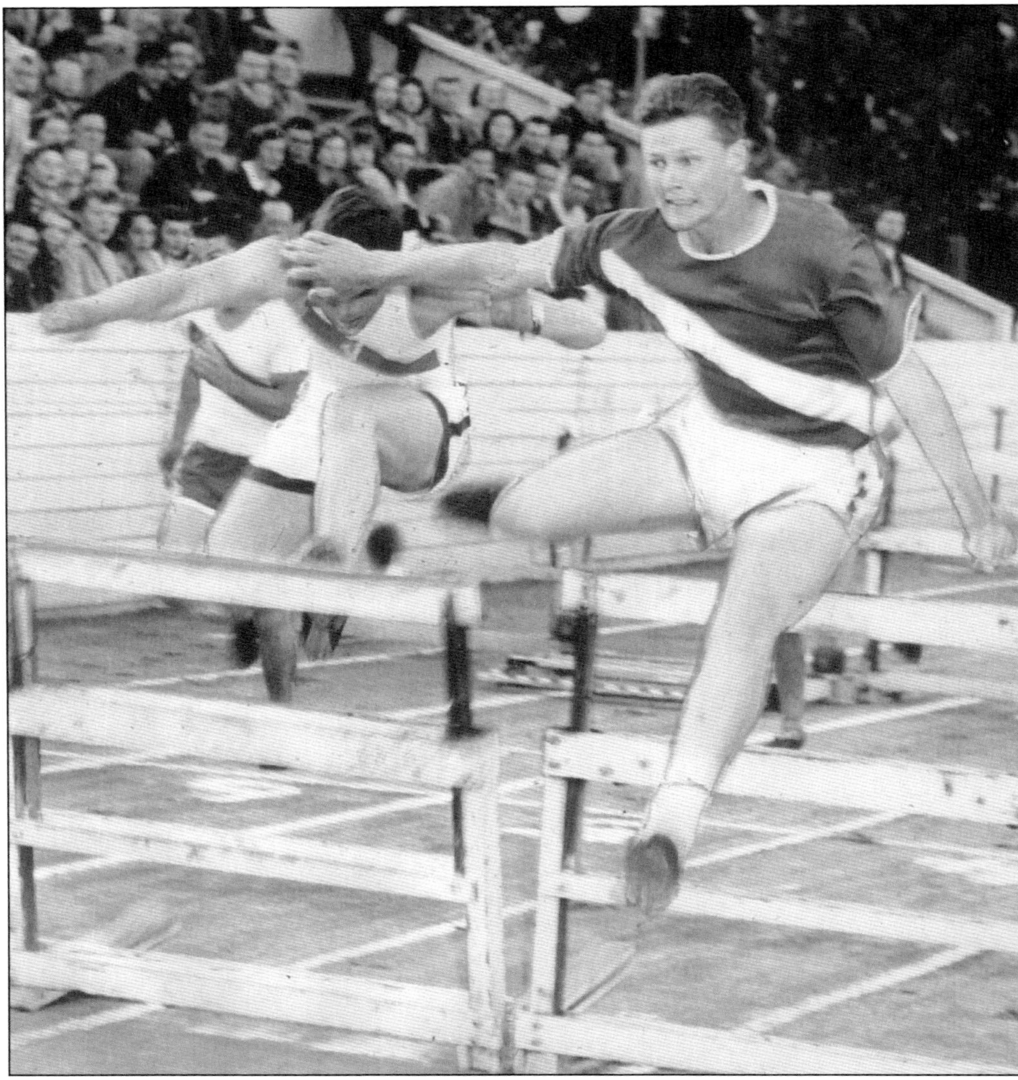

Analy's Bill Scheidecker raced to a 120 high hurdles victory in the North Bay League meet in 1950. Trailing, from left, were Mac MacPherson of Petaluma and Russ Ellis of Vallejo. Scheidecker led a double life in the spring, pitching baseballs and then competing in track meets later in the day. John LeBaron photo.

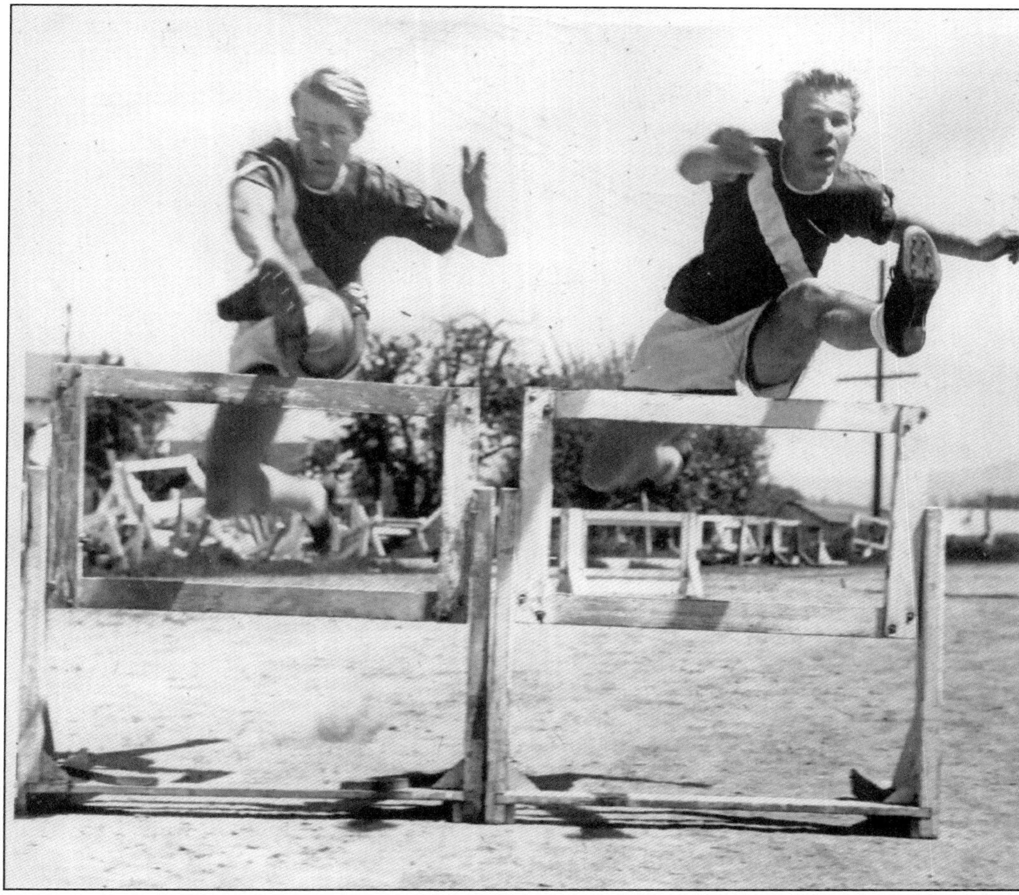

Hurdling twins Dick and Bob DeVilbiss worked on their form in 1950 practice session on the Analy track in Sebastopol. Courtesy of the Foster collection.

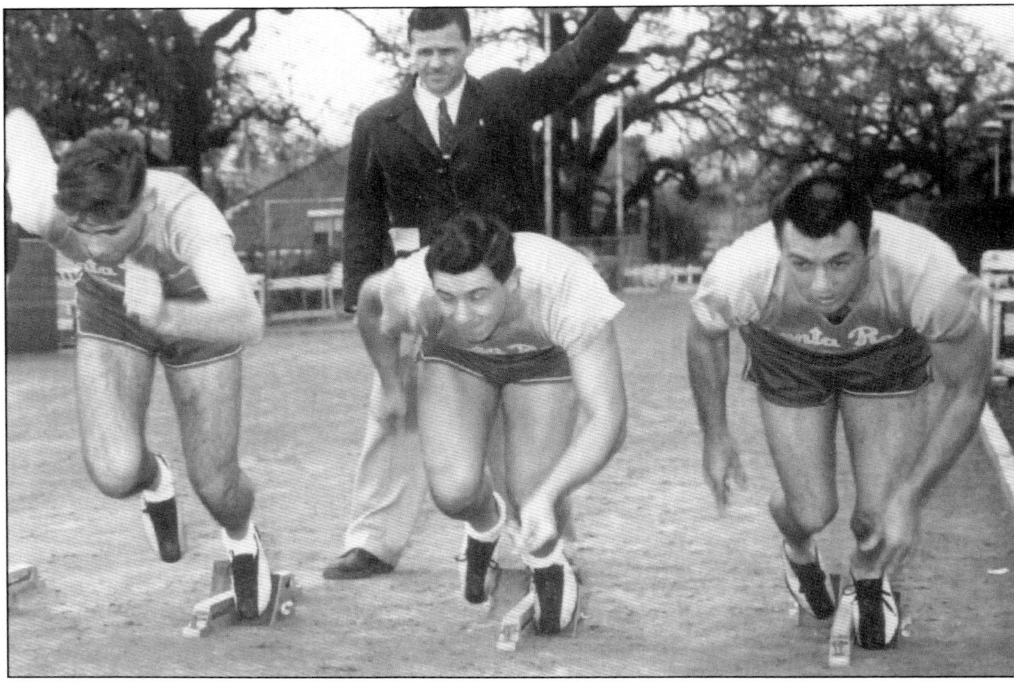

Timer Jack Cooper declared a fair start as runners broke from the blocks under the oaks at Bailey Field, a locale used for many of the major track meets in Sonoma County in the 1940s and '50s. Courtesy of the SRJC collection.

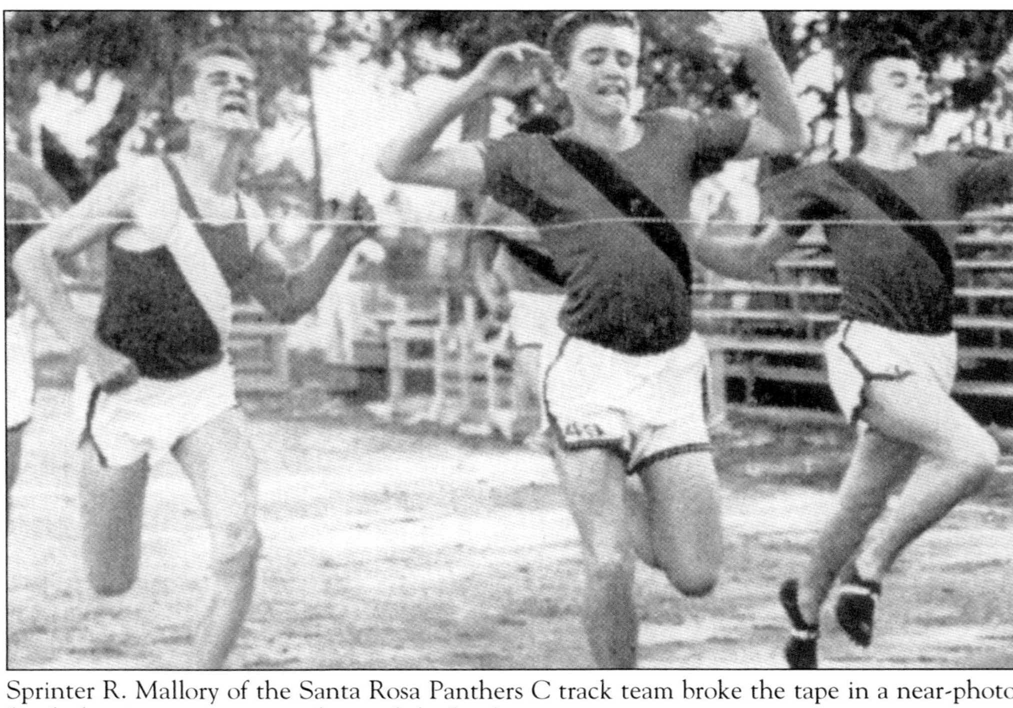

Sprinter R. Mallory of the Santa Rosa Panthers C track team broke the tape in a near-photo-finish, leaving two straining foes to fight for the runner-up spot.

Six

Basketball

Women's basketball teams were playing as early as 1902. In 1905 a Healdsburg high school delegation traveled to Santa Rosa to "to obtain valuable information on how the game should be played." Following the boys' Thanksgiving Day football game that year, the girls played an exhibition game at Truitt's theater. Literature teacher Vesta Cornish and dentist Fred Kinley provided the inspiration and coaching for the team. Petaluma came to town December 16 and won 21-14. Dr. Kinley, serving as referee, was reportedly called "a liar" by a Petaluma girl at a tense moment in the game.

By 1908, Healdsburg's women claimed a major northern California title with a team that handled high school and college opponents with ease. While Ed Beeson was making his name in track, Elva Beeson was becoming a star on the girl's team. The squad included Elva Beeson Grant, Bera Mothorn (later the wife of Ed Beeson), Gertrude Field, Aubry Butler, Kathleen Swisher Poppe, Una Williams Anderson, and Audry Walters Huedry.

The Healdsburg women became champions of the Academic Athletic League by edging Cogswell Polytechnic College in Oakland 16-14.

When Santa Rosa's girls started out for Sonoma to play a basketball game one Friday in 1910, it turned into an adventure. Some of the girls crammed into a car but when the vehicle broke down shortly after leaving Santa Rosa, they were forced to switch to a buggy for the rest of the trip. Those in a smaller auto had another breakdown near Sonoma, walking into the gym at 9 p.m. The girls in the buggy arrived a half-hour later and the game started at 10 p.m., well past the scheduled tip-off time. Putting their stressful day behind them, Santa Rosa's girls beat Sonoma 18-10.

Boys' high school sports took a major leap forward when the Union Basketball League was formed in 1907, featuring five teams: Healdsburg, Santa Rosa, Santa Rosa Business College, Petaluma, and San Rafael. Santa Rosa won the title and Healdsburg was runner-up.

Petaluma hosted Sonoma at the Dreamland Rink in 1907, and whether it was the home court advantage or superior skill, the Egg City team scored a 69-6 victory, after leading 40-1 at the half. After whipping Ukiah twice and Cloverdale once, the Petaluma lads lost a rough and tumble scrimmage to Santa Rosa Business College. The Santa Rosans were criticized for their "rough style...A team that starts out to win by any possible means, no matter how, is not the kind of team Petaluma desires to play," contended a Petaluma yearbook writer.

The 1908 Echo reported that SRHS beat Petaluma 50-1, Ukiah 50-3, Mission 54-1, Healdsburg 24-13, and Lowell. The boys lost the Bay Area finals to Oakland, 22-13.

By 1912, Healdsburg's girls' team was slipping. The girls played only four games "because of a lack of spirit on the part of a few." A couple of years later, there was no team at all.

Healdsburg gave up boys' basketball for a while, but Santa Rosa kept playing and developed one of its best cage teams in 1915, winning 11 of 12 games. The Panthers' victims included Tomales 62-3, Sonoma 73-8, and Healdsburg 71-17. Team captain Hewitt was the team's best shooter.

Early in the 1916 season, Healdsburg's boys had trouble getting the season started. The team had only one practice before taking on Santa Rosa High, and it showed. Santa Rosa won the first half 75-0 and the second half 8-6 for an 83-6 victory.

When Major Victor Hodge became athletic director and teacher in 1918-1919, SRHS fielded both unlimited and lightweight cage teams. Hodge attracted a large number of students to try out for the squad and the rooting section was enthusiastic. The basketball team got off to a good start, beating Analy 26-22, but the flu epidemic caused the school to shut down twice for more than two months. While a number of schools gave up sports because of the flu, Santa Rosa managed to play five games, winning two and losing three.

The up and down days of Santa Rosa basketball ended when coach Orb Fortier succeeded Olympic track star Morris Kirksey as Santa Rosa coach. An "incident" involving principal Gardiner Spring and Coach Kirksey in the school basement one spring day in 1925 led to Kirksey's departure the same afternoon. Some say Kirksey socked the principal, leading to his immediate dismissal.

Orben Fortier, a Midwestern lad who attended Northland College on Lake Superior, coached briefly after college. After working a while for an oil company, he was asked to return to coaching to help save the situation in Santa Rosa, and save it he did. By 1927-28, he began routinely collecting championship trophies. The varsity lost to Analy by one point in the title game but the B and C teams topped their leagues that year.

In 1928-29, Fortier had three cage teams and three titles. It was the first crown for the varsity since basketball had become a major sport at the school. The 1929-30 team won the league and also captured a first North Coast title with a victory over Eureka.

In his 25 years, his C basketball team at SRHS won 22 titles; his B team were tops 9 times in 13 years and his A or varsity teams 13 times in 18 years. The Panthers beat mighty Lowell High from San Francisco two years in a row, and also subdued the Stanford Freshmen, Santa Rosa Jr. College, and College of Marin.

Fortier got a leg up on the opposition by using the zone defense, which he had seen used in Wisconsin. When he tried it out on Ukiah, the opposing coach stopped the game. "He said it wasn't fair," Fortier said.

One of Orb's best boys was lean guard Jack O'Sullivan. The experts told O'Sullivan, who wasn't quite 6 feet tall, that he was too short to play college basketball. O'Sullivan, a stubborn fellow when he had a basketball in his hand, ignored the criticism and began working on a jump shot. His coach, Everett Dean, told him it would never work, but the young Santa Rosan perfected the shot that led him to an illustrious career down on the Farm.

At Santa Rosa High School, O'Sullivan was a benchwarmer as a freshman and a B team player as a sophomore and junior, finally making the varsity in 1945, his senior year. He played one year at Santa Rosa Jr. College and then went to Stanford, where he played for three years. He was captain and MVP of the 1950-51 quintet.

At Santa Rosa Jr. College in the early 1920s, the basketball teams had their ups and downs. The team lost to Geyserville High School, among others, in 1923. Volunteer Clarence (Red) Tauzer became coach the following year when the Cubs won 7 of 12 games. In 1931, the cagers won 14 games and in 1932 went 13 and 9.

In 1950, Coach Bob Mastin turned out one of his best teams, capturing the Modesto Tournament and running off an impressive 10-4 record in league play. Lorne Swanets provided much of the scoring punch, while George Moscone, future mayor of San Francisco, handled political discussions in the locker room.

Vesta Cornish was credited with inaugurating the girl's basketball program at Healdsburg High in 1905 when she joined the faculty after "teaching in the East." She taught History, Civics, and English, and also encouraged young ladies at the school to take part in the basketball program.

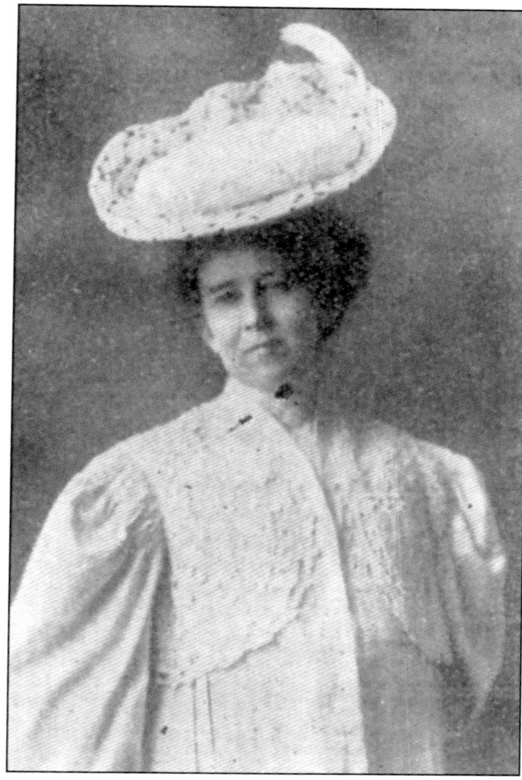

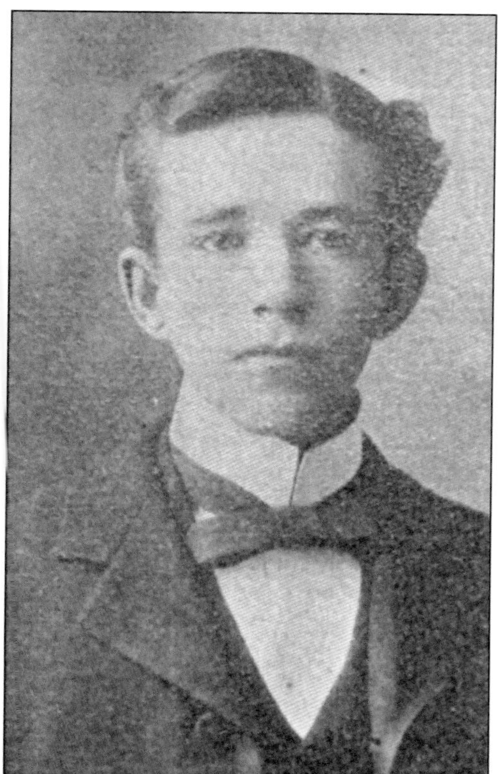

Young dentist Fred Kinley, who moved from Santa Rosa to Healdsburg around 1906, offered his services as coach and referee. He worked with boys in track, football, and basketball and girls in basketball. Kinley scheduled three rigorous practices a week for the young ladies.

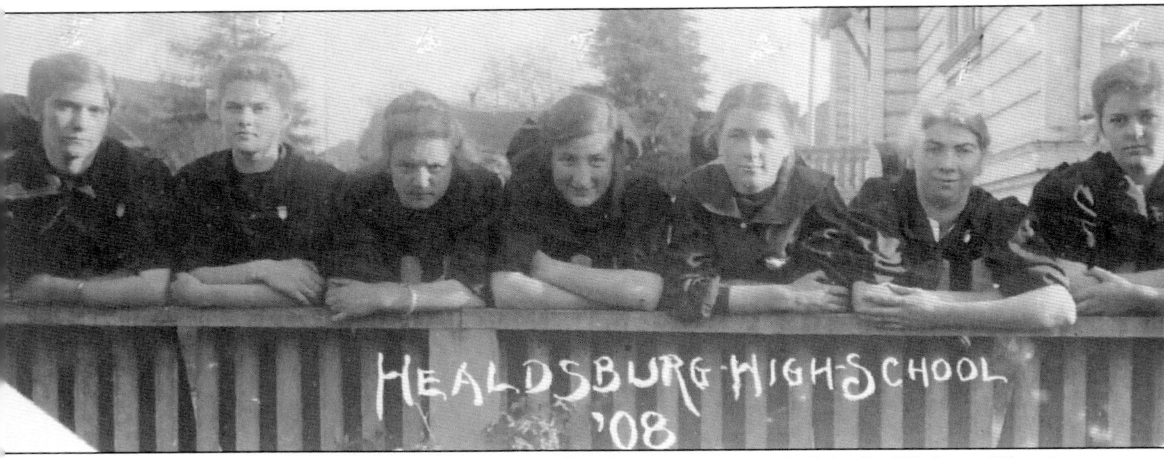

Healdsburg High's basketball juggernaut of 1908 was composed of Audry Walters, Elva Beeson, Aubry Butler, Kathleen Swisher, Gertrude Field, Una Williams, and Bera Mothorn. Losing only two games, the girls defeated Cogswell Polytechnic College of Oakland in the Academic Athletic League championship game 16-14. Courtesy of the Healdsburg Museum.

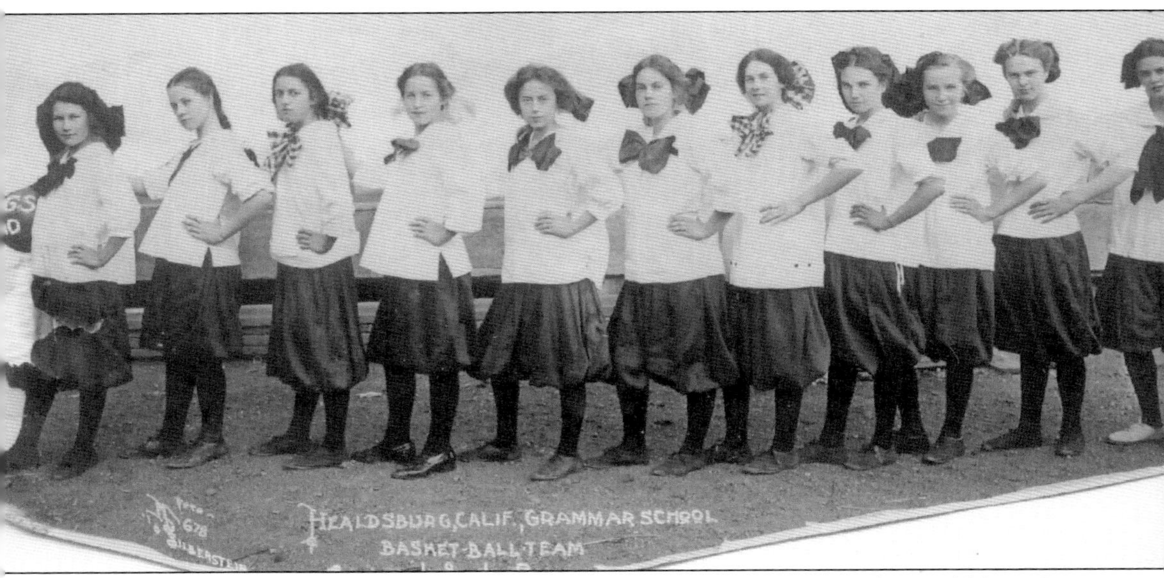

This is what the fashionable young female cager was wearing in 1910. The Healdsburg Grammar School team featured, from left, Laura Destruel, Marian Whitney, Helen Hilgerloh, Mildred Coffman, Lucille Byington, Edna Haigh, Jean Tevendale, Juanita Banks, Claire Schwab, Eda Beeson, and Loraine McDonough. Courtesy of the Healdsburg Museum.

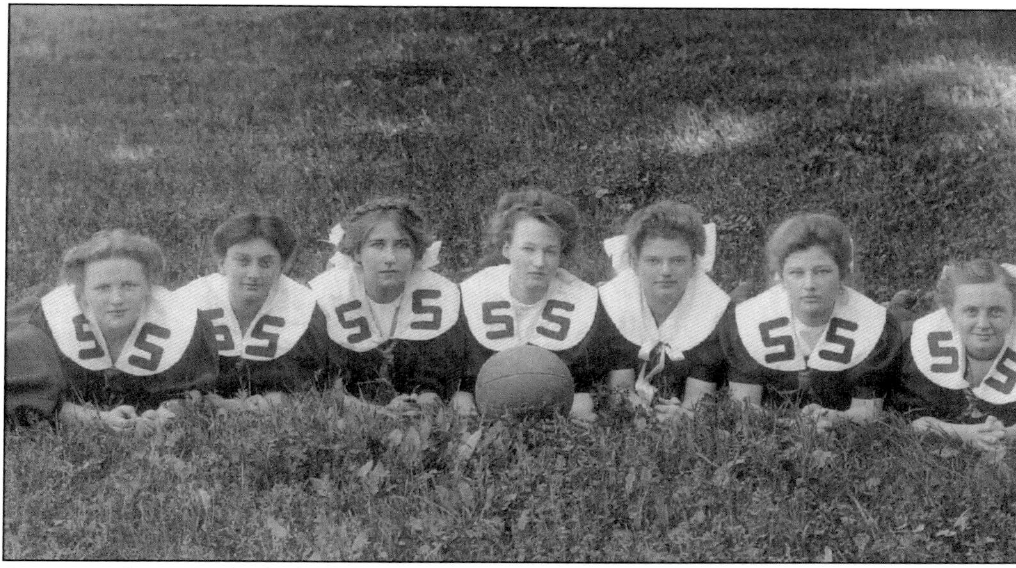

Sonoma girls caught the basketball fever in 1909 and 1910, playing numerous teams in the North Bay. After beating Mill Valley in 1910, the Sonoma girls lost to Santa Rosa 18-10 in their first league game. The starched-collar team of 1909 includes the following: Gertrude Calderwood, Marie Clewe Taylor, Marjorie Buchan Fisk, captain. Edna Cooper, Olive Trowbridge, Eva Dresel, and Emily Poppe Grimstead. Courtesy of the Sonoma Depot Park Museum.

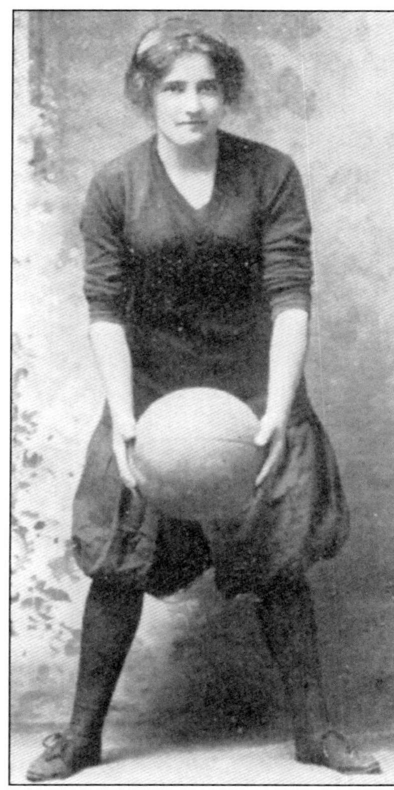

Elsie Parrott was the upbeat team captain of Healdsburg's girls' team in 1911-12, but the girls played only four games "because of the lack of spirit on the part of a few."

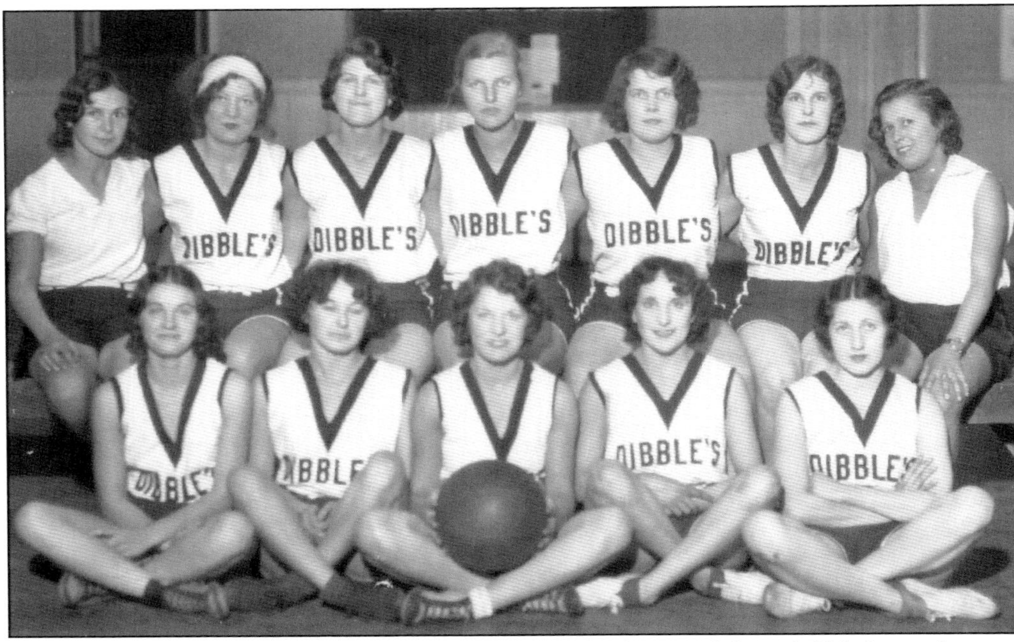

Dibble's basketball team, sponsored by a Santa Rosa women's apparel shop, dribbled onto the scene in 1931, playing teams from Healdsburg, Cloverdale, and Petaluma. The ladies beat Healdsburg 8-3 in the season opener but lost their finale on a last-second shot by Lee Main of the Petaluma Spartans 14-13. The team played games at the Annex Gym on Humboldt Street and at the Company K Armory, where the team picture was taken. The members pictured here are as follows: (back row) Theresa Togneri, Angelina Toscani, Carolyn Barbieri, Marion Bolden, Ethyl McBain, Leonora Bartolomei, and Leonora Slusser; (front) Angelina Peretta, Rose Togneri, captain Edna King, Inez Stefani, and Elsie Novelli. Courtesy of the LeBaron collection.

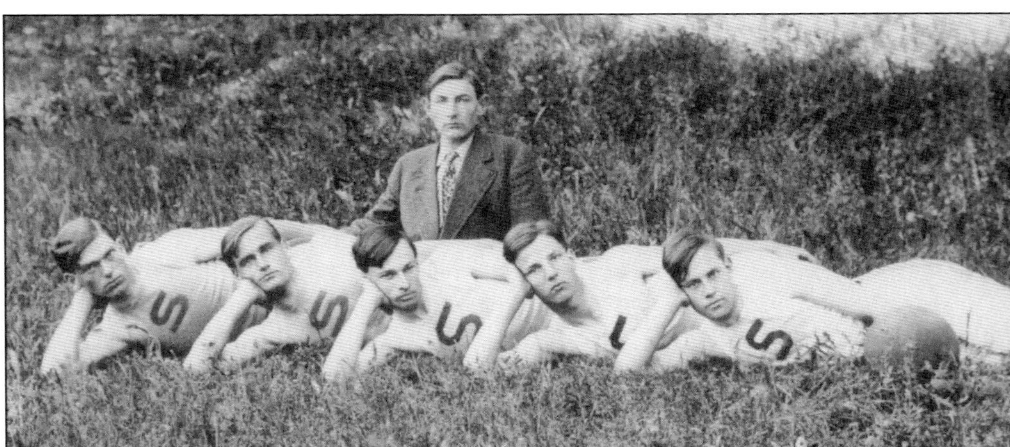

Sonoma High School sent a boys' team to the court for the second time in 1909. Forward Western Logan scored 114 of the team's 204 points as the Dragons went undefeated. Unfortunately, because several players had academic problems, they were not allowed to take part in league play. Team members included, starting from the left, Seymour Trowbridge, Raymond Poppe, Raymond Cooper, Otto Dresel, Logan, and manager Reuben Woodworth. Courtesy of the Sonoma Depot Park Museum.

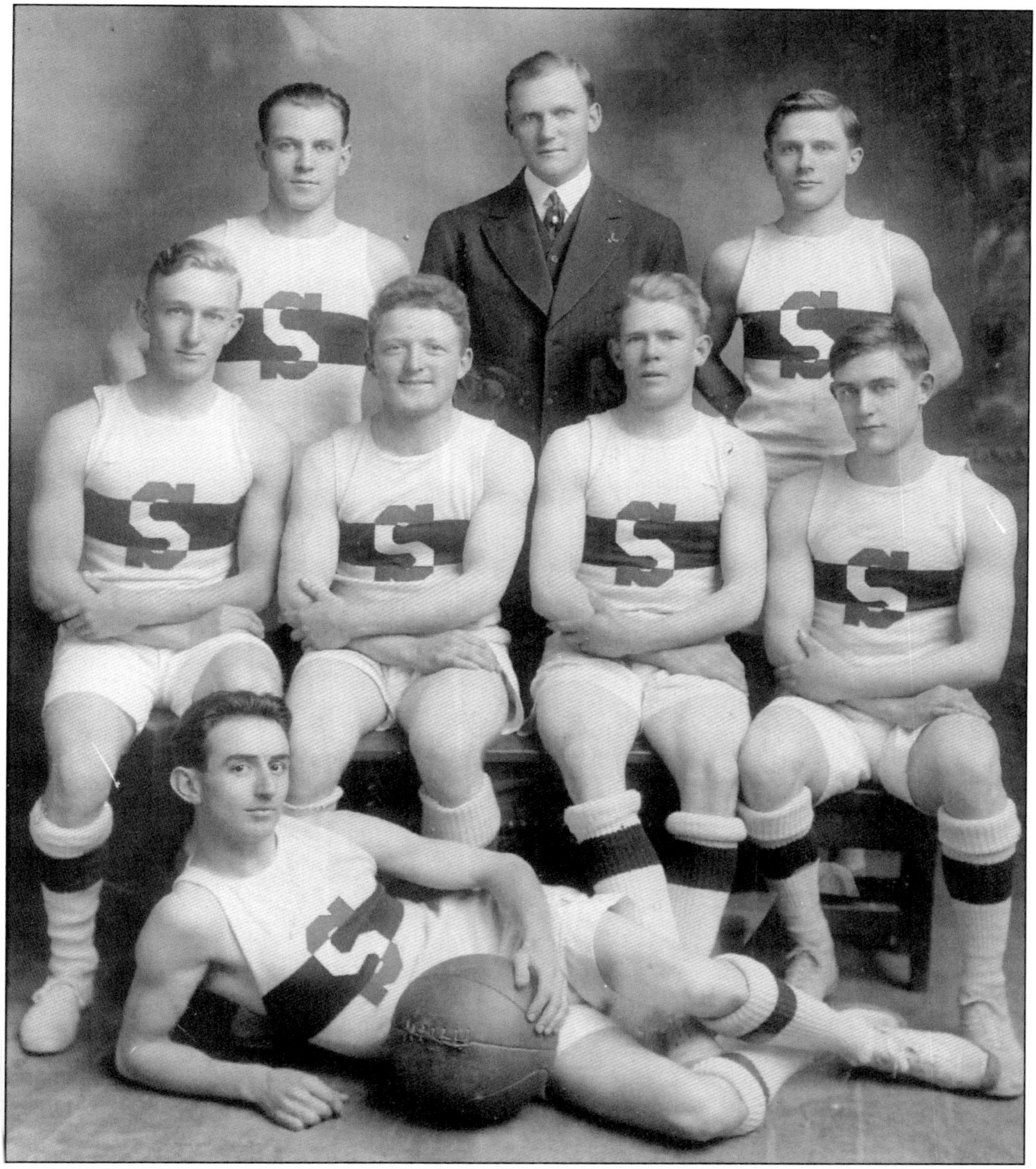

Petaluma's original 1910-11 Spartans basketball team featured "Dimp" S.S. Peck, Marty Sandvig, manager Marty Walters, Homer Green, Carlton Dorroh, Glen Page, Moore Sweetman, and captain Roy Evans. Courtesy of the Petaluma Museum.

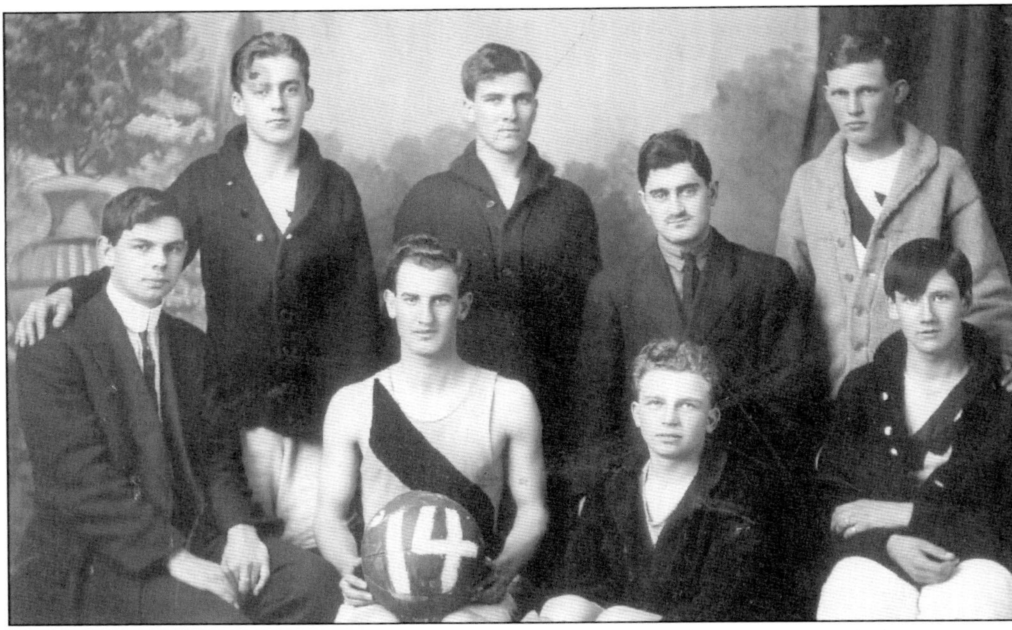

The 1914 Healdsburg High School basketball team won 6 of 11 games, including a victory over traditional rival Santa Rosa in the 1913-14 season. Team members included forwards Hilgerloh and Dewey, center Burke, guards Sanborn and Albert Hoskinson, and substitute Parker. Hoskinson is in the back row, second from the left. Enthusiasm for basketball apparently slipped badly the following season as Healdsburg lost 71-17 to Santa Rosa High. Courtesy of the Healdsburg Museum.

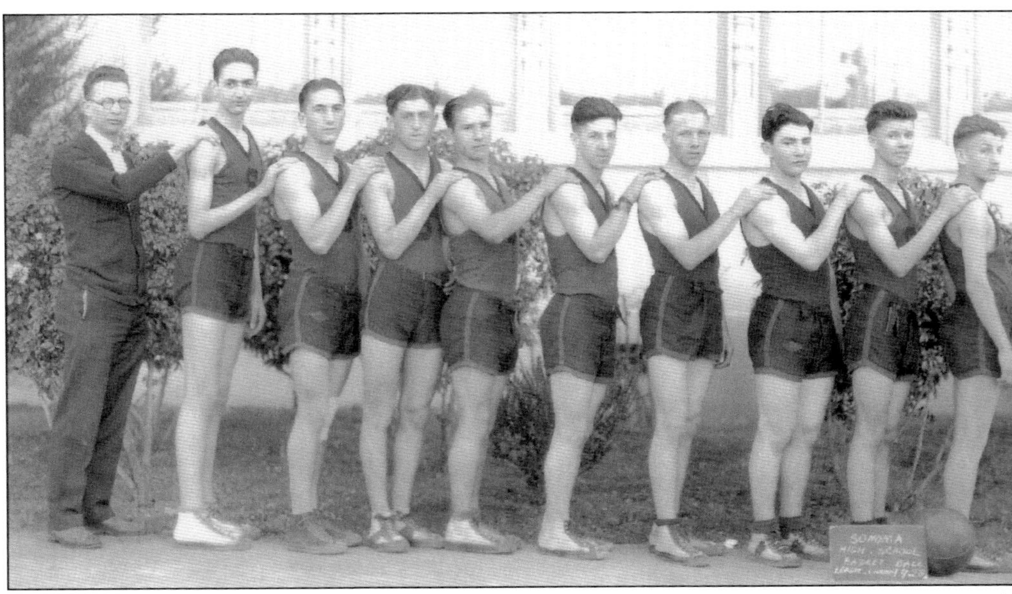

The Sonoma High School B team, playing solid team ball through the season, swept to the League championship in 1928. Team members pictured here, from left, are: Coach Phieffer, John Mohr, Louie Panendini, "Pin" Mazza, Forrest Remy, Louie Minelli, John Hoeft, Ray Barrachi, "Ding" Hoeft, and Owen Neiman. Courtesy of the Sonoma Depot Park Museum.

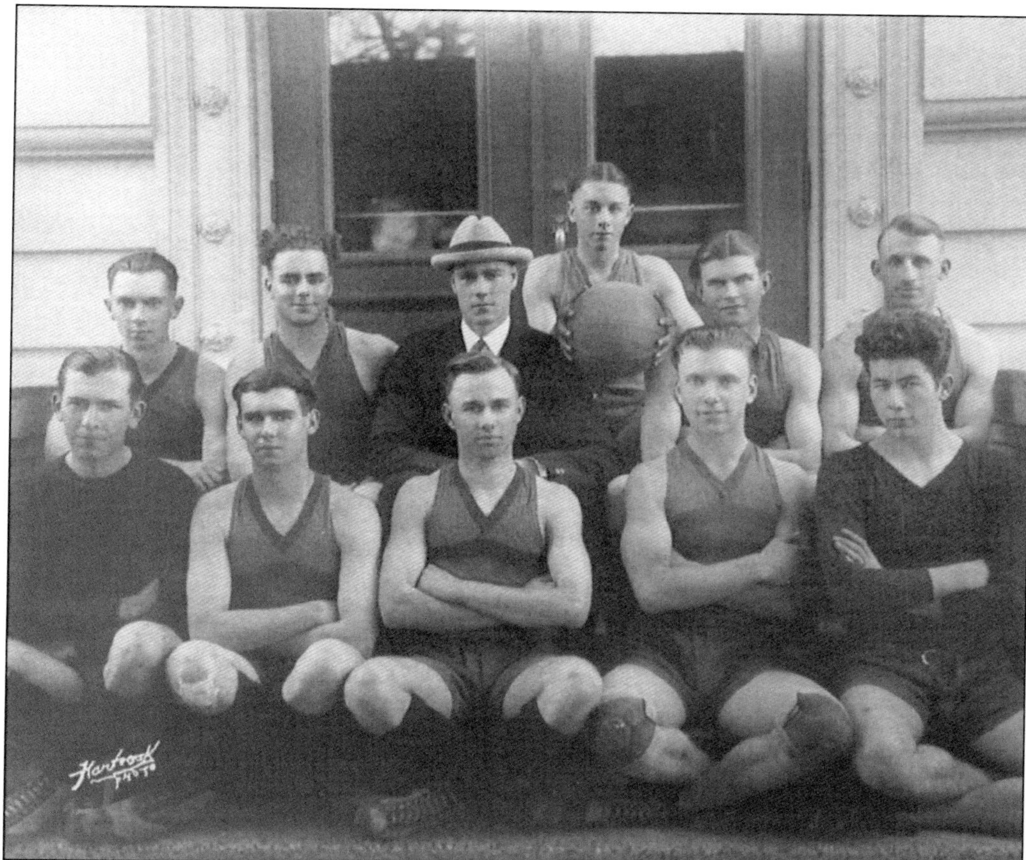

With a volunteer coach in young lawyer C. J. (Red) Tauzer, Santa Rosa JC entered basketball competition in 1923. The team played only two games that year but expanded its schedule and competed against a variety of teams, including high schools, until the end of Tauzer's reign in 1927. An upset of San Jose Teachers' College was the high point of Tauzer's tenure as coach. Although he rode crew and threw the discus on the track team at Stanford, he ended up coaching football and basketball at the junior college. Tauzer started out with the Geary law firm in Santa Rosa, became an SRJC trustee, and later a state senator. He remained a loyal fan, sitting on the bench at every football game. The 1923-24 team members, pictured here, are: (back row) Gardner, captain Joel Mallory, Coach Tauzer, Bath, and Wilson and Howard Fry; (front) Harvey Sullivan, Bryant Forsyth, Alan Evans, Ken Shaffer, and Plover. Courtesy of the SRJC collection.

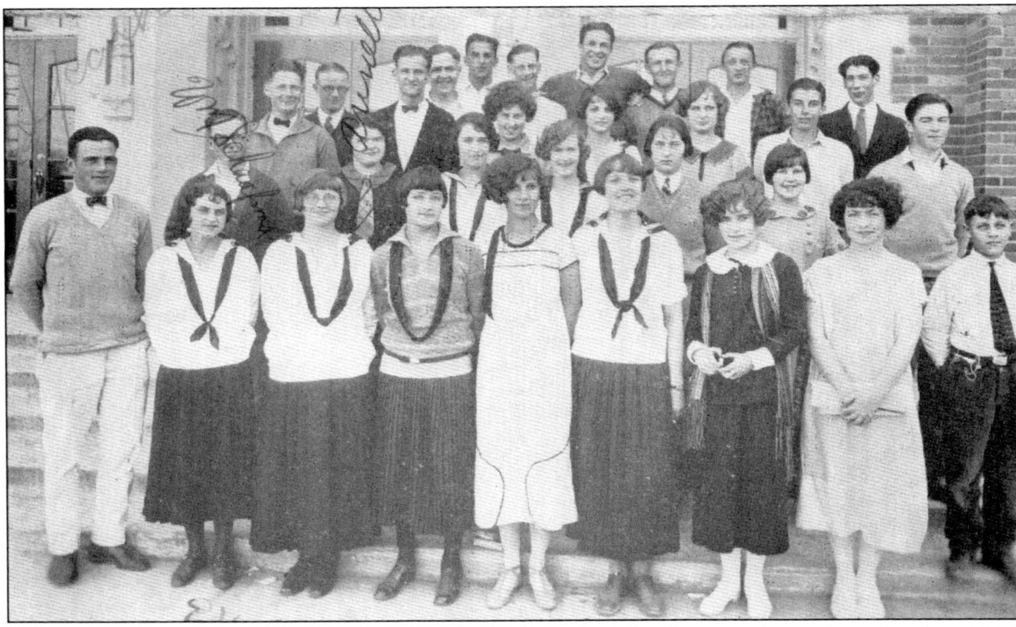

Santa Rosa High School boosters reorganized after a fire that burned down the school in 1921. By 1924-25 the group engaged in many activities, including providing basketball players with sandwiches, cake, and chocolate after each game.

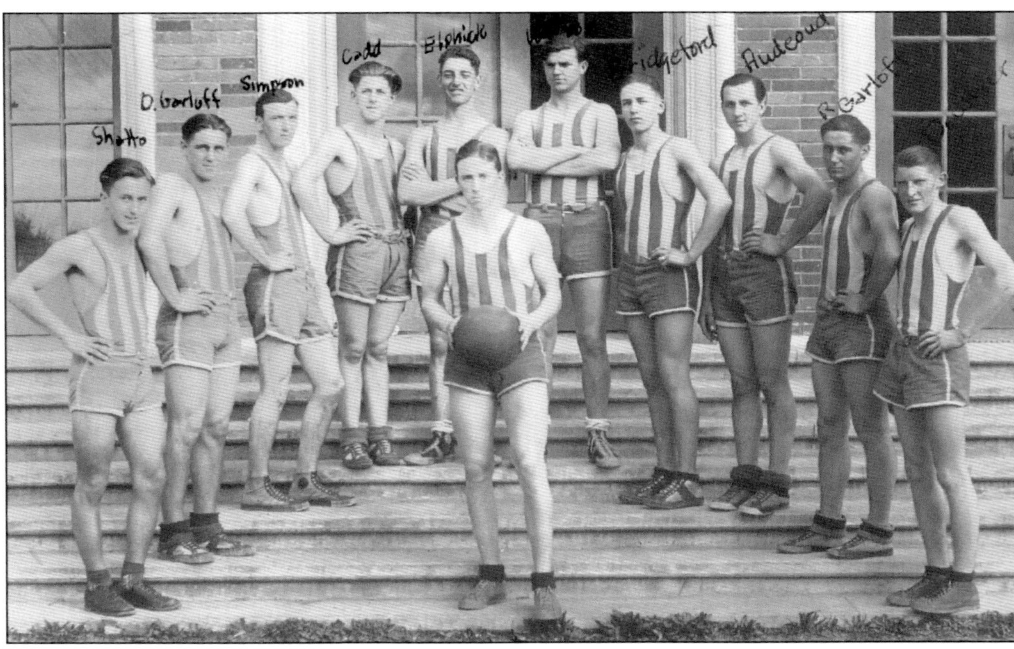

The 1931 Analy B cage team wore its flashy striped uniforms with pride. Team members included, clockwise from left: Shatto, D. Garloff, Simpson, Cadd, Elsnick, Wilson, Bridgeford, Audcoud, R. Garloff, and Downer, with Walt Foster in the middle. Foster was a longtime coach at Analy High School. Courtesy of the Foster collection.

Orb Fortier made history as Santa Rosa High School's basketball coach from the mid-1920s, winning a string of varsity, B, and C crowns. He won 80 percent of his league games and was 252-127 overall.

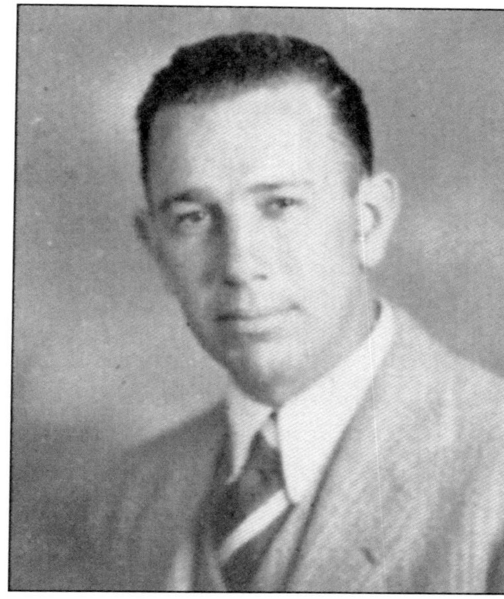

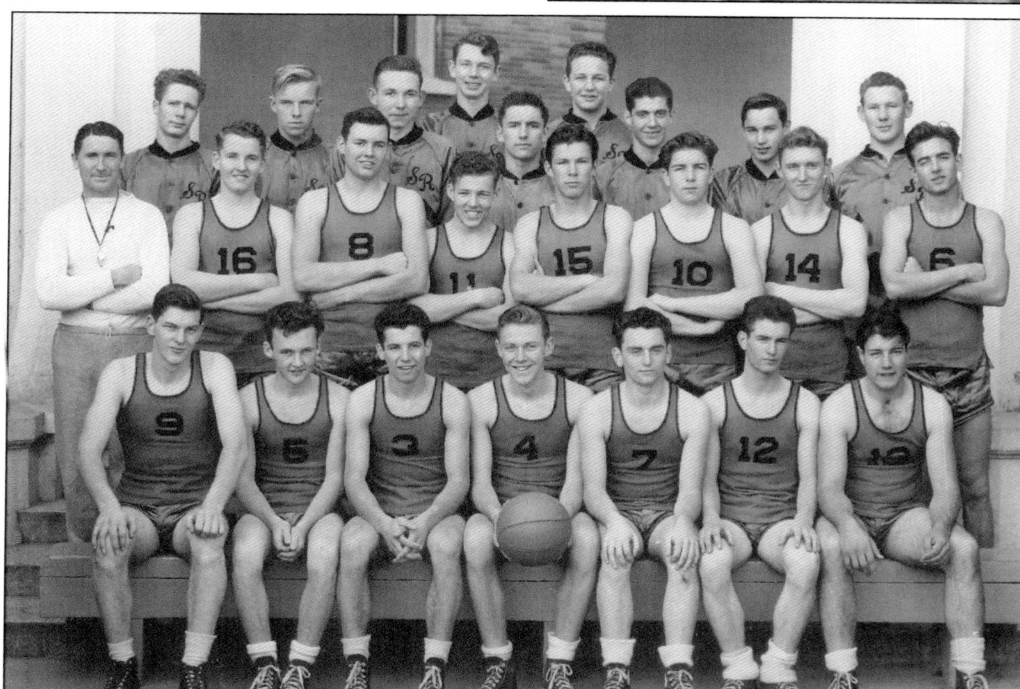

When Fortier retired, Jim Dardis became coach and led the 1947-48 team to a league title. Team members included, from the left: (back row) T. Moss, D. Cordson, C. Wulf, Bob Becklund, Gene Malvino, R. Buffi, G. Sumner, E. Cameron, and B. Epple; (middle) Coach Dardis, Ward von Tillow, C. Toscher, D. Miller, B. Slivkoff, Ron Goode, Art Liebscher, and L. Waters; (front) D. Carico, J. Maghetti, M. Sullivan, Lorne Swanets, Bill Noonan, B. Cromie, and Nate Del Querra. Swanets and Noonan provided much of the team's scoring punch. The 6-foot 1-inch Swanets was a leading scorer on the 1948-49 team but graduated at mid-year and joined the SRJC quintet in the second half of the season.

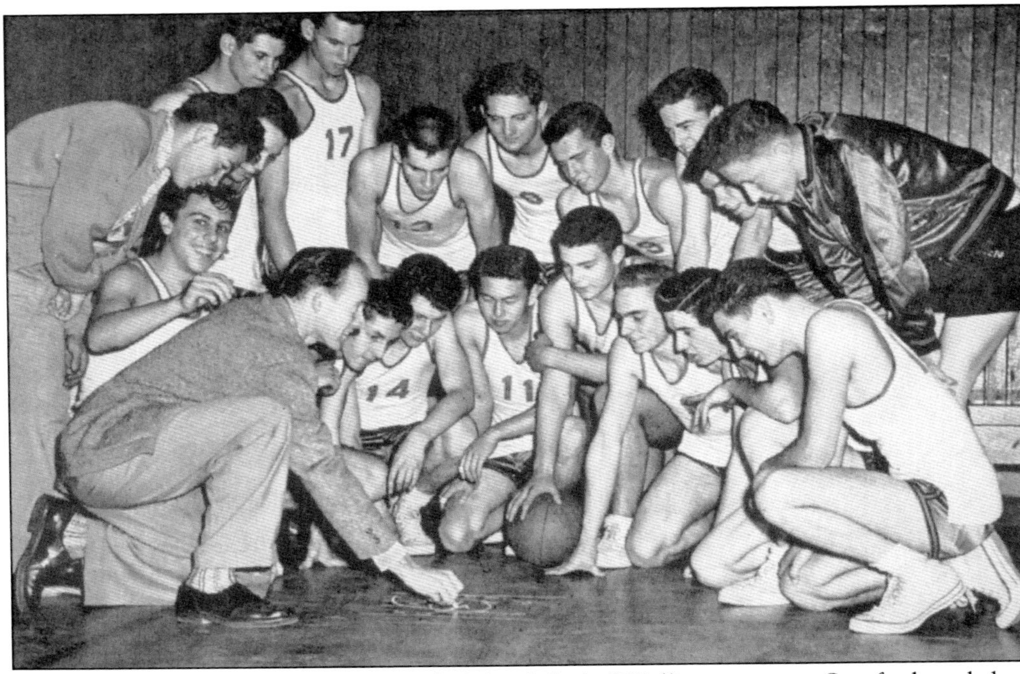

A basketball player at Santa Rosa High School, Jack O'Sullivan went to Stanford, and then returned home to teach and coach basketball. He chalked a play on the hardwood for his 1952-53 team, which won nine games and lost five. Pictured here are: (front row) O'Sullivan, W. Ahr, D. Sumner, Chet Hamamoto, Doug Camilli, V. Borbe, Q. Furia, and H. Stefanelli; (back row) manager A. Conley, Fred Giannini, B. Foley, Len Read, L. Mayer, V. Crownover, Mel Flohr, J. Thiederman, J. Hyde, C. Gore, and L. Jorgenson. Courtesy of the 1953 Echo Yearbook.

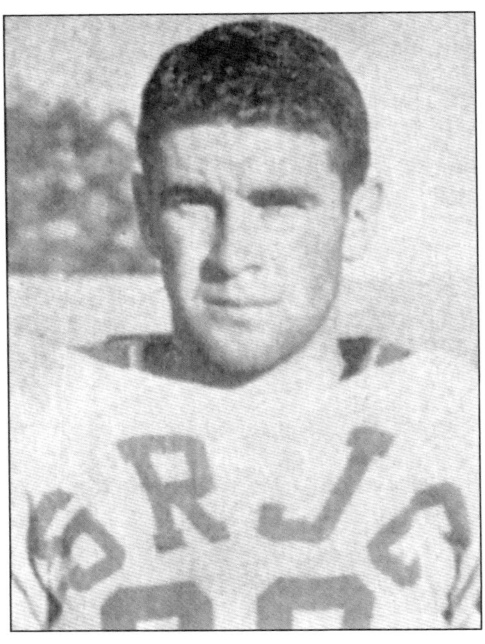

Bob Mastin, an all-around athlete who attended Santa Rosa Jr. College in 1937-38, came back in the 1940s to coach basketball and other sports.

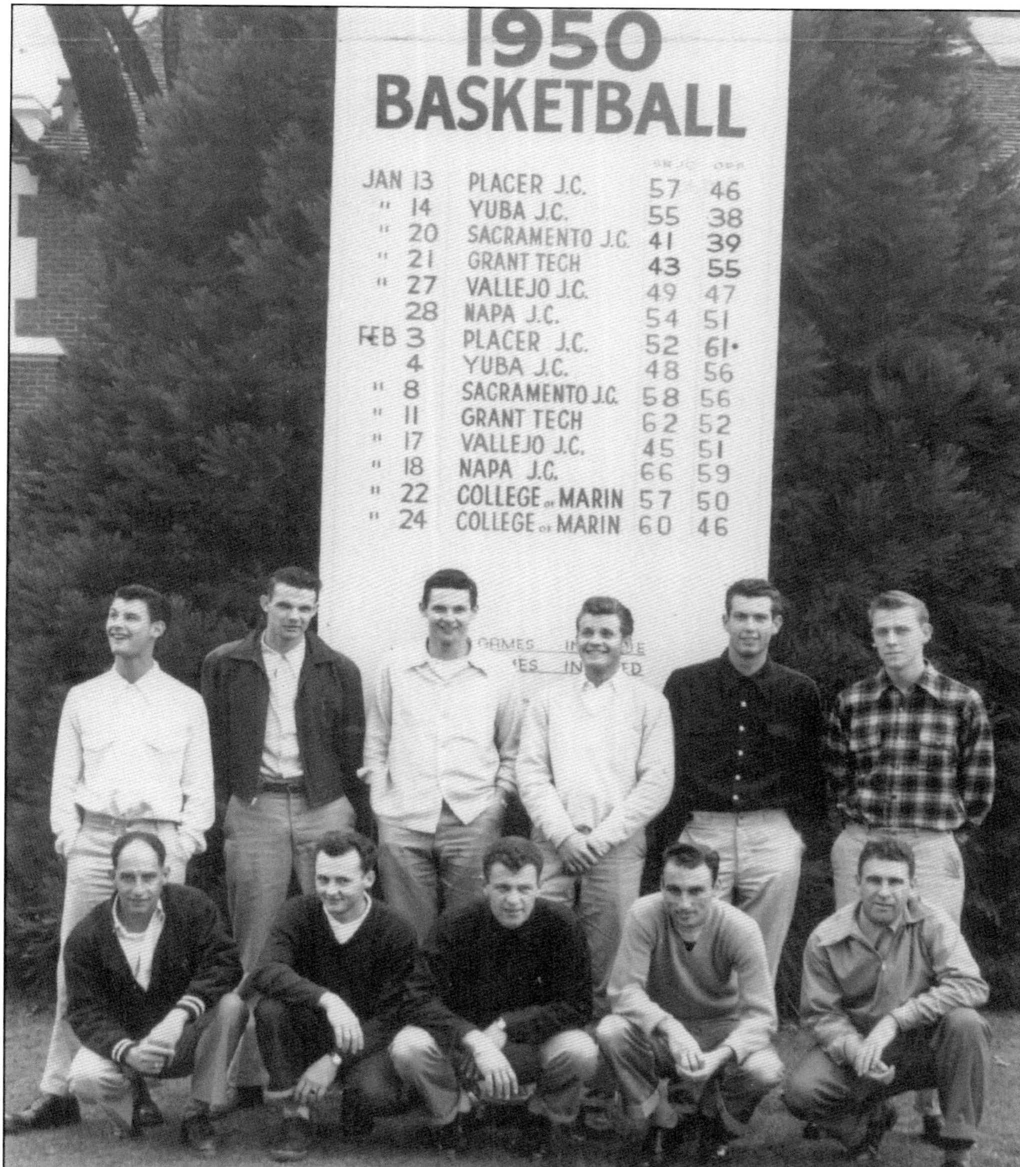

Playing tough all season, the Santa Rosa Bear Cubs 1950 basketball team won the Modesto Tournament and made a strong bid for the title in league play, finishing with 10 wins and 4 losses. Team members pictured here are, from left: (back row) future San Francisco mayor George Moscone, Roland Irvine, Roger Irvine, Gordon Brown, Will Turner, and Lorne Swanets; (front) assistant coach Bill Neel, manager Gerald Maghetti, Tom Dufor, Jim Ellis, and coach Bob Mastin. Courtesy of the Swanets collection.

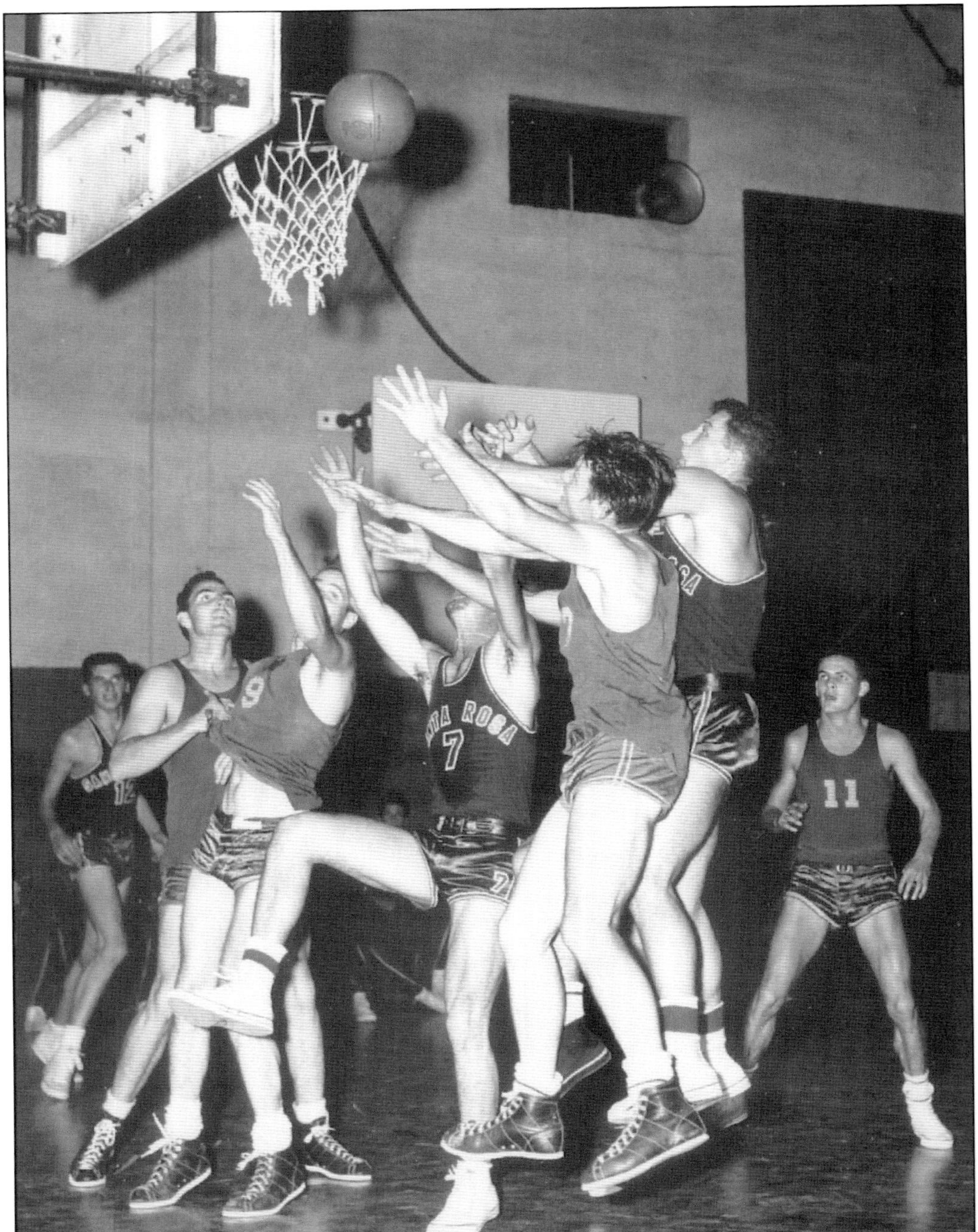

There was a crowd under the basket as five players soared for a rebound in rugged SRJC basketball action in 1950. Player # 9 would have joined the scramble, but was held back by a hand grabbing his shirt. Courtesy of the SRJC collection.

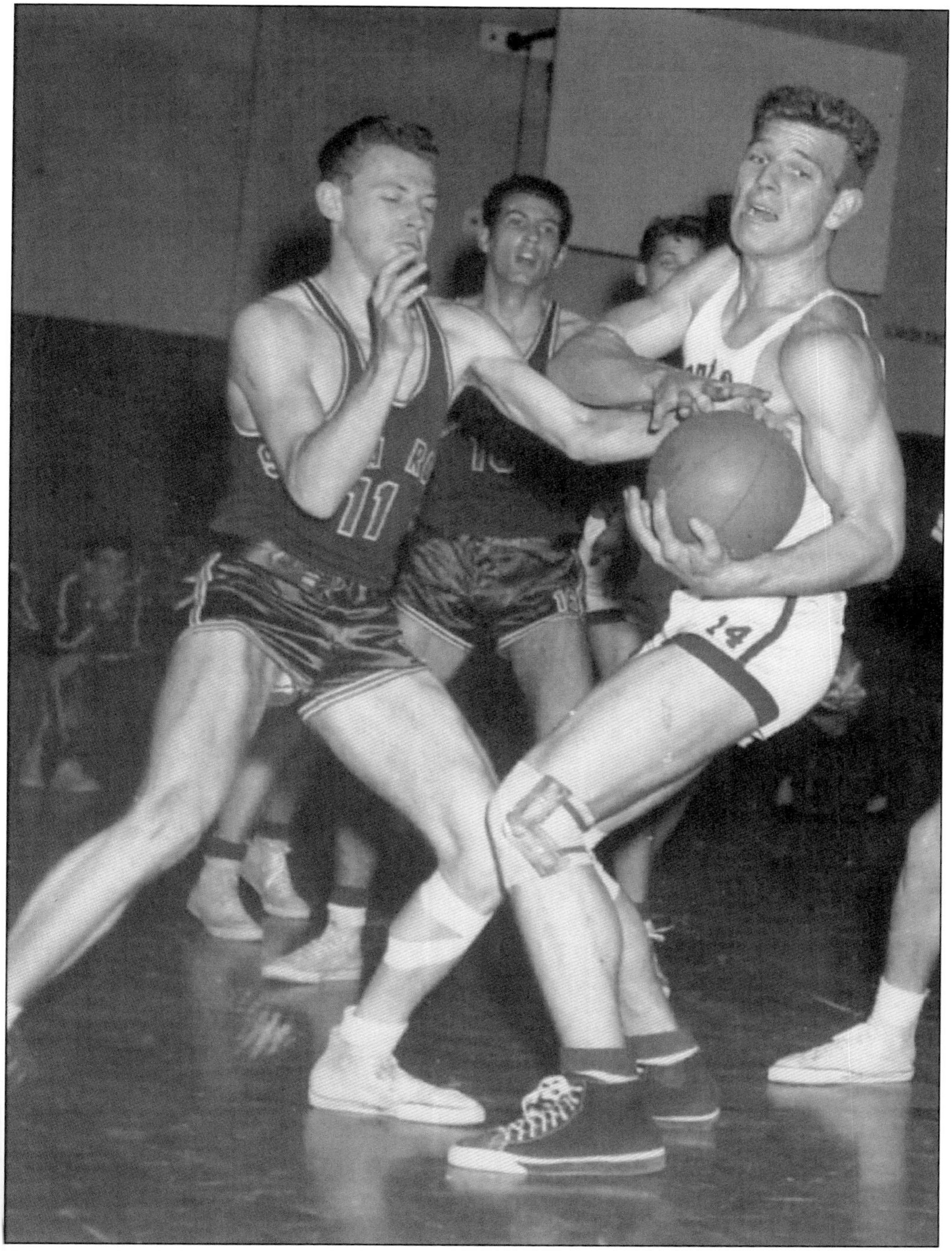

"Mommy, this bully's taking my ball away," grimacing Jim Loscutoff of Grant Tech seemed to complain to the referee during a game against Santa Rosa Jr. College in 1949-50. "Give it to me or else," Bear Cubs defender Lorne Swanets responded during a tense moment at Tauzer gym. Santa Rosa won 62-52. Center Loscutoff went on to a pro career as the enforcer on the Boston Celtics team in the Bill Russell years. Courtesy of the SRJC collection.

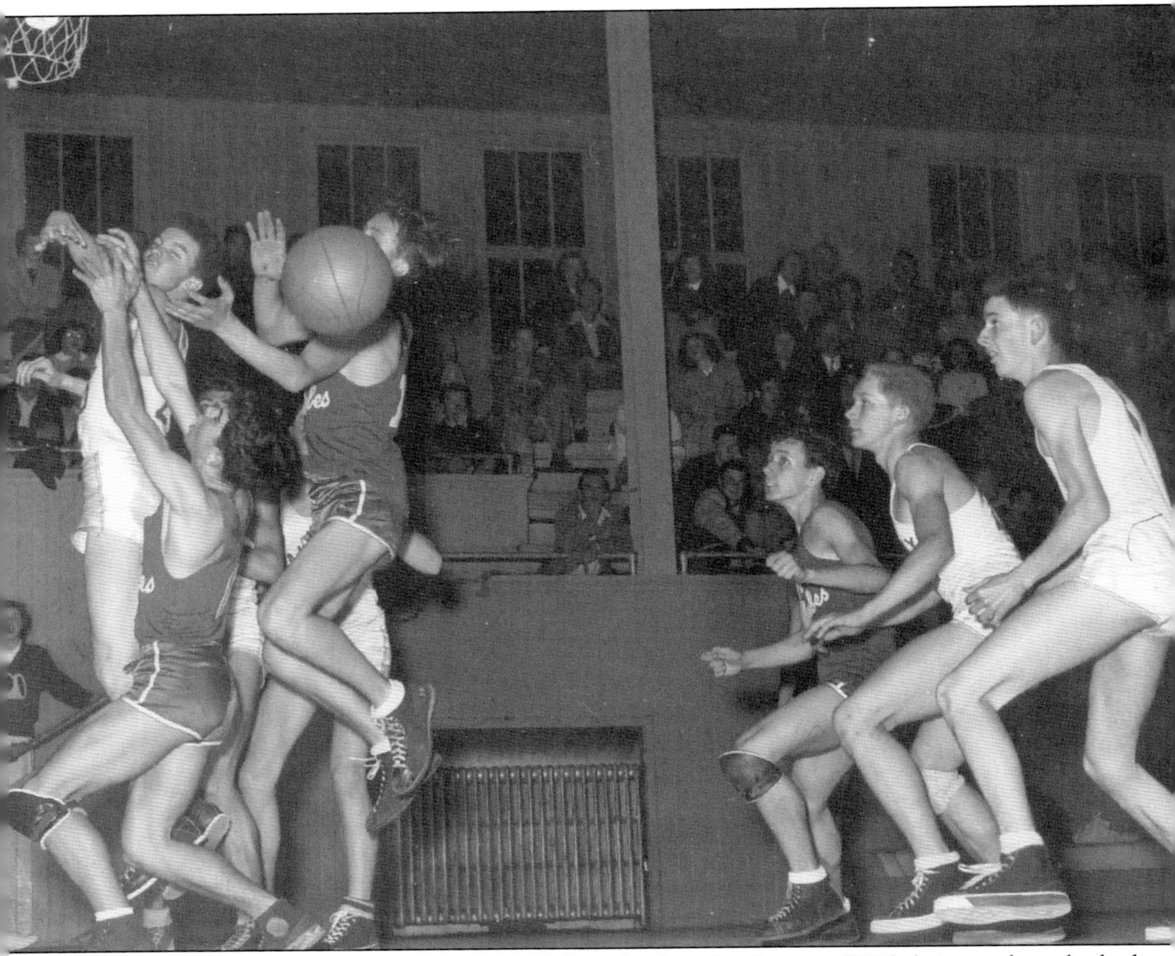

Are these guys basketball players or candidates for the school musical? While it may have looked like a dance recital, these players were busy fighting for position during an Analy-Petaluma game in 1949. Courtesy of Kay Dee Reynolds.

Seven

TENNIS

Charles Frost and Floyd Darby became Healdsburg High School's first tennis team in 1914. They played on a new court constructed in the shadow of the high school.

Well before Frost and Darby came on the scene, Healdsburg had a tennis tradition of sorts. Healdsburg-born Helen Hotchkiss Wightman had won the triple crown of women's tennis three straight years: 1909, 1910, and 1911. Helen Hotchkiss, born December 20, 1886, on the family ranch on Eastside Road near Windsor, never played a game of tennis in Healdsburg, but became one of the female superstars of the early 20th century.

Wightman, barely 5 feet tall, competed with four brothers in pickup games of baseball and football on the farm. When the family moved to Berkeley in 1900, Hotchkiss Wightman and her brothers started playing tennis on a gravel court in their backyard.

Since the ball didn't bounce well on gravel, "we tried to hit the ball in the air as much as possible," she said. Hotchkiss Wightman later became known for her ability to volley.

Wightman shocked spectators with her attire. She was first to wear sleeveless dresses and jaunty head scarves instead of the traditional ankle-length skirts and broad-brimmed hats. She persuaded her mother to make dresses that gave her freedom to move her arm to make overhead volleys.

In 1902, at age 15, she won her first tournament. In 1909, she went east to play her first tournament on grass, in the process winning her first triple crown. She won the singles, women's doubles, and mixed doubles titles. She was a repeat winner the next two years.

She didn't forget her childhood home, showing up in 1909 to play an exhibition during the Sonoma County Tennis Championships. Still Miss Hazel Hotchkiss at the time, she played a singles match and two doubles matches, winning both against male competition. The games were played at the courts in Santa Rosa and it was all very civilized.

"The courts were lined with spectators, the ladies, in their bright gowns, and flower-decked millinery giving the place a dash of color. In the clubhouse a number of young ladies served delicious punch and altogether the afternoon was a delightful one."

A banquet and dance was held at the Hotel Overton that Saturday evening. As the men filed into the room, the ladies, seated at a second table, "welcomed the gentlemen with songs and waving of flags and the evening's program began." Guests included the famous teacher Miss Frances O'Meara, later credited with shaping Robert "Believe It Or Not" Ripley into a world-famous celebrity. Hilliard Comstock, E. L. Finley, and other Sonoma County notables attended the affair.

The female tennis star married George Wightman of Boston in 1912. Winning numerous titles, Wightman also donated the "Wightman Cup" to develop international competition between Great Britain and the U.S.

The net sport also appealed to the social elite in Petaluma. Mixed doubles was the order of the day in a tournament held at the Whitney Court on Sixth Street in Petaluma in October 1902. Easily identifiable names included William Early, Rodney Putnam, Mr. and Mrs. Wesley Putnam, and Elly Cavanaugh.

Santa Rosa hosted county tennis tournaments in 1908 and again in 1909. When Major Victor Hodge came to Santa Rosa High School as athletic director in 1919, the school fielded its first tennis team, borrowing the courts of the Santa Rosa Tennis Club. The flu epidemic complicated matters but the team returned to the courts in 1920.

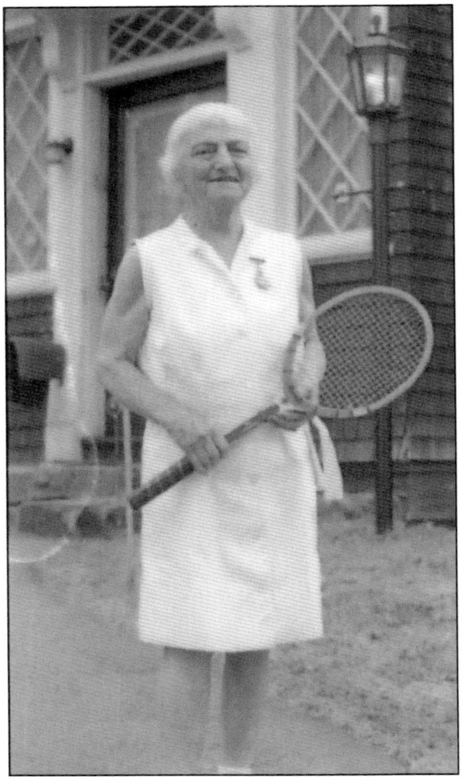

After growing up in Healdsburg, Helen Hotchkiss Wightman moved away, learned how to play tennis, and gained fame and fortune as an internationally-heralded tennis star. She spent much of her time encouraging young people to take up the sport. In 1970, at age 83, she could still wield a mean racket. Courtesy of the Healdsburg Museum.

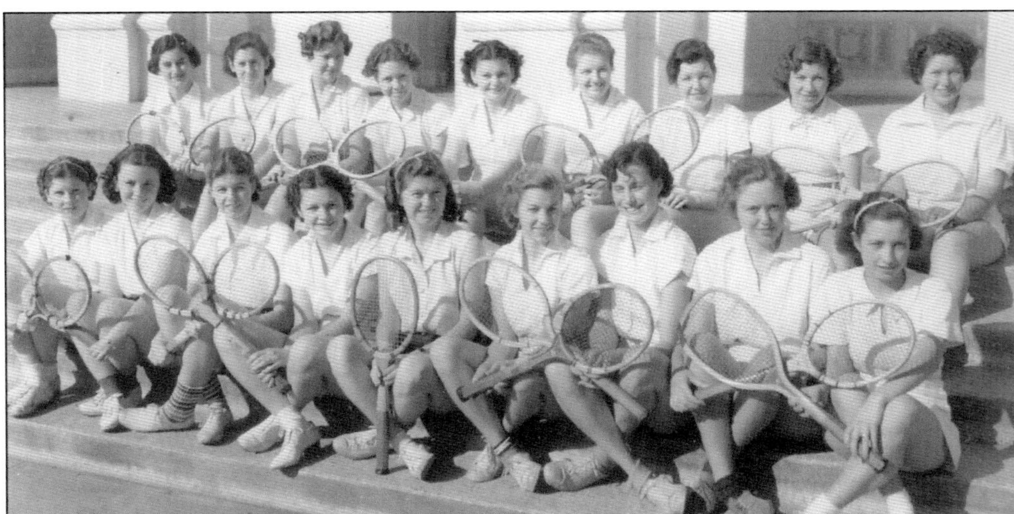

In the 1930s, Santa Rosa High School girls mainly engaged in in-school sports activities, including tennis. The 1936-37 competitors included: (back row) Gloria Genesa, Alice Good, Florence Cace, Hazel Richardson, Jane Violetti, Thelma Carner, Ruth McDonald, Peggy Hudson, and Alice Maxwell; (front) Barbara Montgomery, Jane Schiber, Bobbe Austin, Carmella Plamandosi, Heidi Schmidt, Doris Owens, Margaret Kursten, Barella Pittman, and Adean Anderson. Courtesy of the Santa Rosa High School Foundation.

Eight

Ice Hockey

Sonoma had grapes, Healdsburg had prunes, Sebastopol had apples, and Petaluma had chickens. What was Santa Rosa's claim to fame? During two magical years, from 1939-1941, it was ice. During that span, Santa Rosa Junior College became one of the major ice hockey capitals of the world. Of course, it took a little help from the outside world, since the young men who played during these championship seasons were imported from far away places, either Canada or the more frigid portions of the United States.

During Prohibition, Grace Brothers Brewery, headed by Joseph T. Grace, made money by operating the Union Ice Co. in an age when iceboxes were as common as refrigerators. They also made money by icing boxcars carrying fruit out of Santa Rosa. Grace Brothers went back into the beer-making business in the 1930s, but kept the ice-making operation as well. When he heard that somebody else might build an ice-skating rink, Grace created his own ice-skating facility ("large, unlovely, barn-like") near the brewery.

Before the ice hockey season started, Grace found ways to lure crowds to the ice rink. By March 1939, the facility was open for skating and five-man broomball teams took to the ice in April. An ice revue, heavy on pretty ladies in scanty costumes, opened in April. But that wasn't enough.

Grace talked with Julius Schroeder, the ice hockey coach at UC Berkeley, to see what could be done to build interest in his new ice palace. He connected Schroeder with SRJC's already over-committed football, rugby, and baseball coach Cook Sypher, who knew very little about ice hockey. But he knew a challenge when he saw one, and when Schroeder promised to deliver him a youthful all-star team, 12 from Canada and 4 from the Pacific Northwest and Minnesota, ages 17-18, Sypher agreed, and went out to buy a book on how to coach hockey. Schroeder got a farm club, Santa Rosa merchants provided jobs, and Sypher got the team enrolled at SRJC.

Sypher recalled that the hockey team drove in private cars to games the first year, then money came in so "we moved in buses (after that)." Sypher, who had only seen a couple of ice hockey games before he was provided with a near-perfect collection of players, said it was the "most amazing thing to ever happen in my life." The coach recruited merchants for money and looked for lodging for his team. He found a storage building that was converted into a varsity house for students.

The season ran from October to March, which meant Sypher coached football in the afternoon and ice hockey at night, rugby in the afternoon and ice hockey at night, and baseball in the afternoon and ice hockey at night. His pay remained the same. For all the agony, Sypher was thrilled that his little rural junior college team could beat sports giants like "USC, UCLA, and Cal, one, two, three, right in a row."

"The night we played UCLA at that Grace Brothers rink there were 2,500 people inside and 1,000 standing outside—in the rain."

Jobs paid the athletes something like 35 cents an hour, not much even for end of the Depression years. They got huge crowds but "didn't make enough to pay the heat bill in the dressing room to dry the players' underwear."

He wasn't the first referee but Santa Rosa High School coach and NFL official Jimmy Underhill boned up on hockey rules and took his turn refereeing games. Accountant Jack Liebau donated a trophy and hockey equipment sold briskly at Mailer-Frey Hardware store. By 1941, Great Britain was at war and the two-year reign of the Polar Bears came to an end, probably forever. Cartoonist Charles Schulz built his ice arena well after World War II but there were no more young, unshaven Canadians to go out on the ice and make monkeys of their elders.

Some of the main names of these two legendary teams were Ray Gillman, Larry Silvestri, Ross McIntyre, Pinky Carter, Jack Sindall, Joe McCutcheon, Al Johnson, Tommy Meagher, and Art Green. Over the years, McIntyre, a business executive, came back for occasional golf games with coach Sypher.

The Santa Rosa Junior College hockey team may have been put together as a farm team for Cal but when the two teams met for the first game in Santa Rosa in 1939, the Polar Bears knocked off the Golden Bears 5-2. Three SRJC players left the games with injuries, including goalie Jack "Eagle Eye" Sindall, who knocked himself out on the goal pole diving for a flying puck. Larry Silvestri, a center from Minnesota, took the lead on offense, scoring two goals. He led the team in scoring for the season.

When UC and SRJC met again in mid-November, the Berkeley team won 3-2 before a crowd of 3,000. The icemen held their own against Bay Area teams through December, losing only to Cal a second time.

After joining the California Hockey League, the Polar Bears lost only to the Pacific Club of Oakland. The winning goal was disputed when an Oakland player popped the puck in the net while other players were popping each other with sticks, fists, and helmets during an on-ice altercation. The Cubs beat Cal twice and won the Maxwell and Liebau trophies after beating Golden State. Santa Rosa claimed the mythical state title after icing UCLA 5-1 in March 1940.

In the second season in 1940, the Cubs reeled off eight wins before losing to Illinois and USC in a tournament of top teams in December; in those wins, they scored 48 goals to 13 for the opposition.

Back in league play in January, the Polar Bears beat a string of opponents to win the state title and the Liebau cup. As baseball season began, Sypher went on another two-a-day coaching schedule. His schedule included planning the trip to Southern California for the season-ending ice hockey tournament. The student body provided minimal funds, and houses were found to provide sleeping accommodations. The high-scoring Silvestri made two goals in a 4-2 win over Bakersfield, but San Diego Rowing Club slapped down the Cubs 4-2. The key play of the game turned out to be a goal that didn't count. Silvestri hit a shot into the net but it bounced back out so quickly that officials did not count it. The failure to count the score was important because the number of goals a team scored counted toward the title in case of a tie. The next day, the Polar Bears won by two goals in regulation time, which forced overtime with San Diego. The south state team scored two goals to win. If the Silvestri goal had counted the night before, there would have been no overtime and Santa Rosa would have won. It was the end of the season and the end of ice hockey in Santa Rosa.

Sypher was the second paid coach at the junior college. Dick Blewett, fresh from UC's great Wonder Teams of the 1920s, was hired in 1929. He was joined in 1936 by Sypher, who stayed until 1964. When he retired, the tireless Sypher claimed 22 titles in various high school and junior college sports.

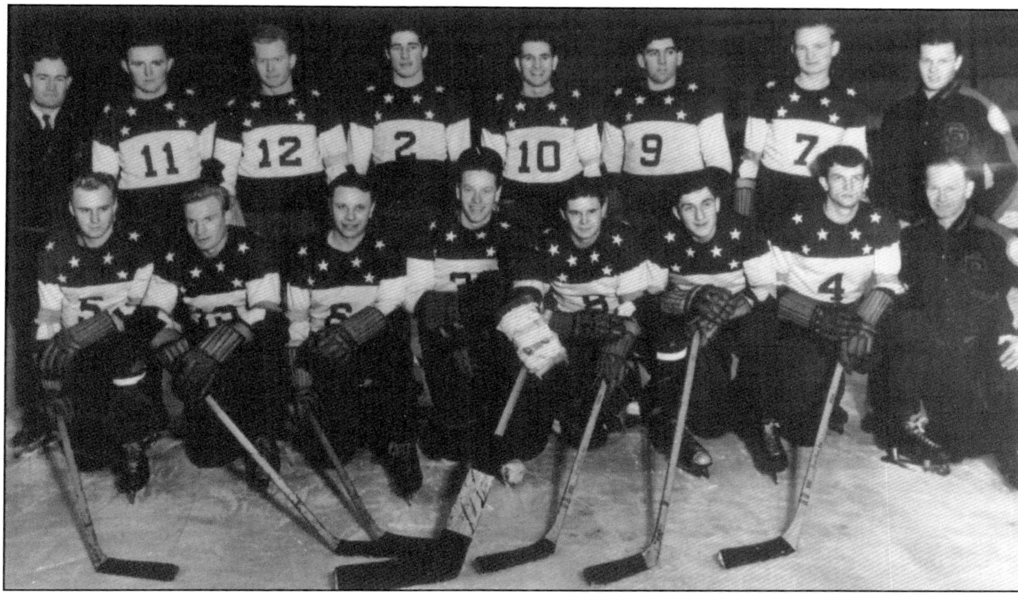

Santa Rosa's Polar Bear Cubs walked off with championships during two magical seasons in 1939-40 and 1940-41. The Cubs were set up as a farm team for UC Berkeley, but ended up beating the East Bay university team on numerous occasions. The 1940-41 Santa Rosa team, from left, included: (back row) coach Cook Sypher, Mack, Gillman, Charlton, McIntyre, Houx, Malin, and manager Gregory; (front) Green, Carter, Brandreth, Sindall, Holdsworth, Silvestri, Kempton, and trainer Meagher. With the approach of World War II, the team disbanded. Courtesy of the LeBaron collection.

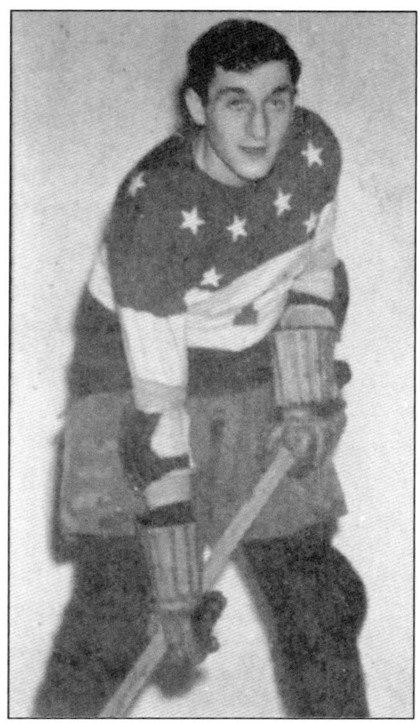

Larry Silvestri was the leading scorer on the Polar Bear Cubs hockey team. He once scored a goal that bounced out of the net so fast it was not counted by the referee. The "failed call" cost the team a possible state championship.

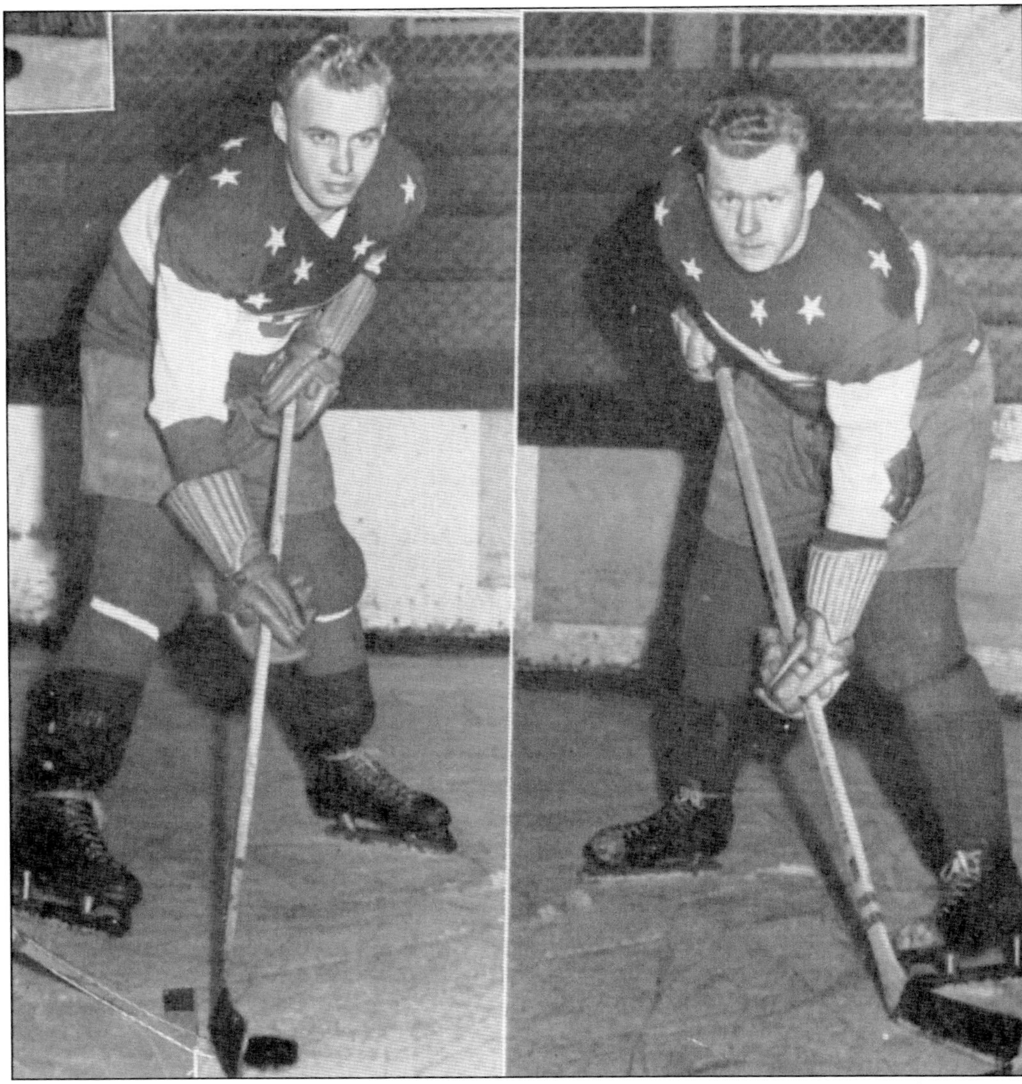

Art Green and Ray Gillman were two of the young men who came to Santa Rosa for a magic two years on the ice before World War II.

Nine

Boxing

During the first half of the 20th century, Sonoma County boxing promoters came and went. As early as 1909, the Sonoma Valley Athletic Club offered 40 rounds of boxing with two preliminaries and a "double main event" in Santa Rosa. The Sonoma County Athletic Club turned out to be "a local saloonkeeper, who recently came (to Santa Rosa) from San Francisco. By what right he advertised as the Sonoma Valley Athletic Club nobody seems to know."

In 1929, the Petaluma Spartans and Santa Rosa Athletic Club promoted boxing programs in Sonoma County, as did Frank Scaler who organized weekly boxing programs at the Athletic Club on Fifth Street in Santa Rosa. There was a mix of local boxers and others from outside the area, including Tiger Cline of Fresno, Frank Waters of Santa Rosa, Pedro Luna and Johnny Murray of Healdsburg, Billy Toth of Santa Rosa, and a black Vallejo heavyweight named Dusty Miller. It was back in the days when fighters had monikers like "Kid, Sailor, Tiger, Young, and Fighting Dutchman."

By 1931, Benny Wagner did the promoting, and wrestling was mixed in with boxing events.

Boxing programs had been dormant in Santa Rosa for a number of years when Ike Mendoza and Lou Basso did a series of amateur boxing and wrestling cards at the Sports Club at the corner of Fourth and Washington Streets in 1939 and beyond. Drawing mostly from local talent for the boxing, all shapes and sizes were represented at the matches. In one preliminary in September 1939, 70-pounders Jackie Stewart and Pliney Johnson fought to a draw.

Mendoza was a local boxing trainer, and Basso owned the Sports Club.

George Duke of Petaluma was a boxer with heart, in and out of the ring. Starting as a youngster with the Spartan Athletic Club in the late 1930s, Duke fought as an amateur for a number of years before turning professional. After he retired from the ring, he spent many hours training youngsters in junior boxing programs in Vacaville. In 1988, he was inducted into the Bay Area Boxing Hall of Fame.

Over his career, Duke fought more than 70 professional matches. A clever boxer, he avoided punishment and, well into his career, had only a cut over his eye to show for his many years in the ring. In his amateur days, under Bill Bojorques of the Spartan Club, Duke boxed in the 147-pound welterweight division, winning many awards and participating in Golden Gloves and Diamond Ring matches.

Duke built up his local reputation fighting in Santa Rosa in 1939 against popular Billy Nordyke. Duke and Santa Rosan Nordyke had fought to a draw in an earlier bout, but this time it was no contest. Duke stopped Nordyke in the second round of the main event at the Santa Rosa Sports Club before 250 fans.

Turning pro meant commuting to San Francisco daily to train, since there was a lack of adequate gyms in the area. As a pro, he fought three world middleweight champions, including Fred Apostoli and Carl "Bobo" Olson. Duke gave Apostoli a good test but was knocked out in the ninth round of their bout.

At one point, Duke had only 11 losses in 69 fights and was still considered a contender when he took on slugger Antone Raadik in 1948. Duke fought well early, but the slugging Raadik was too tough in the clinches. He knocked the Petaluman down 3 times in the 10th round, earning a TKO victory.

Duke settled in Vacaville where he taught young men to box and played the seasonal role of Santa Claus for children in the area. When Vacaville opened a new sports center around 1990, they named it after the Petaluma boxer.

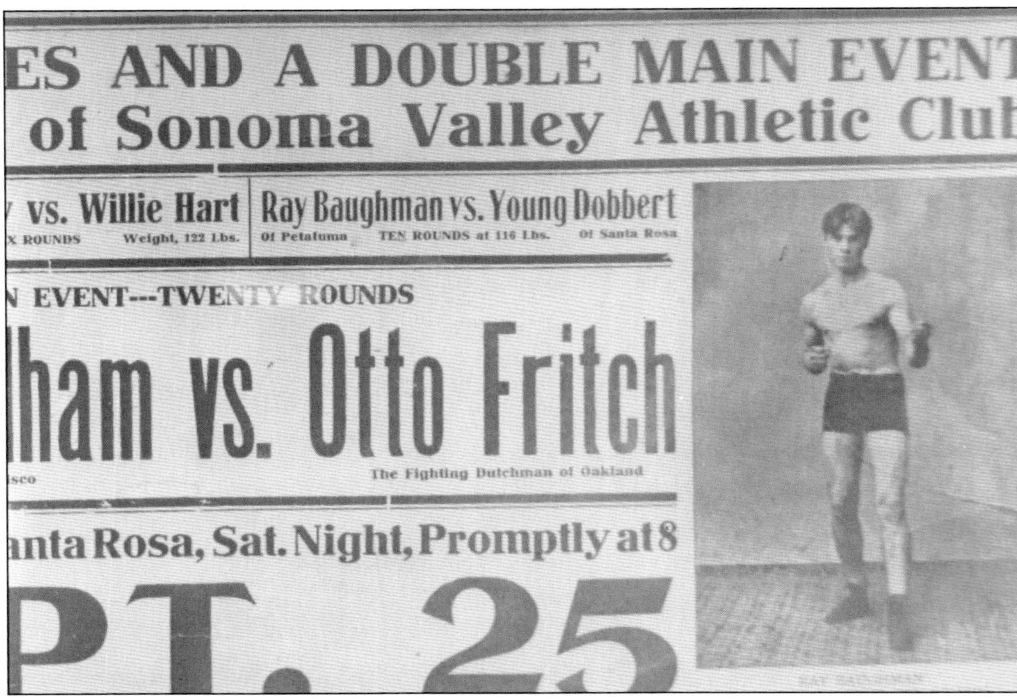

Various promoters put together boxing programs in Sonoma County through the first half of the 20th century, with mixed results. One of the early programs teased fans with a placard offering 40 rounds of boxing, including a double main event, Sept. 25, 1909. The *Press Democrat* gave the following report the next morning: "The so-called prize fight at the Pavillion rink Saturday night attracted only a fair crowd...young (Ray) Baughman knocked out Dobbert in the third, Mike Nolan won from Kid Noriel in the fourth on a foul, bets being declared off, and Willie Hart knocked young Perry out in the third. The 'contest' was advertised as being given under the auspices of the Sonoma Valley Athletic Club. As a matter of fact, it was given by a local saloonkeeper, who recently came here from San Francisco. By what right he advertised as the Sonoma Valley Athletic Club nobody seems to know." Courtesy of the Sonoma County Museum.

Middleweight Jimmy Britt met many leading fighters of his time on the west coast. As early as 1902, he kayoed ex-champion Frank True in San Francisco and showed his stamina, decisioning a boxer named Cannole in a 25-rounder in 1903. After he retired, he opened a popular cocktail lounge in Guerneville. Courtesy of the Sonoma County Museum.

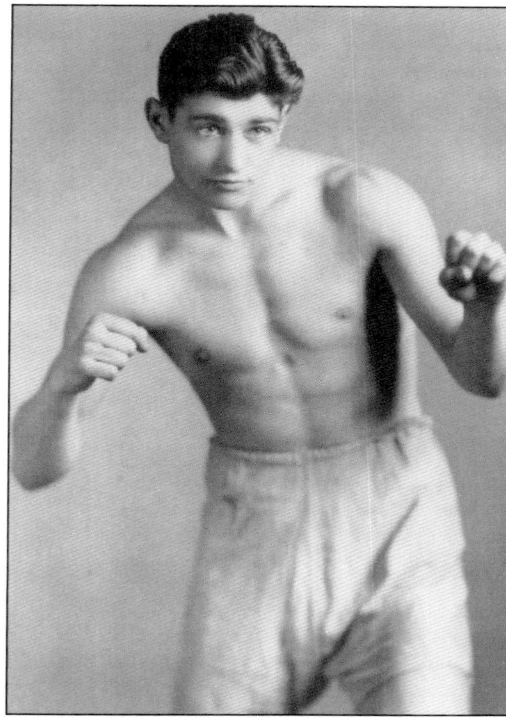

Britt and wife Betty retired to the peace and quiet of Guerneville where they greeted visitors and swapped old boxing stories at their cocktail lounge. Courtesy of the Sonoma County Museum.

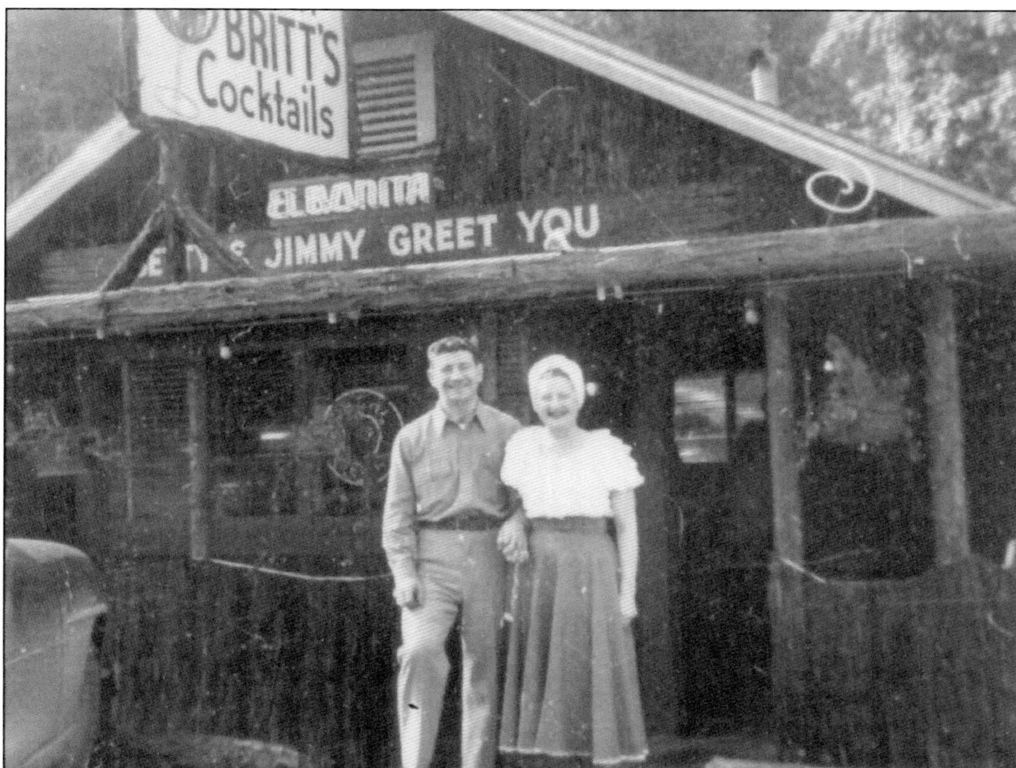

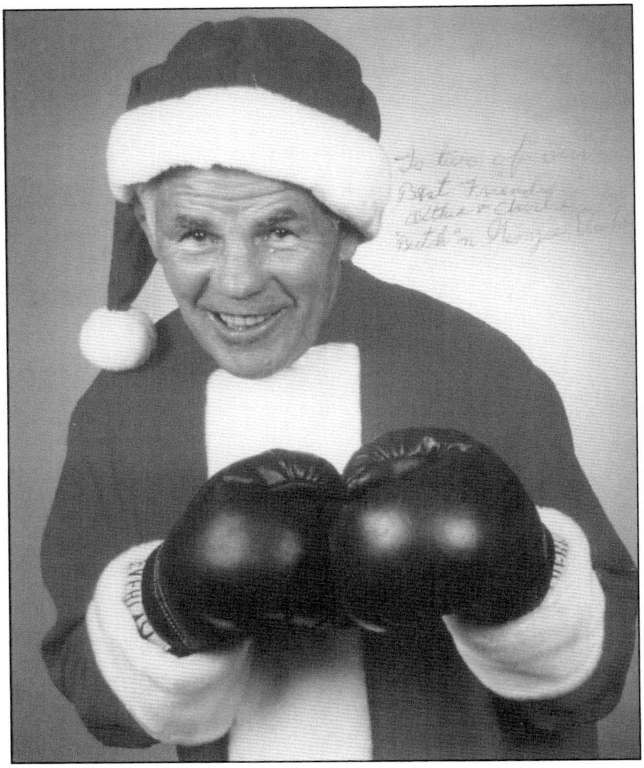

George Duke of Petaluma fought Fred Apostoli and other leading boxers in a career that began in the 1930s and extended through much of the 1940s. When he retired, he taught boxing to dozens of young people and even played a Santa Claus with gloves on Christmas cards. Courtesy of the Torliatt family collection.

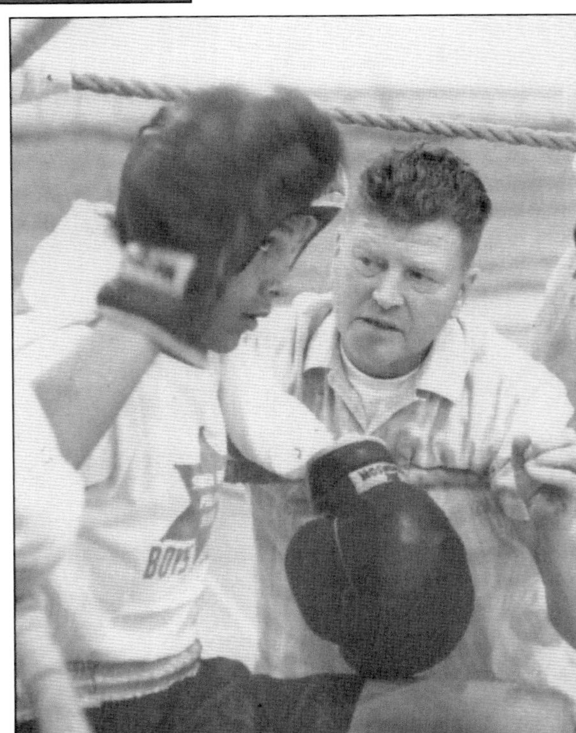

Encouraged by Police Chief Melvin (Dutch) Flohr to start a program for youngsters, coach Andy Wallstrum brought boxing to Santa Rosa High School after World War II. Working in the corner, he gave advice to one of his promising young boxers. The youngsters, sometimes 20 or more of them, mixed it up at Father's Nights in the late 1940s. Courtesy of the Wallstrum collection.

Ten

OUTDOORS

Hunting and fishing were among the earliest sports activities in Sonoma County. Many of the hearty settlers of the 19th century were far more comfortable with a rifle, shotgun, or fishing pole than they would have been with a bat or ball. Farmers in the area often used their guns to kill the bears or mountain lions that attacked their stock. They also put fresh meat or fish on the table by going off into the nearby river or woods.

Some people made a living shipping their kill down the Petaluma River to the bustling market in San Francisco. The commercial hunters and fishermen often faced criticism for taking more than their "fair share" of fish or game or because of the methods they used to "bring home the bacon." Dynamiting in the rivers led to the wholesale slaughter of salmon and other fish and protests from a growing number of rod and gun groups that formed in the late 19th century. In 1907, two men were given jail time for dynamiting fish—one sentenced to three months and the other to 175 days. The latter's plea that he wasn't there when the fish were dynamited but merely gathered dead fish floating in the water fell on deaf ears.

For 40 years, from 1948 to 1988, Walt Christensen kept a watchful eye on the outdoor sports scene for readers of the Santa Rosa *Press Democrat*. Here are some excerpts from early Walt's Rod and Gun columns:

January, 1948: "It is estimated that at least 2,000 anglers lined the banks of the Russian River over the past weekend. This is, without a doubt, the largest number of fishermen ever to fish a stream in a single day...The fish were probably so busy dodging sinkers they didn't have time to bite."

February 15, 1948: "If you are figuring on doing a bit of illegal deer hunting, it would be a good idea to stay clear of the Willits (Mendocino County) area...Charles Boyce of Fort Bragg was picked up in Santa Rosa recently and returned to Willits to stand trial for the illegal slaying of a spike buck." Boyce and a companion were found guilty, and paid $800 fines in lieu of six-month prison terms.

June 18, 1948: "Halibut fishing at Bodega Bay continues to be the main attraction for anglers. Over the weekend upwards of 50 boats of all sizes and descriptions took advantage of an extremely calm ocean to troll and bait-fish the waters inside and outside the bay. Trolling whole sardines is the most popular method of taking halibut..."

August 17, 1948: "To upper Rincon Valley (just east of Santa Rosa) goes the credit for the largest buck so far in the current season. Hunting in the hills above Rincon Valley, Mike Bastoni bagged the big buck, a four-pointer that tipped the scales at a record-breaking 173 pounds. Mike attributes the size of the buck to the diet of grapes, prunes, and apples he has been eating the past several years."

September 26, 1948: "Hunting in the rain, some snow, and weather cold enough to freeze a layer of ice two inches thick in the water bucket each night, Alexander Karkov of Jenner brought down the buck he has been searching for, for many years. The big buck with nine points on one side and seven on the other tipped the scales at 305 pounds.

November 11, 1948: "Salmon fishermen turned out in full force over the weekend from Tomales Bay to the Eel River for a try at the silvery fighters...we can vouch for the fact that there are plenty of salmon in the (Tomales) bay because any time yours truly can land a limit there must be scads of them."

November 21, 1948: "An army of upwards of 100,000 hunters entered the two big valleys of central California for the opening of pheasant season Friday morning and as usual some nimrods bagged their limits with little effort while others hunted hard all day for their two birds or less."

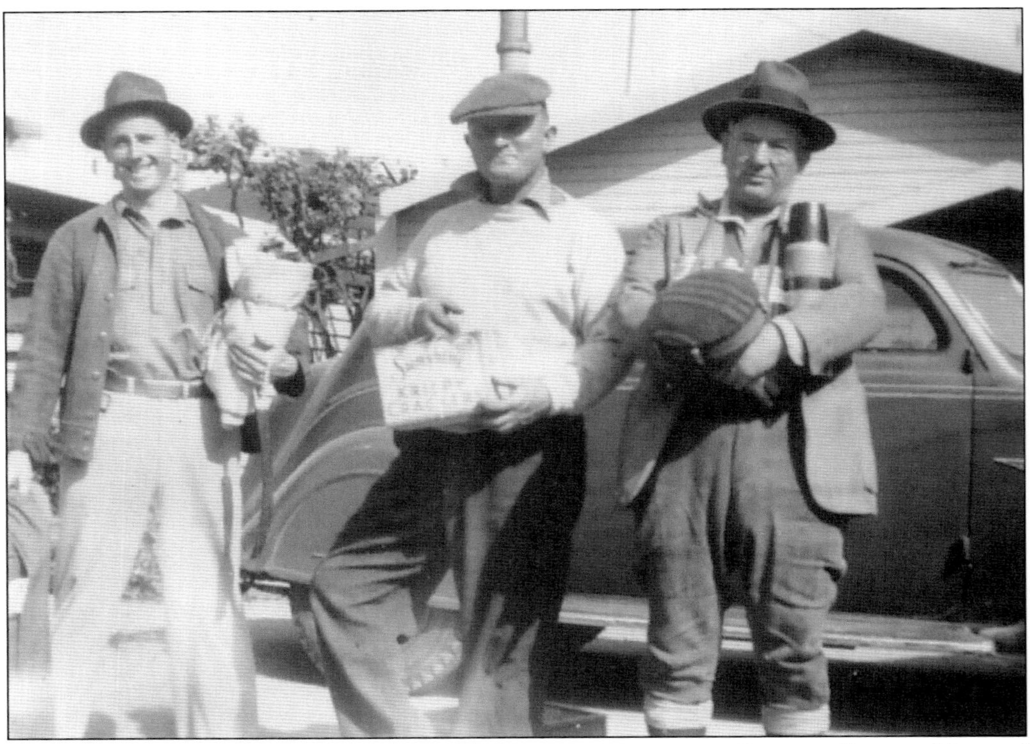

Hunting and fishing were among the earliest sports activities in Sonoma County. Many of the earliest settlers were far more comfortable with a rifle, shotgun, or fishing pole than they would have been with a bat or ball. Armed with sleeping bags, crackers, canteens, and thermos, Petaluma laundryman Lucien (Red) Libarle, auto repairman Pete Torliatt Jr., and banker Al Tomasi prepared for a Russian River fishing trip in 1937. Courtesy of the Torliatt collection.

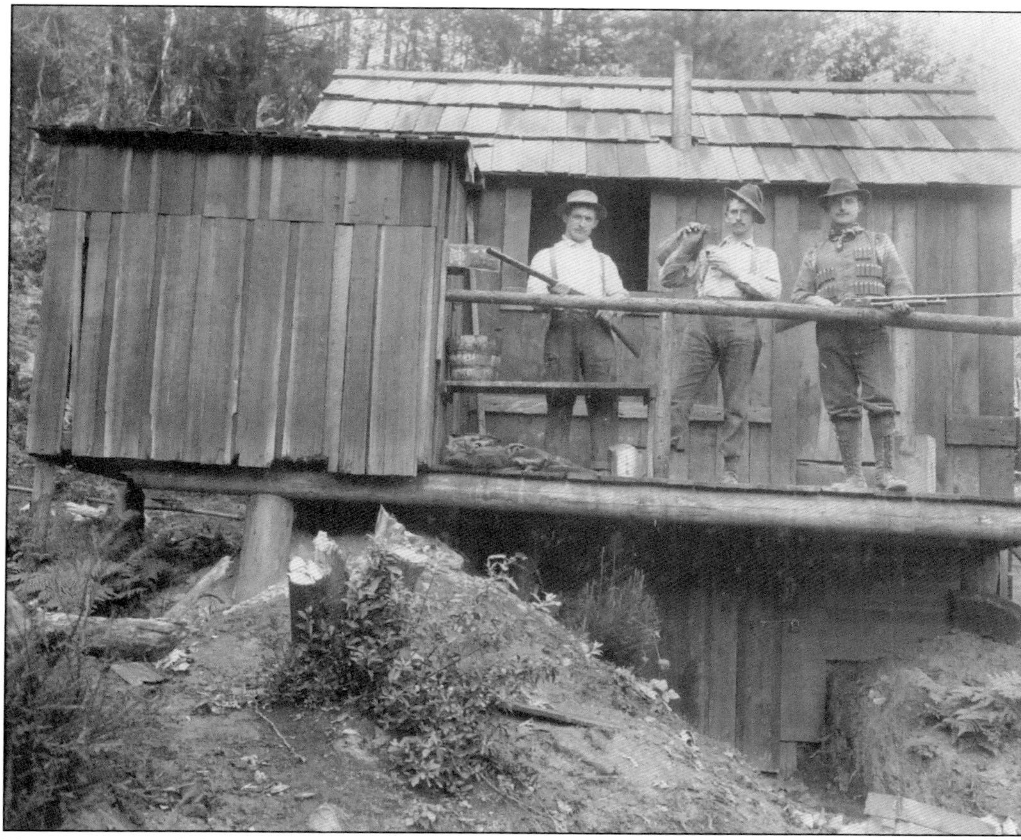

Hunters enjoyed the pleasures of the rustic outdoor living at Big River, Mendocino County *c.* 1910. The man in the middle put down his rifle to take a swig from a jug while another, Ralph Mazzotti (right), showed off his cartridge vest. Courtesy of the Sonoma County Museum.

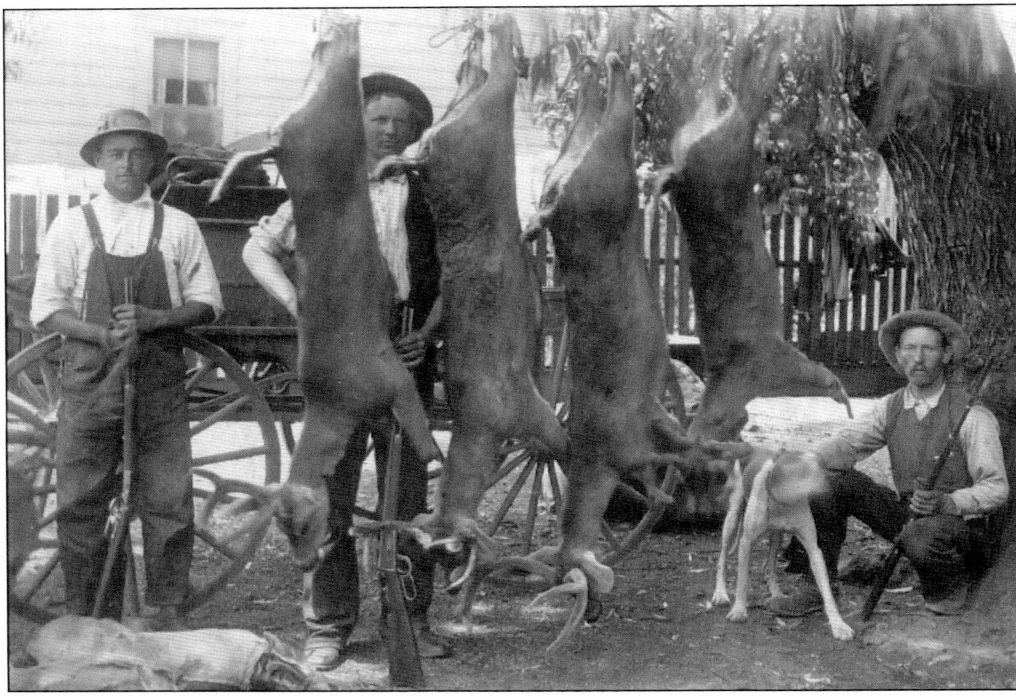

Deer hunters came home with their kills in scene from early in the 20th century. The hunters included Paul Noonan who lived on Beaver Street in Santa Rosa. Courtesy of the Sonoma County Museum.

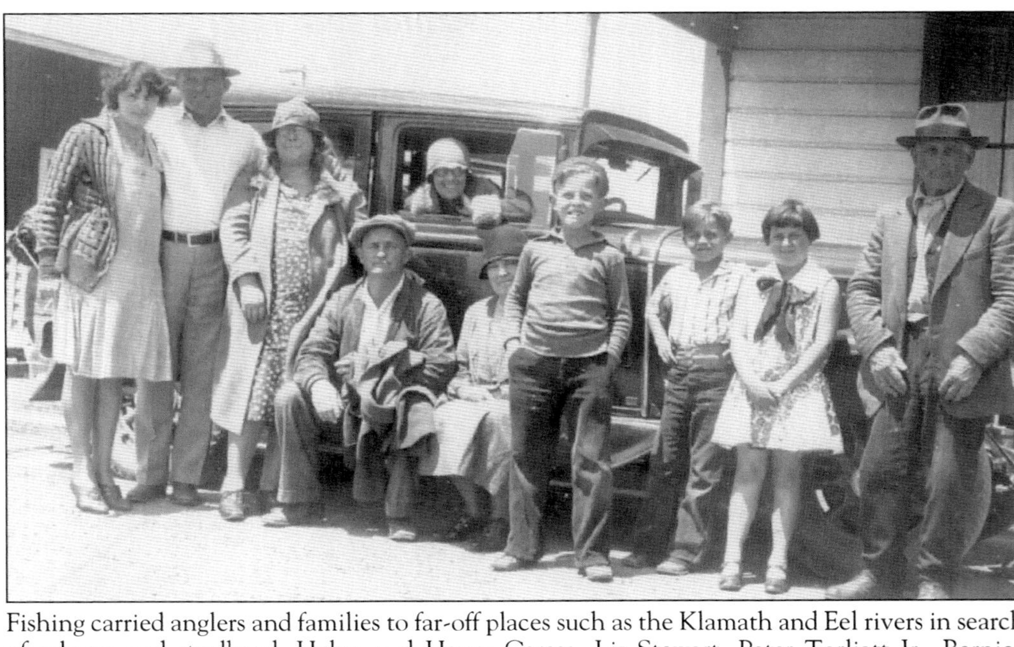

Fishing carried anglers and families to far-off places such as the Klamath and Eel rivers in search of salmon and steelhead. Helen and Henry Ceresa, Liz Stewart, Peter Torliatt Jr., Bernice Torliatt, and several unidentified travelers stopped for food and liquid refreshment at the Swiss Hotel in Crescent City during a fishing trip in 1926. Courtesy of the Torliatt collection.

Eleven

Photo Gallery

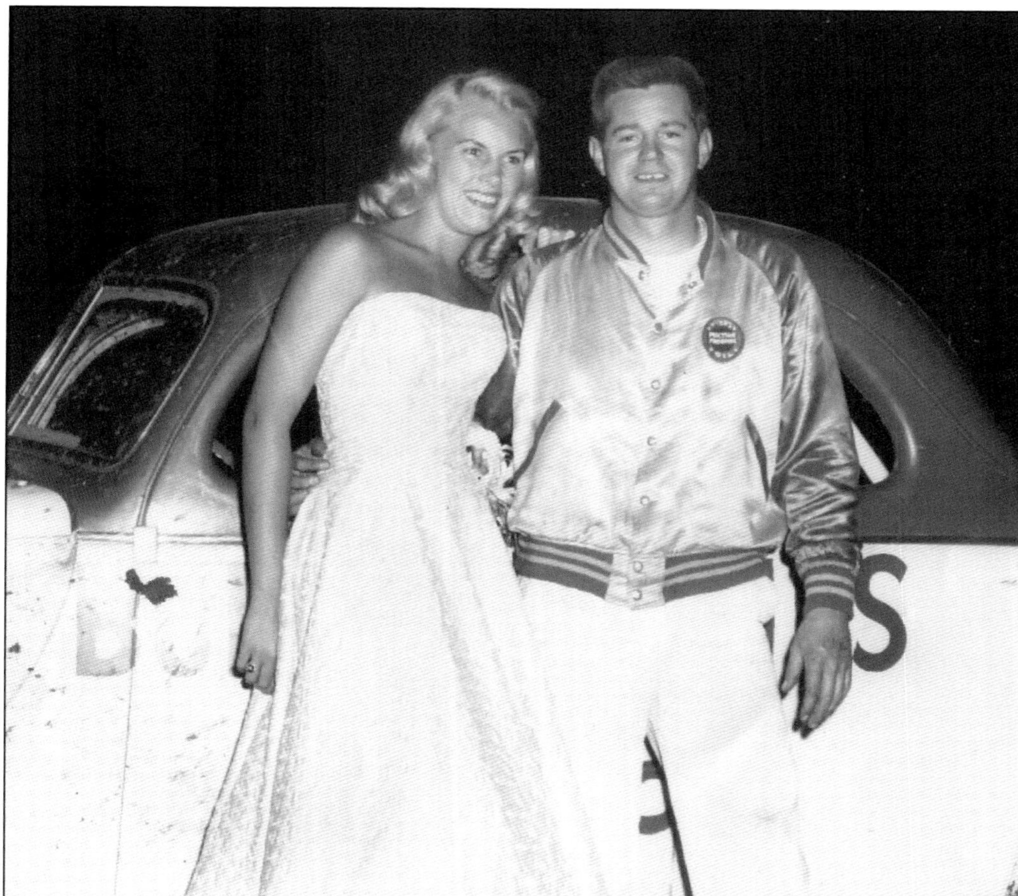

Rick Henderson started tinkering with motors in his father's garage when he was 13, started hardtop racing in Sonoma County when he was 18, won a race of car versus horse shortly thereafter, and became a national modified stock car champion. In the summer of 1952, Henderson and the horse Sleepy, ridden by Bob Offutt, raced 200 yards from a standing start, with Henderson coming out the winner. Henderson, Rod Zanoline, and the Rogers brothers from Healdsburg were among the leading drivers on the hardtop circuit in the early 1950s. In addition to fame and financial rewards, winning a race usually meant a hug and a kiss from a comely trophy girl. The unnamed beauty had a big smile for race winner Henderson. Courtesy of the Henderson family collection.

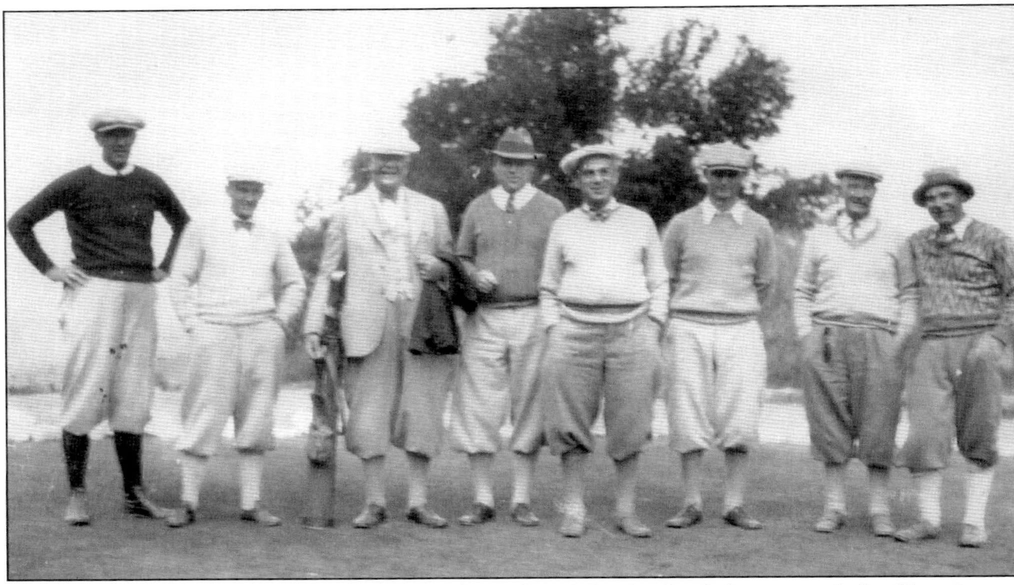

Back in the 1920s and '30s, knickers were the order of the day for fashion-minded golfers. In step with the times were members of the Petaluma Golf Club, pictured here starting from the left: captain William Thomas, H.C. Scrutton, Dolph Hill, Eric Nissen, Grover Stone, Jack Olmsted, Emmett Olmsted Jr., and Jack Cavanaugh. Courtesy of the Petaluma Museum.

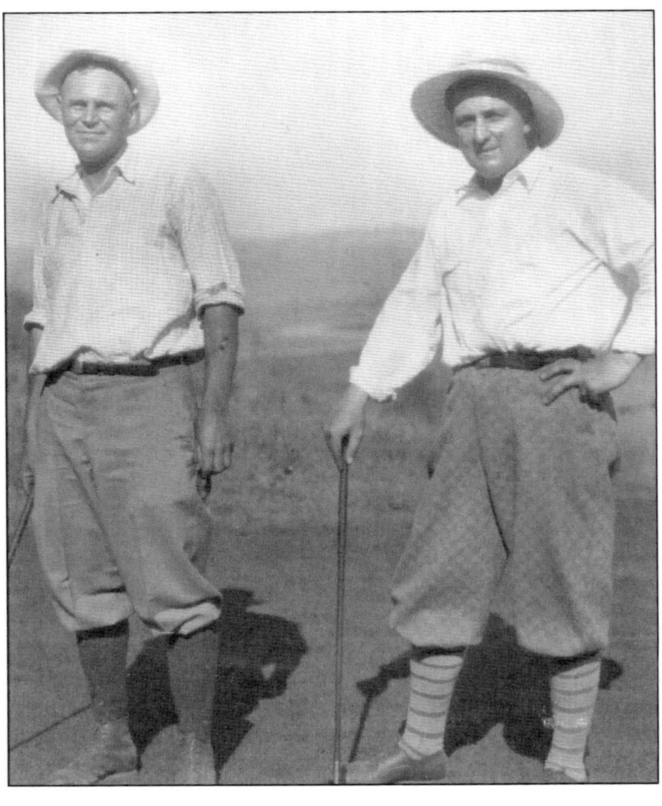

No, they're not out on safari—they were just trying to break par on the hilly, challenging Petaluma golf course. Eric Nissen and Grover Stone were among the more active Jazz Age golfers at the Petaluma Golf and Country Club. Courtesy of the Petaluma Museum.

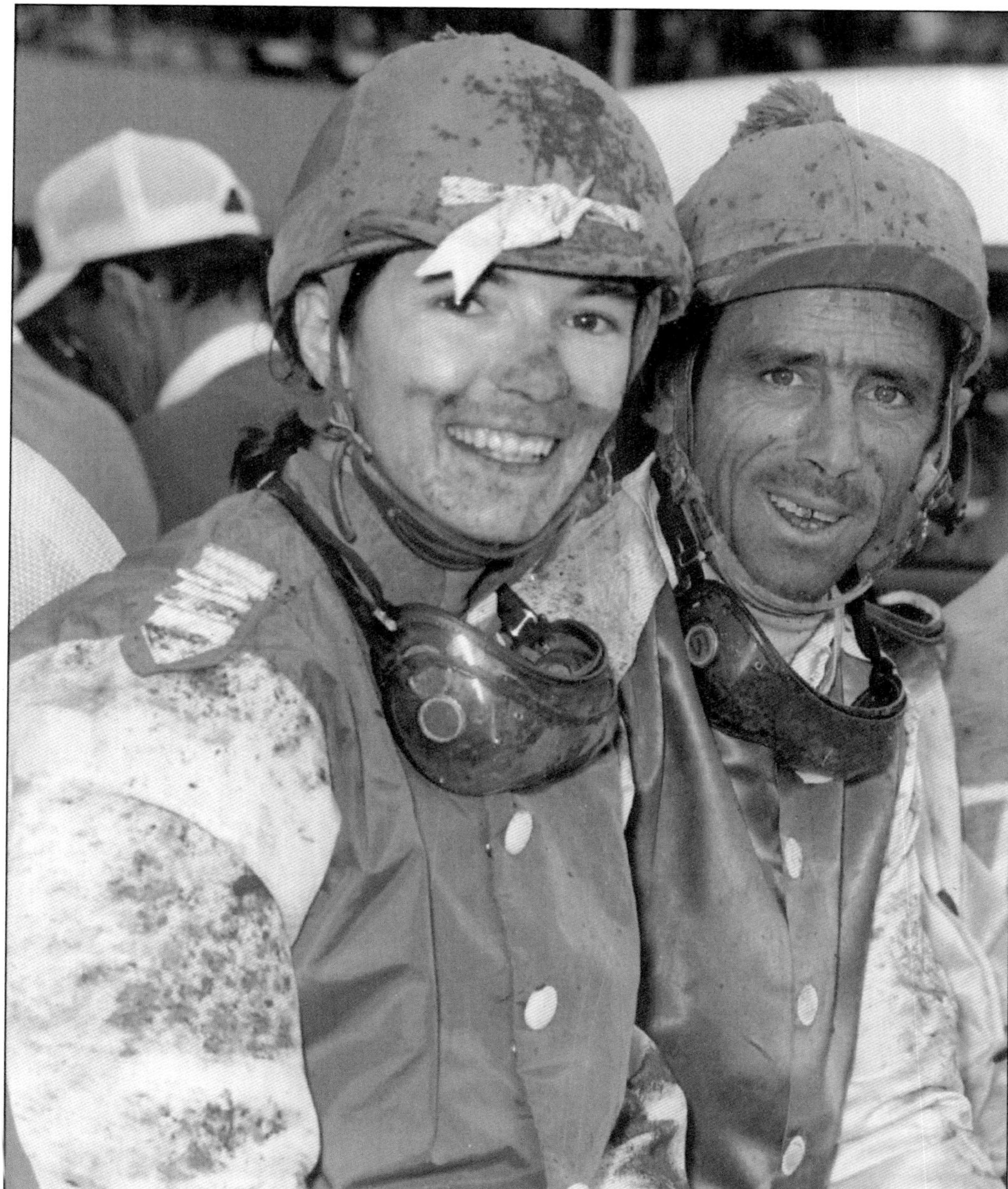

Uniforms full of dirt and mud, two jockeys still manage a smile after a hard day on the track at the Sonoma County Fairgrounds. Racing purses, totaling $7,400 in 1936, had swollen to $54,200 by 1950. Courtesy of the Sonoma County Fair.

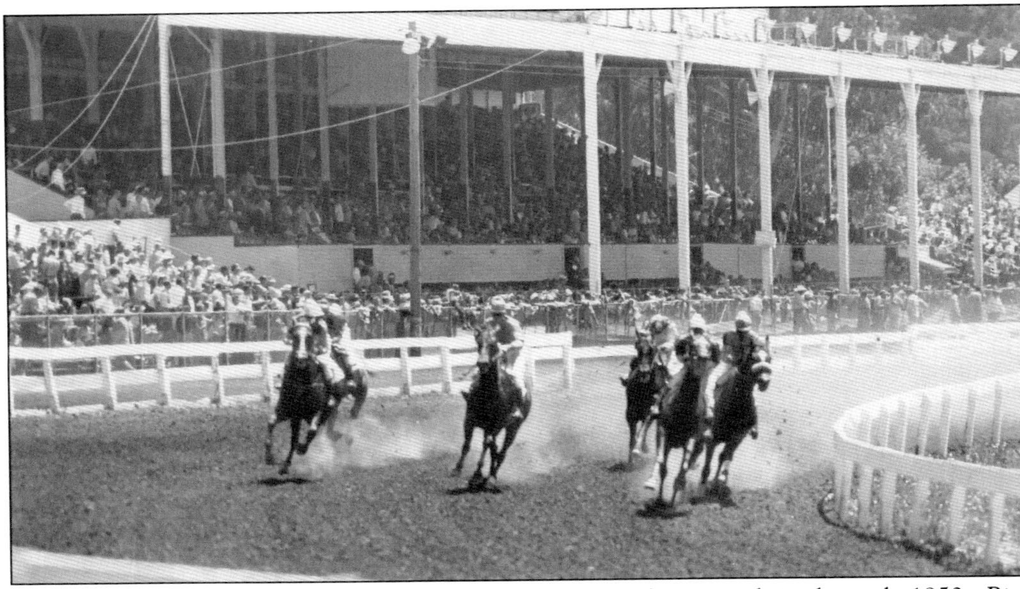

They're off and running at the Sonoma County Fairgrounds racetrack in the early 1950s. Big-time fair racing started in 1936 and except for a couple of war years has been a popular feature of the annual event ever since. Courtesy of the Sonoma County Fair.

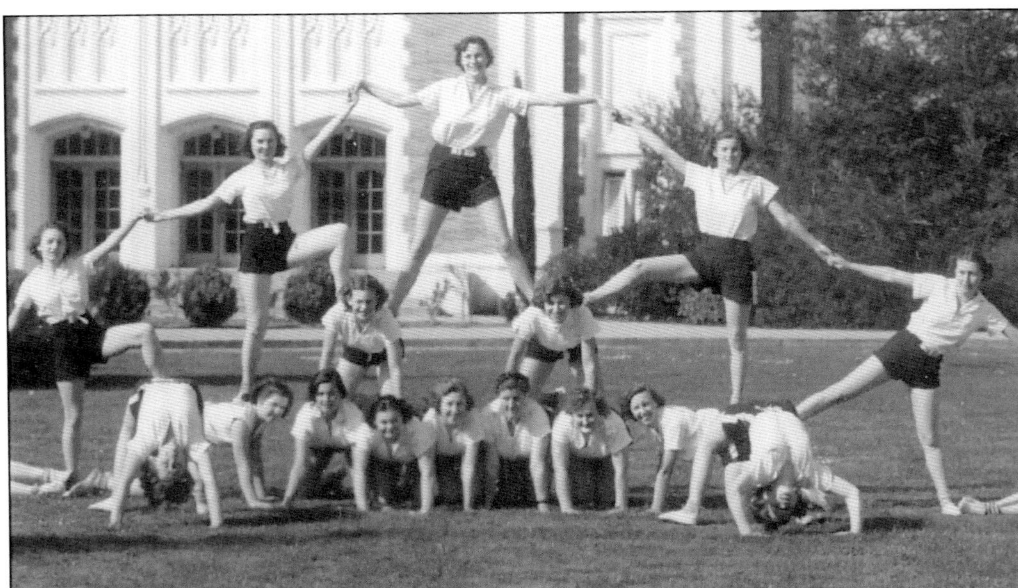

Good balance was mainly what it took to do a fancy pyramid at Santa Rosa High School in 1936. An array of talented and flexible young ladies took their show to the front lawn of the campus where pedestrians and passersby in cars could view the proceedings. Included in the performance, but not in order, are: Shirley Frey, Eileen Norton, Ann Withnels, Margaret Karsten, Phyllis Laughlin, Beatrice Clarke, Jeanne Saul, Evelyn Hayes, Vivian Bacca, Ramona Call, Anna Maggiora, Virginia Downing, Ruth Johnson, Katherine Steele, Jane Violetti, Naomi Call, Margaret Hudson, Inez Howry, Caroline Williams, and Lars Young. Courtesy of the SRHS Foundation.

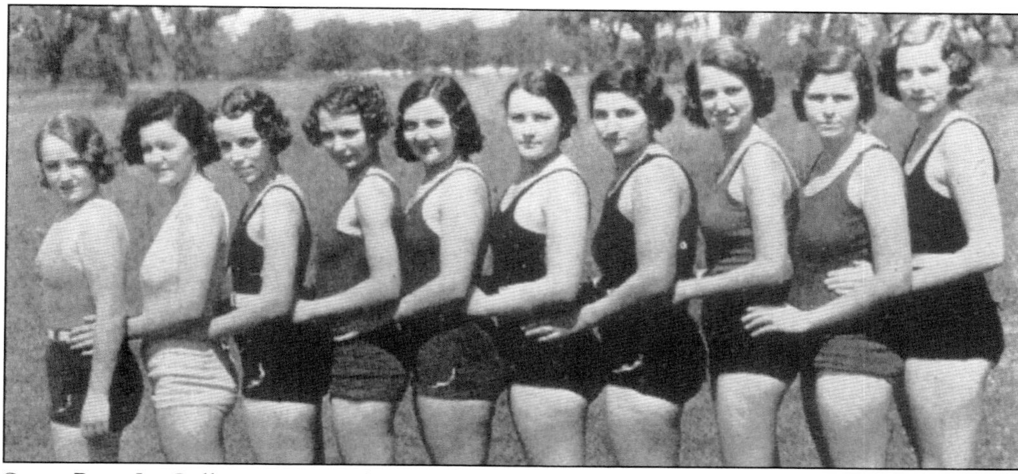

Santa Rosa Jr. College women played six sports, including six basketball games with outside teams in the 1932 season. Swimming began when the "muni tank" opened May 1. Girls competed in 50 and 100-yard races at the annual picnic on the Russian River near the end of the school year.

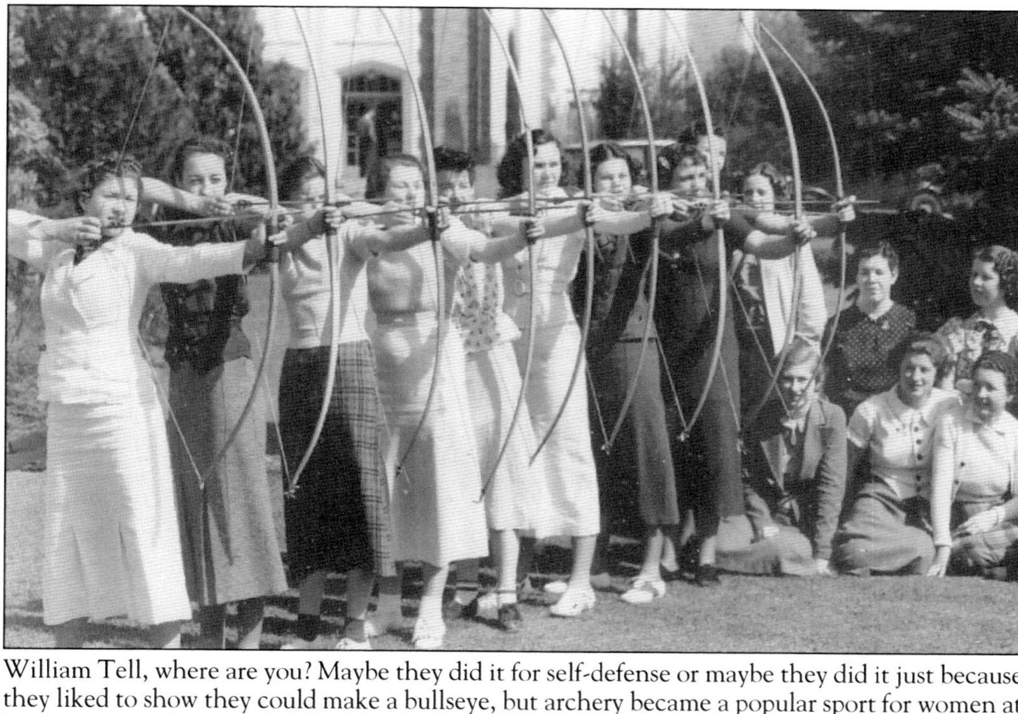

William Tell, where are you? Maybe they did it for self-defense or maybe they did it just because they liked to show they could make a bullseye, but archery became a popular sport for women at Santa Rosa High School in the 1930s. The 1936-37 SRHS archers included: (standing) Peggy Hudson, Keitha Jamison, Grace Close, Vivian Chuhart, Mary Macdonell, Anne Withnell, Jane Violetti, Lucy Gioletti, Betty Randell, and Louise Tiernan; (sitting and kneeling) Frances Chihart, Edith Antoliola, Marjorie McDowell, Ruth McDonald, and Alice Tinker. In the early years in Sonoma County schools, women's sports were low-key, often focused on intra-mural programs rather competition with other schools. Courtesy of the SRHS Foundation.

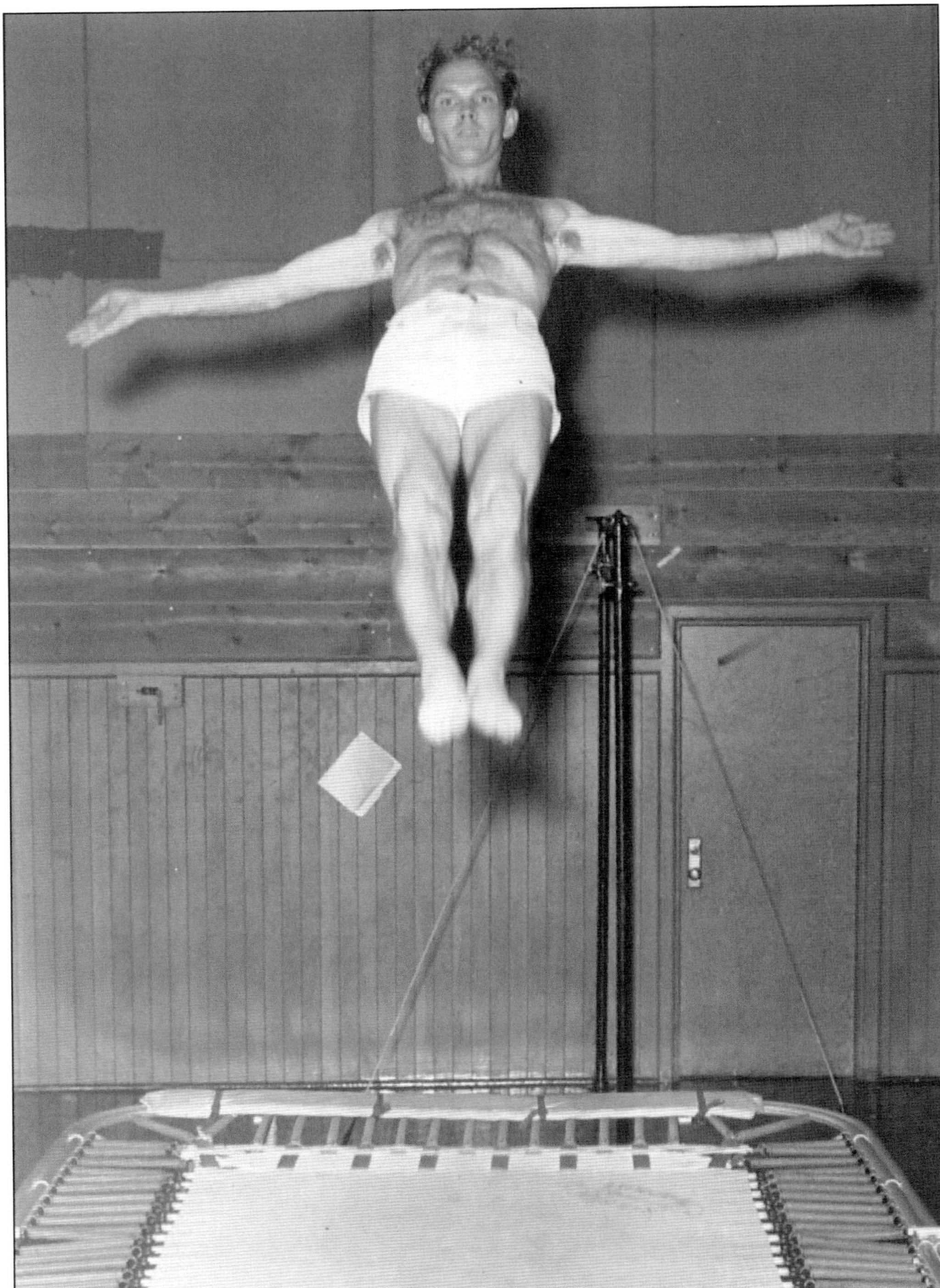

When new equipment was acquired, gymnastics and tumbling became a popular sport in the early 1950s at Santa Rosa Jr. College. On this trip, a young tumbler bounced high off the mat, missing the ceiling, but not by much. Courtesy of the SRJC collection.

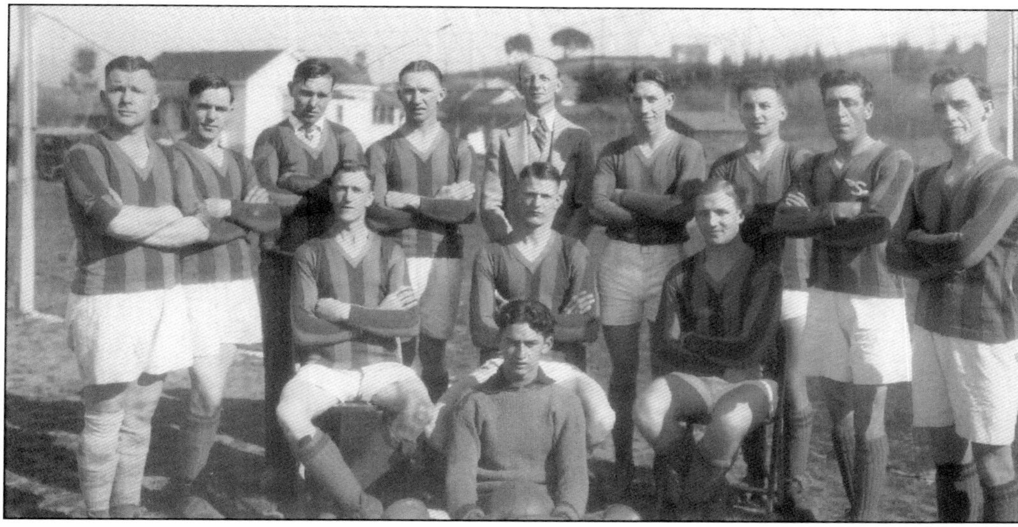

Those who liked to get their "kicks" out of sports in Sonoma County generally turned to football. But there were other games, such as soccer and rugby that required expert footwork. Healdsburg won a soccer game at Nagle Field in Santa Rosa in 1922. Later, the Petaluma Spartans Athletic Club fielded a strong team, winning a league championship in 1928. In the back row (but not necessarily in order) are: M. Campbell, Jack Barron, Mike Giblin, George Holmes, Aldo Baccala (third from right), Jim Gilbert, and Jack Batey; (second row seated) Robert Taylor, Walter Taylor, and G. Sturm; (front) goalkeeper Phil Talamantes. The team played at McNear Park. Courtesy of the Fratini collection.

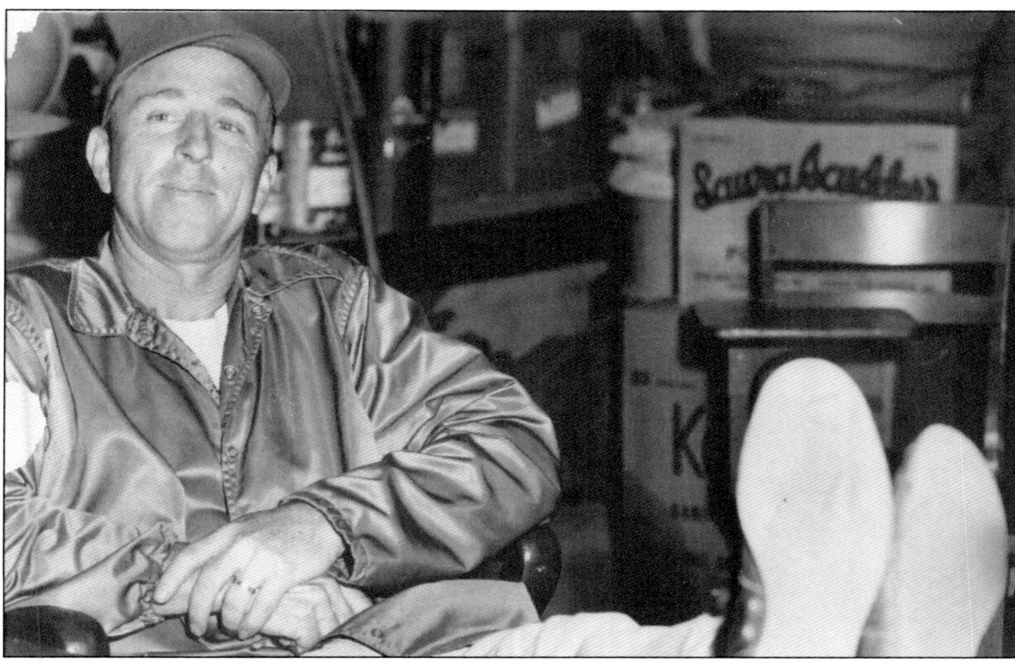

When the games and practices ended, it was time for a break. Analy coach Walt Foster, a hard-working player and coach, put his feet on the desk and kicked back after a long day on the practice field. Courtesy of the Foster collection.

INDEX